THE MANAGER'S GUIDE TO FINANCIAL STATEMENT ANALYSIS

SECOND EDITION

The Manager's Guide to Financial Statement Analysis

Second Edition

Stephen F. Jablonsky
Noah P. Barsky

JOHN WILEY & SONS, INC.

New York • Chichester • Weinheim • Brisbane • Singapore • Toronto

Library of Congress Cataloging-in-Publication Data:

Jablonsky, Stephen F.
   The manager's guide to financial statement analysis / Stephen F. Jablonsky, Noah P. Barsky.—2nd ed.
      p. cm.
   Includes bibliographical references and index.
   ISBN 0-471-40274-5 (cloth : alk. paper)
   1. Financial statements—United States. 2. Managerial accounting. 3. Business enterprises—United States—Valuation. 4. Corporations—United States—Valuation. 5. Business enterprises—United States—Finance. 6. Corporations—United States—Finance. 7. Wal-Mart (Firm) I. Barsky, Noah P. II. Title.

HF5681.B2 J23 2001
658.15′12—dc2100-061961

Printed in the United States of America.

10 9 8 7 6 5 4 3 2 1

Contents

Preface

In today's marketplace, digital technology is having a profound effect on the way that people think about and conduct business. Information technology is changing job descriptions and expectations in all occupations and professions. Information technology and the Internet make it possible for people to access an overwhelming amount of information "on-demand" and at little or no cost. At many firms, traditional scorekeeping and reporting activities are now embedded in technology. Financial managers are now expected to play a greater role in achieving business objectives. These changes in the business environment demand new skill sets and mindsets to succeed in the competitive marketplace.

Despite changes in information technology, reliance on financial information to evaluate business performance remains timeless. Managers need to know how to read financial statements and use that information in the formulation and implementation of business strategy. Managers also need to know how the expectations of creditors and shareholders influence business strategy. Once managers understand how to make sense out of the financial statements and market information about their firm, they will be able to function more effectively as members of their management teams.

In writing this book, we have emphasized the need for managers to be able to communicate with one another in order to accomplish their shared objectives. It is one thing to be able to develop a personal understanding of how to read financial statements. It is quite another thing to be able to communicate that understanding to other members of the management team. In each chapter, we provide concrete examples of how to explain what you have learned to co-workers who have similar interests in understanding more about business.

In the Introduction, we provide a framework for helping managers understand the business through financial information. We consider a firm in terms of a business strategy, management control, and shareholder accountability cycle. Based on our experiences working in executive development programs, managers find the context of strategy, control, and accountability to be a useful way of thinking about financial information. This context helps managers see the value of using financial information for decision making without dwelling on the technical aspects of financial reporting.

In Part One of this book, we show you how to make sense out of the information found in a firm's financial statements using two business strategy models: a Strategic Profit Model and a Strategic Financing Model. We have found these models to be extremely effective in helping managers develop a shared understanding of the business and a common framework for discussing the financial aspects of their business.

In Part Two, we show you how to make sense of the key measures of financial performance that reflect the market's assessment of a firm's past and expected future performance. We define and explain the meaning of these key performance measures as we work through the mechanics of how the market values a firm's debt and common stock. After explaining how the market valuation process works, we revisit the Strategic Profit Model and extend that model to include information about the market valuation process.

To reinforce how the information found in the financial statements and market information about a firm relates to the firm's overall business strategy, we focus our analysis on one firm, Wal-Mart. As the world's largest retailer, managers from the United States and around the world know of Wal-Mart. If you read this book cover-to-cover, you will see how all of the pieces of financial information fit together for one firm. An alternative strategy for using this guide to financial statement analysis is to analyze your own firm's financial statements as you read the book.

The two parts of this book represent a journey to understanding the business through financial information, which comes full circle in the last chapter and ends back where we started—visualizing the firm through the Strategic Profit Model. The first trip through the material provides the foundation for developing a management understanding of how to use financial statements. By taking a second trip through the book, you will be able to gain additional insights into Wal-Mart and your own company because you will have a better grasp of the financial terminology you learned on the first journey.

In addition to taking individual trips through this book, we recommend taking several group trips through the chapters with members of your management team. The group trips provide a chance for all managers to practice their communication skills. As previously mentioned, it takes practice to see if you can translate what you have learned into words.

Acknowledgments

The following organizations have played a significant role in helping us write this book from a management perspective.

Penn State Executive Programs has provided us with the opportunity to help managers understand a business through financial information. The organization of the chapters and the materials presented in each chapter reflect its feedback on the best way to learn how to understand the business through financial information.

The Financial Executives Research Foundation (FERF) has provided us with the opportunity to study the changing roles of financial management in major U.S. corporations. Over the past twelve years, we have had the opportunity to interview senior corporate executives and financial and nonfinancial managers at all levels throughout our case study firms. The strong emphasis on management communications throughout the book is based primarily on our interviews with all of the executives and managers at the case study firms. In particular, we wish to thank Bob Moore, Roland Laing, and Bill Sinnett for supporting our research efforts.

Stephen F. Jablonsky would also like to thank the W. K. Kellogg Foundation and the Kellogg National Fellowship program for providing fellowship support to develop a different, more people-oriented approach to teaching and doing research in accounting and finance. Although the practices of accounting and finance are technically grounded, the importance of these disciplines is grounded in how they affect human behavior. The Kellogg fellowship experience is reflected in our emphasis on "insight and understanding" versus "prediction and control." We wish to thank the fellows and advisors of KNFP Group IV for all of their commitment to helping individuals expand their horizons beyond the traditional academic disciplines.

Noah P. Barsky would like to thank the University of Connecticut Ph.D. Program for providing support and an intellectual environment conducive to personal and professional growth. In particular, the insights of Mo Hussein, Garry Marchant, Doug Heckathorn, and Stan Biggs have been instrumental in the development of my approach to thinking about business and social issues.

The second edition of this book would not have been possible without the many valuable insights and feedback from participants in the Villanova University MBA program. Last, we are very grateful for the editorial support provided by Sheck Cho, Lea Baranowski, Michelle Mutchnik, and Kiki Peterson.

Introduction

People often refer to accounting as the "language of business." As with any language, when we understand accounting, we can communicate with anyone else who speaks that language. Knowledge of any language offers unlimited opportunities to communicate with other people.

Communicating is imparting information through speaking, writing, or visual representation. Communication implies the exchange of information through face-to-face interaction or through more impersonal channels, such as written reports and computerized data exchange. Communicating is structuring information to promote a shared understanding between speaker and listener, author and reader. The words—and, in our case, numbers—must be meaningful to everyone involved in the communication process.

In his autobiography, Sam Walton includes communication as one of his ten rules for running a successful company:

> RULE 4: COMMUNICATE everything you possibly can to your partners. The more they know, the more they'll understand. The more they understand, the more they'll care. Once they care, there's no stopping them. If you don't trust your associates to know what's going on, they'll know that you don't really consider them partners. Information is power, and the gain you get from empowering your associates more than offsets the risks of informing your competitors.[1]

This book has been written in the spirit of open communications underlying Sam Walton's quote.

In his book *The Great Game of Business,* Jack Stack, CEO of Springfield Remanufacturing Corp. (SRC), expresses a similar commitment to increasing understanding through open communications:

The more people know about a company, the better that company will perform. This is an iron-clad rule. You will *always* be more successful in business by sharing information with the people you work with than by keeping them in the dark.

Information should not be a power tool—it should be a means of education. Don't use information to intimidate, control, or manipulate people. Use it to teach people how to work together to achieve common goals and thereby gain control over their lives. When you share the numbers and bring them alive, you turn them into tools people can use to help themselves as they go about their business every day. That's the key to open-book management.[2]

In explaining SRC's approach to managing the business, Stack contrasts its open-book management philosophy with closed-book management:

After all, numbers are simply a way of telling stories about people, as well as a means of keeping score. If you're keeping score, there must be a game going on somewhere. The only issue is whether or not the players know it. (That's the absurdity of traditional closed-book management: it's based on getting people to play a game without telling them.)[3]

As discussed more fully later in the Introduction, it is one thing to extol the virtues of open communications; it is another thing to actually create an environment of open communications within a business. In order to make the transition from inspiration to implementation, managers need to know how their actions affect the overall financial performance of their firms. They need tools for translating theory into practice. That is where this book comes into play. Some universal tools for helping managers understand their business through financial information are provided in this book.

Fortunately, we do not have to worry about having enough raw material to help managers begin to understand their business through financial information. In a market economy populated by publicly held corporations, there is more than enough information available to begin the process. Every publicly held corporation is required to include a complete set of financial statements in its annual report to shareholders. These annual reports may be obtained on request by writing or calling the firm's investor relations department. For many firms, all of the information needed to start understanding the business may be accessed through the firm's World Wide Web site.

Financial statements, particularly the balance sheet and the income statement, provide a touchstone for understanding any business. These statements summarize the financial performance of the firm at a particular time (the balance sheet) and over some time period (the income statement). Whether managers know it or not, the score is kept through these financial statements. After working through the material presented in each chapter of this book, managers should have a better understanding of the relationship among their actions, the outcomes reported in the financial statements, and their firm's overall business strategy.

Managers know that a score is being kept for their firms. They also know that they are involved in their firm's economic game plan. What they lack is a better understanding of how the score relates back to the game plan. They want to know how to adjust their actions in order to generate a better performance score for themselves and their firm. This book has been developed to fill the gap between playing the game and generating a better performance score.

MOST MANAGERS ARE QUITE HAPPY THEY ARE NOT ACCOUNTANTS

Managers, particularly nonfinancial managers, are quick to point out that they do not want to become accountants or financial analysts. Managers want to understand how to use financial information to improve the financial performance of their firms. They do not want to become preparers of financial information. They want to learn the language of business to become more effective in their current and future positions but stop well short of becoming accountants and financial analysts. They are more than happy to leave the technical work to the experts. In developing the approach to understanding the business through financial information presented in this book, we have taken these nonfinancial managers at their word. We have placed understanding in the foreground and moved most of the technical issues into the background.

ACCOUNTING IS THE "LANGUAGE OF BUSINESS"

Learning the language of business is like learning any other language. A certain amount of written material is needed to get the process started, but practice improves performance. It is one thing to be able to complete the exercises at the end of each chapter of a Spanish, German, or Japanese language book; it is another thing to engage in a meaningful conversation with individuals who speak the language fluently. Practice makes perfect.

This book has been developed in a manner similar to the model followed in intensive language programs. Even though you will be able to benefit from reading each of the chapters in sequence, you can benefit even more by applying the concepts presented in each chapter to your own company or a company in which you have a personal interest and by practicing your language skills with other managers within your own company or other managers you know on the outside. As previously stated, only practice makes perfect.

As we shall see, the financial information included in this book comes from the firm's annual reports to shareholders, the *Wall Street Journal (WSJ)*, the *Value Line Investment Survey (Value Line)*, *Business Week,* and other business periodicals. We will rely exclusively on financial information that is available to the public (either free by request, through public libraries or on a subscription basis through online computer services). We encourage you to use the tools presented in each chapter to develop a better understanding of your own firm. What better place to start than to use the financial statements for your own firm?

Our primary emphasis will be placed on the financial information found in the firm's balance sheets and income statements. This information will then be supplemented by information that can be found in other sections of the firm's annual report, the *WSJ, Value Line,* and *Business Week.* This additional information will allow us to look at the financial performance of a firm from a broader economic perspective.

IS A BROADER ECONOMIC PERSPECTIVE REALLY NECESSARY?

With the advent of individual retirement accounts (IRAs), 401(k) plans, discount brokerage services, and mutual funds, most of the readers of this book will probably be investors in the global economy as well as managers in particular firms. When each of us steps into an investor role, the typical concern is the return (dividends plus stock price appreciation) that has been earned, or can be expected to be earned, by investing in a specific firm or portfolio of firms. We want to know if the managers of the firms we have invested in have created *shareholder value.*

When we play both manager and investor roles, we come full circle. As managers, we need to know what we must do to create shareholder value. As investors, we want to know if managers have, in fact, created any value. The tools presented in this book allow us to have it both ways. As managers, we look at the firm in terms of its business strategy. We try to think in terms of what managers have to do to make the firm a success in the future. As investors, we look at the firm in terms of shareholder accountability. We try to think in terms of what management has done for us in the past to create shareholder value. We also want to know what management is doing to create shareholder value in the future.

WHY DID WE WRITE THIS BOOK?

Although we have used the approach to understanding the business presented in this book for many years, the interest in going public with this approach was stimulated by our observation of a number of changes occurring in the financial management practices of major U.S. corporations. Based on a series of research studies sponsored by the Financial Executives Research Foundation (FERF), we have been able to identify two models of financial management that reflect underlying differences in management operating philosophies.

We use the terms *Business Advocate* and *Corporate Police* to refer to the two models of financial management. This book has been written from a Business Advocate perspective that is consistent with an open-book management operating philosophy. Since the Business Advocate model reflects a management operating philosophy that differs radically from the Corporate Police model, we believe it is worth taking some time to explain the differences between the two models.

Business Advocates and Corporate Police

While studying the financial management practices at six major U.S. corporations (AT&T, Boeing, Citicorp, Ford, Merck, and 3M), we discovered that the work performed by financial professionals can be described in terms of three orientations to financial work:

1. Command and control
2. Conformance
3. Competitive team

Even though all of the firms were required to meet similar external financial-reporting requirements (e.g., SEC regulations and Financial Accounting Standards Board pronouncements), the manner in which they met these requirements and met the financial information needs of senior management and line management differed dramatically. No two financial organizations functioned in exactly the same manner, yet each financial organization could be described in terms of a combination of command and control, conformance, and competitive team orientations.

A short description of the three orientations to financial work is provided in the following list. Even though the descriptions are brief, managers usually have no trouble identifying with the orientation that characterizes their financial organization.

- *Command and control orientation.* This orientation to financial work stresses the vertical flow of financial information up and down the corporate hierarchy. The financial organization serves top management by providing an independent review, evaluation, and commentary on the operating and capital investment plans of the business units.
- *Conformance orientation.* This orientation to financial work stresses the external flow of information prepared in accordance with externally imposed reporting requirements. The financial organization serves regulators, analysts, and other external parties by complying with the rules and regulations established for demonstrating external accountability.
- *Competitive team orientation.* This orientation to financial work stresses the horizontal flow of information among all managers within the firm. The financial organization serves the business units by providing the sophisticated analytical and accounting support necessary for achieving the firm's strategic business objectives.

In subsequent studies involving over 2,500 managers (910 financial managers and 1,632 nonfinancial managers), two distinct models of financial management emerged from the research: (1) the Business Advocate model and (2) the Corporate Police model.[4] The Business Advocate model represents a combination of the command and control and competitive team orientations to financial work, while the Corporate Police model represents a combination of the command and control and conformance orientations.

Figure I.1 presents the two models of financial management and three orientations to financial work as a triangle with the command and control

Figure I.1   Models of Financial Management: Business Advocate and Corporate Police

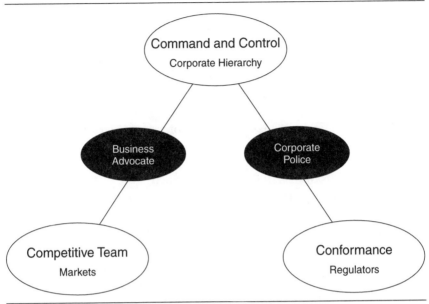

orientation at the top. All of the managers we have worked with over the years know that someone has to be in charge. Some formal control structure must be in place if the organization is to function effectively. The question is, do we combine the necessary control function (command and control orientation) with a conformance orientation or a competitive team orientation?

When managers in executive development programs describe the financial management practices of their firms, the differences between the Business Advocate and Corporate Police models of financial management could not be more striking. In a Business Advocate environment, open communications are encouraged and financial information is integrated directly into the fabric of the business operations. In a Corporate Police environment, communications are tied to position in the corporate hierarchy on a "need to know" basis, and financial information is used to enforce compliance with corporate policies and procedures.

The differences between the two models are almost as stark as the difference between day and night. The differences may be summarized in terms of the expectations established for the financial professionals working in each type of financial organization. In the Business Advocate model, financial professionals are expected to

- Know the business and be involved
- Think in terms of service and involvement
- Encourage wide use of financial information
- Integrate business operations throughout the firm
- Provide financial discipline for the business operations

In the Corporate Police model, financial professionals are expected to

- Administer the rules and regulations
- Think in terms of oversight and surveillance
- Limit access to information on a need to know basis
- Enforce compliance with policies and procedures
- Monitor the collection and disclosure of information

In a Business Advocate environment, a premium is placed on being able to communicate. A Business Advocate environment is typically a team-based, high-involvement setting. All managers are held mutually account-able for achieving the business objectives and hitting the financial targets set for the business. In this type of environment, everyone needs to know how business strategy, financial control, and shareholder accountability interrelate.

In a Corporate Police environment, need to know access to financial information works against open communication. Information is typically restricted to specific budget categories within functional areas of responsi-bility. Financial personnel are seen as scorekeepers and evaluators rather than educators and integrators. No attempt is made to link business strat-egy to shareholder accountability through the financial control system.

BUSINESS ADVOCATE PERSPECTIVE OF THIS BOOK

This book has been developed with a vision of the ideal Business Advocate financial organization in mind. In a Business Advocate environment, the concepts contained in this book may be used by individual managers to increase their personal understanding of the business through financial in-formation and by management groups to develop a shared understanding of the business.

Even though we have developed the book with the ideal Business Advocate financial organization in mind, managers from Corporate Police environments are often the most appreciative of our efforts to help them increase their understanding of the business. In these cases, we have been able to make a contribution to their personal development. However, we have not been able to help them develop a shared understanding of the business along with other members of the management team. Unfortunately, open communications are not a cornerstone of the Corporate Police model.

Figure I.2 presents an overview of the Business Advocate perspective we use to help managers understand the business through financial information. The Business Advocate perspective consists of three major components:

1. Business strategy
2. Management control
3. Shareholder accountability

Figure I.2 **Understanding the Business through Financial Information: Business Advocate Perspective**

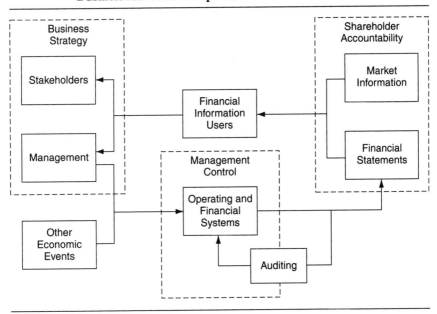

In a Business Advocate environment, financial information provides the thread that ties the firm's business strategy to shareholder accountability through the firm's management control system.

As we can see from Figure I.2, a gap exists between the worlds of business strategy and shareholder accountability. This gap is filled by people, financial information users. Of all the possible financial information users who may exist in the business environment, we identify most closely with the managers who need to know how to bridge the gap between business strategy and shareholder accountability.

The *business strategy* component of the framework emphasizes the interrelationships between managers and stakeholders in the firm. *Stakeholders* include customers, suppliers, employees, shareholders, creditors, taxing authorities, regulators, and the communities where the firm's operations are located. As we shall see throughout this book, business strategy begins with the customers and ends with the shareholders. Customers provide the primary source of financing for any business, while shareholders own the business and expect a return on their investment. Management is responsible for incorporating the needs of the other stakeholders into an effective business strategy without losing sight of the needs of both customers and shareholders. In firms such as Wal-Mart and SRC, keeping employees informed about the performance of the business is a key part of management's overall strategy.

Other economic events are changes in the broader environment, which, although not the result of conscious business strategy, affect the financial performance of the firm (e.g., floods, earthquakes, prolonged economic recession). Whether managers and other stakeholders in the firm like it or not, the effects of economic events beyond the control of the firm must be included in the financial control system.

The *management control* component of the framework represents the point where information about all of the economic events affecting the firm enters into the firm's operating and financial control systems. In this book, we are concerned primarily with the part of the management control system that generates the information contained in the firm's financial statements.

Auditing is seen as part of a feedback loop that ensures that financial information is reported in accordance with generally accepted accounting principles (GAAP). The penalties for violating GAAP (a qualified opinion or a disclaimer of opinion) are typically so severe that managers are more likely to play the game according to the rules.

The *shareholder accountability* component of the framework emphasizes that financial statements provide a foundation for assessing management's accountability to the firm's shareholders. However, in a market economy, shareholder accountability does not end with the financial statements. Financial statements provide a starting point for assessing management's performance.

As we can see, shareholder accountability also includes the market information about the firm's financial performance that does not flow through the firm's management control system. Information about stock prices, dividend yields, interest rates, and so on, along with analyst reports and economic forecasts, are all factored into the assessment process.

Based on our experiences working with managers, we know that it does not take much to become overwhelmed by all of the information found in the financial statements and available from the marketplace. In filling the gap between shareholder accountability and business strategy, we have found that managers need a way of getting their arms around the information, so they can put it to good use.

STORYTELLING AND MODEL BUILDING

This book is about helping managers tell a story about the financial performance of their firm. In order to tell a convincing story, managers need to have some idea of what users of financial information consider to be important performance indicators, and they need to know how their actions affect those performance indicators.

In helping managers develop this storytelling capability, we have found it useful to begin by learning to tell a story about the past performance of a single firm that virtually everyone knows and considers to be highly successful. Over the past several years, we have used Wal-Mart to show managers how to link business strategy to shareholder accountability through financial information. Information about Wal-Mart's financial performance during the 1990s provides the basis for integrating all of the material presented in this book into a single comprehensive management framework.

Our ultimate goal is to help managers tell a similar story about the financial performance of their own firm, a story that can be told to and shared with other members of their management team. In working your way through Chapters 1 through 12, we recommend that you apply these financial statement analysis techniques to your own firm.

ORGANIZATION OF *THE MANAGER'S GUIDE*

This book is organized into two parts. Part One, "Financial Statements and Business Strategy," begins the process of understanding the business through financial information by focusing on the profitability relationships found in the firm's balance sheet and income statement. Our first business strategy model, the Strategic Profit Model (SPM) is used to structure the information found in these two financial statements into a more visually oriented communications framework. As discussed in this part, the SPM is based on the logic underlying the DuPont model, which was first developed and introduced as a major management innovation in the early 1900s. All of the information contained in the balance sheet and income statement is discussed in terms of the margin management, asset management, and financial management concepts embedded within the logic of the SPM.

After using the SPM to understand the relationship between business strategy and profitability, a second business strategy model is introduced—that is, the Strategic Financing Model (SFM). The SFM is used to explore the interrelationships between the firm's long-term investment needs and sources of long-term debt and equity financing.

Profitable firms can get themselves into financial trouble if they do not develop a long-term financing and investment strategy to support their overall business plan. In this discussion, we also address the charge that managers sacrifice the long-run future of the firms in their pursuit of short-term performance measures.

Any discussion of the financial performance of a firm cannot ignore the question of whether management has created value on behalf of the shareholders. In Part Two, "Market Valuation and Business Strategy," we look at the market valuation process in terms of the investors' expectations about interest rates and required returns on investments in common stock. In this part, we show how "time value of money" concepts are applied to the firm's actual and expected future cash flows to determine a current market value for the firm.

After showing how market information and a multi-year time horizon are factored into the market valuation process, we revisit the SPM and extend that model to include market-based performance measures. The SPM, as extended, provides a comprehensive framework for integrating all of the firm- and market-based performance measures into a comprehensive management performance evaluation system.

In Chapter 1, we begin our journey by examining Wal-Mart's financial statements and introducing our first business strategy model, the Strategic Profit Model.

NOTES

1. Sam Walton and John Huey, *Sam Walton, Made in America: My Story* (New York: Doubleday, 1992), 247.
2. J. Stock, *The Great Game of Business* (New York: Currency Doubleday, 1994), 71.
3. *Ibid.,* p. xv.
4. The Business Advocate and Corporate Police profiles have been developed from a twenty-nine-question research instrument, the Management Communication and Control Systems Diagnostic Questionnaire (DQ9). More than 3,500 managers participating in the research studies have completed the diagnostic questionnaire. For more information, please see www.mamag. com/strategicfinance/2000/06h.htm or www.mamag.com/strategicfinance/ 1999/11i.htm for other articles.

PART ONE

Financial Statements and Business Strategy

CHAPTER 1

Financial Statements and Business Strategy

The amount of information available to anyone about publicly held U.S. corporations is staggering. Any one of us can contact the investor relations department at one of these firms and receive a copy of the annual report to shareholders, a proxy statement, and annual and quarterly filings with the Securities and Exchange Commission (SEC). We can also obtain comparative information about hundreds of companies through business periodicals (*BusinessWeek, Fortune, Forbes,* etc.) and investment advisory services (*Moody's, Standard & Poor's, Value Line,* etc.). And if this type of information access were not enough, we can go to our firm's World Wide Web site and obtain even more information instantaneously. If we are not careful, we can drown in a sea of financial information.

For many managers, their own firm's annual report to shareholders contains more information than they know what to do with. They do not need more information to become more confused. To a certain extent, their financial statements are about as intelligible as the optical illusion presented in Figure 1.1. On first glance all they see is a black-and-white inkblot, with the largest concentration of black appearing on the left side of the image. When asked to identify what they see, they think we are pulling their legs.

We typically respond by saying that they are looking at an animal, with the head appearing on the left side of the image. Given this hint, a few managers will begin to see the shape of an animal emerge from the inkblot. For those managers who still have not seen the animal, we provide a second hint. The animal makes the following sound: "moo." With

Figure 1.1   Inkblot Test

Source: © 1998 Imaginary Studio.

that hint and a little coaching from their colleagues, more managers begin to see the cow.

For those managers who have trouble seeing what the rest of us see, we outline the shape of the cow. The cow's head appears on your left, with its body (excluding the hindquarters) extending to the right. The white triangle (in the shape of Africa) is on the cow's head. The cow's left ear extends out of the "northeast coast" of Africa. The cow's right ear is black and can be found just "west" of Africa. The small white dot off of the "southeast coast" of Africa represents the cow's left eye. The white spot somewhat below Africa is on the cow's nose. The very large black spot due east of the cow's face is the cow's left side.

After everyone sees the cow, we point out that most people cannot *not* see the cow in the future. After not seeing the image for some time, it may take someone a few seconds to refocus and see the cow, but he or she knows the cow is there.

To a certain extent, helping managers understand the business through financial statements is like going on this kind of cow hunt. Initially, the financial statements look like our optical illusion. Half of the battle involves convincing managers that the financial statements actually do contain valuable information. The other half of the battle involves helping them see the valuable information contained in those statements.

FINANCIAL STATEMENTS

Our starting point for helping managers understand the business through financial information is the balance sheet and income statement. Although firms are required to include a statement of cash flows and a statement of shareholders' equity in their annual reports to shareholders, the key financial performance indicators that we will use to begin understanding the business are typically found in the balance sheet and income statement.

Throughout this book, we will use Wal-Mart's balance sheets and income statements as our touchstone for understanding the business.

- *Balance sheet.* The balance sheet lists all of the assets, liabilities, and shareholders' (owners') equity in the company at the end of the year or at the end of a shorter reporting period. *Assets* represent the economic resources controlled by the company. *Liabilities* and *shareholders' equity* represent the claims on the company's assets by creditors (liabilities) and owners (shareholders' equity).
- *Income statement.* The income statement lists all of the company's revenues, expenses, and net income for the year or shorter reporting period (quarter or month). The net income (or net loss) tells us how well management performed on behalf of the shareholders during the year.

We could have used the income statements and balance sheets for any company to illustrate how managers can analyze a company's financial statements, but we chose Wal-Mart because this company is one of those American success stories and has held the public's attention ever since going public in 1970. By focusing on a single firm such as Wal-Mart to introduce the concepts and models presented in this book, we will be able to show how different aspects of the business may be integrated into a comprehensive framework for understanding the entire business.[1]

Figure 1.2 presents Wal-Mart's balance sheets for the fiscal years ended January 31, 1990 and 2000.[2]

Figure 1.2 Wal-Mart Balance Sheets (for the Fiscal Years Ended January 31, 1990 and 2000 – Amounts in Millions)

	1990	2000
Assets		
Current Assets		
Cash and Equivalents	$13	$1,856
Receivables	$156	$1,341
Inventory	$4,428	$19,793
Other	116	$1,366
Total Current Assets	$4,713	$24,356
Productive Assets		
Property, Plant, and Equipment	$4,402	$45,348
Accumulated Depreciation	($972)	($9,379)
Net Productive Assets	$3,430	$35,969
Other Assets	$55	$10,024
Total	$8,198	$70,349
Liabilities and Shareholders' Equity		
Liabilities		
Current Liabilities		
Accounts Payable	$1,827	$13,105
Current Debt Due	$24	$2,085
Other	$995	$10,613
Total Current Liabilities	$2,846	$25,803
Long-Term Liabilities		
Long-Term Debt	$185	$13,672
Long-Term Lease Obligations	$1,087	$3,002
Deferred Income Taxes and Other	$115	$759
Minority Interest	$0	$1,279
Total Long-Term Liabilities	$1,387	$18,712
Total Liabilities	$4,233	$44,515
Shareholders' Equity		
Common Stock	$237	$1,160
Retained Earnings	$3,728	$25,129
Other Equity Adjustments	$0	($455)
Total Shareholders' Equity	$3,965	$25,834
Total	$8,198	$70,349

Figure 1.3 presents Wal-Mart's statements of income and retained earnings for the fiscal years ended January 31, 1990 and 2000.[3] These statements represent our first financial optical illusion.

Figure 1.3   Wal-Mart Statements of Income and Retained Earnings (for the Fiscal Years Ended January 31, 1990 and 2000 – Amounts in Millions)

	1990	2000
Net Sales	$25,985	$166,809
Total Revenue	$25,985	$166,809
Costs and Expenses		
Cost of Sales	$20,070	$129,664
Operating Expenses	$4,070	$27,040
Interest Expense	$138	$1,022
Other Expense (Income)	$0	$368
Total Costs and Expenses	$24,278	$158,904
Income before Income Taxes	$1,707	$8,715
Provision for Income Taxes		
Current Portion	$609	$3,476
Deferred Portion	$23	($138)
Total Provision	$632	$3,338
Net Income	$1,075	$5,377
Dividends	($124)	($890)
Adjustments to Retained Earnings	$0	($99)
Retained Earnings, Beginning Balance	$2,777	$20,741
Retained Earnings, Ending Balance	$3,728	$25,129

In virtually every annual report sent to shareholders, the current year's financial performance is compared to the previous year's performance (on the balance sheet) and previous two years' financial performance (on the income statement). As we can see from Figures 1.2 and 1.3, we have chosen to extend the time horizon to ten years by using the financial statements for the fiscal years ended January 31, 1990 and 2000. With a ten-year gap between statements, we can look at both the short- and long-term aspects of running a business such as Wal-Mart.

In order to develop a better understanding of what the words and numbers included in the financial statements mean, we will focus on how Wal-Mart performed for the fiscal year ended January 31, 1990, and for the fiscal year ended January 31, 2000. In the process of learning how to analyze individual balance sheets and income statements, we will also begin to look at how management grew the business between 1990 and 2000. As we shall see in Part Two of this book, investors reward companies for profitable growth by bidding up the price of the company's common stock.

BEGINNING THE ANALYSIS

The definitions of a balance sheet and income statement presented earlier provide accurate descriptions of those financial statements. However, these definitions do not emphasize a management perspective. In order to help managers understand a business through financial information, we have found it helpful to ground the balance sheet and income statement in the underlying economics of the business.

We begin the financial statement analysis process from a management perspective by stressing the following three points:

▶────────────────────────────────

Point 1.   The balance sheet presents the financial relationships between the resources (assets) under management's control and management's responsibility to creditors (liabilities) and owners (shareholders' equity).

────────────────────────────────◀

In trying to understand the business through the balance sheet, we alternate between looking at a firm in terms of the *things* owned or controlled by the firm (assets, liabilities, and shareholders' equity) and economic *relationships* between the firm (as represented by management and employees) and external parties (suppliers, customers, creditors, taxing authorities, and shareholders).

▶────────────────────────────────

Point 2.   The income statement shows the amount of net income (assets−liabilities) that management has earned on the owners' behalf during the year.

────────────────────────────────◀

8

The net income reported in the income statement represents management's contribution to the overall success of the firm on behalf of the shareholders. All things considered, shareholders would prefer management to generate a higher rather than a lower net income.[4]

Point 3.   By linking the financial performance measures in the income statement to the balance sheet, we can get a pretty good handle on how well management has performed on behalf of the shareholders. The balance sheet and income statement may be meaningfully integrated through the concept of return on shareholders' equity (return on equity, or ROE).

Return on equity (ROE) is calculated by dividing net income by shareholders' equity. We use the concept of ROE to help managers (1) develop a basic understanding of how all aspects of the firm's business operations may be integrated into a simple yet comprehensive performance measurement system and (2) link the financial performance of a specific firm to the broader global capital markets for debt and equity financing.

We will begin the process of understanding the business through financial information by taking a closer look at the balance sheet (Point 1), then move on to the income statement (Point 2), and then integrate the balance sheet and income statement through the concept of ROE (Point 3).

Balance Sheets

The balance sheet (also referred to as a statement of financial position) provides a snapshot of where the firm stands at a particular point in time. The relationship between the resources under management control and the firm's obligations to creditors and shareholders is expressed in the following financial control equation:

Assets = Liabilities + Shareholders' Equity

9

In exchange for the right to determine how the firm's resources are used, management promises to be responsible to the creditors and shareholders who have provided the money needed to run the business. That is,

$$\begin{aligned} \text{Resources} &= \text{Obligations} \\ \text{Rights} &= \text{Responsibilities} \end{aligned}$$

In the case of creditors such as lenders, management promises to pay interest and repay principal on the amounts borrowed. In the case of suppliers and employees, management promises to pay amounts owed for goods and services received by the firm. In the case of shareholders, management promises to be held accountable for earning a return on the shareholders' investment.

For the fiscal years ended 1990 and 2000, Wal-Mart's balance sheet equations appear as

$$\begin{aligned} \text{Assets} &= \text{Liabilities} + \text{Shareholders' Equity} \\ 1990\text{: } \$\,8.198B &= \$\,4.233B + \$\,3.965B \\ 2000\text{: } \$70.349B &= \$44.515B + \$25.834B \end{aligned}$$

At the end of 1990, management controlled $8.2 billion of assets on behalf of creditors and shareholders. By the end of 2000, the assets under management control increased to $70.3 billion. Between 1990 and 2000, assets under management control increased by 509%, a 24.0% compound annual growth rate. During that same period of time, liabilities increased at a 26.5% compound annual growth rate, and shareholders' equity increased at a 20.6% growth rate. (See Appendix 1A for a discussion of how compound annual growth rates are computed.)

As seen, even the limited amount of information contained in a firm's balance sheet equations can allow us to make a number of descriptive (and most likely boring) statements about a firm. Fortunately, the importance of financial information lies in its use in the performance evaluation process, not merely in its use in describing the business.

The only trouble with trying to understand the business from two balance sheets is that we know very little about the economic journey management took to get from point A (1990) to point B (2000). Without additional information, it is hard to tell from the balance sheets whether management has been a success or a failure over the past ten years. That's where the income statements come into play.

Income Statements

The amounts reported in the firm's balance sheets do not just happen; they result from management's formulating and implementing a business strategy and then competing against other firms in the global marketplace. The financial success or failure of that business strategy is captured in the income statement.

While the balance sheet provides us with a snapshot of the firm at a particular point in time, the income statement tells us how well management has performed on behalf of the shareholders during the year. Like the balance sheet, the relationships captured in an income statement are best summarized in the following financial control equations:

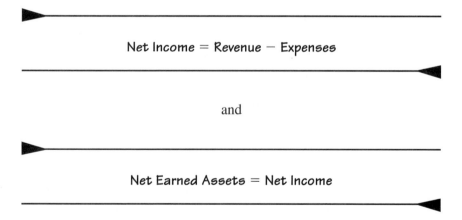

Net Income = Revenue − Expenses

and

Net Earned Assets = Net Income

Given the standard format of a typical income statement, many managers are somewhat familiar with the first financial control equation, but not the second equation. However, it is the second equation that puts teeth into the first equation. Net income equals the amount of net assets (economic resources) that management earned on behalf of the shareholders during the year.

For the fiscal years ended 1990 and 2000, Wal-Mart's income statement equations were:

▶

$$
\begin{aligned}
\text{Net Income} &= \text{Revenue} &- \text{Expenses} \\
1990: \$1.075B &= \$25.985B &- \$24.910B \\
2000: \$5.377B &= \$166.809B &- \$161.432B
\end{aligned}
$$

◀

In 1990, Wal-Mart generated $26.0 billion in revenue and incurred $24.9 billion in expenses. The net income of $1.1 billion represents the increase in net assets (assets − liabilities) *earned* by management on behalf of the shareholders during the year. In 2000, Wal-Mart generated $166.8 billion in revenue while incurring $161.4 billion in expenses. In 2000, management *earned* $5.4 billion in net assets on behalf of the shareholders.

Generating net assets through the earnings process is the name of the management performance game. Over these ten years, Wal-Mart's net income increased at a 17.5% compound annual growth rate, a feat very few firms, especially large firms, have been able to match in recent history.

As impressive as Wal-Mart's increase in net income was during this period, that growth did not keep up with the growth in revenue and expenses. Between 1990 and 2000, revenue (net sales) grew at a 20.4% compound rate, while expenses grew at a 20.5% compound rate. When expenses grow at a faster rate than revenue, net income is bound to suffer. A difference of a mere 0.1% in compound annual growth rates for revenue and expenses had a very dramatic impact on Wal-Mart's net income. Over this ten-year period, the 0.1 percentage point difference had a cumulative effect of 2.9 percentage point difference between the growth in revenue (20.4%) and the growth in net income (17.5%).[5] In Wal-Mart's case, 2.9 percentage points translates into a difference of billions of dollars in net income.

Like our analysis of the balance sheet equation, the analysis of the income statement equation can provide some interesting initial insights into the business (if you are a financial type who likes numbers). Unfortunately, most managers with operating responsibilities are still looking for the cow. They need a more tangible or visceral way of grasping the significance of numbers.

That's where the ROE calculation comes into play. It represents a simple, straightforward point of reference for making our way through the sea of words and numbers found in balance sheets and income statements.

Understanding the Business Through the Concept of ROE

We use the concept of ROE to help managers understand a firm's overall business strategy in terms of the information found in income statements and balance sheets. By dividing net income (taken from the income statement) by shareholders' equity (taken from the balance sheet), we can drive a stake into the ground and begin to develop a more in-depth understanding of the business.

The ROE calculation that links the income statement to the balance sheet is as follows:

Return on Equity (ROE) = Net Income ÷ Shareholders' Equity

Wal-Mart's ROEs for the fiscal years ended 1990 and 2000 were as follows:

	ROE		Net Income		Shareholders' Equity
	ROE	=	Net Income	÷	Shareholders' Equity
1990:	27.1%	=	$ 1.075B	÷	$ 3.965B
2000:	20.8%	=	$5.377B	÷	$25.834B

When asked to explain ROE in their own words, many managers fall into the trap of trying to describe how ROE is calculated rather than explaining what the concept might mean in terms of understanding the business. A typical first attempt to explain ROE goes something like this:

ROE is the percentage relationship you get when you divide net income by shareholders' equity.

This explanation is about as interesting as our description of the compound growth rates associated with Wal-Mart's balance sheet and income statement equations.

Contrast this initial attempt to explain ROE with an explanation that is a little more action-oriented.

In 1990, Wal-Mart generated 27.1¢ in profit for every $1 of shareholders' equity.

In 2000, Wal-Mart generated 20.8¢ in profit for every $1 of shareholders' equity.

If management had been able to maintain a 27.1¢ ROE in 2000, Wal-Mart would have generated an additional $1.624 billion in net income on shareholders' equity of $25.834 billion.

Even at this early stage of learning how to understand the business through financial information, it only seems natural to wonder why Wal-Mart's ROE has fallen by 6.3¢ for every $1 of shareholders' equity. Given this drop in ROE, it would probably not be surprising to learn that Wal-Mart's common stock has not performed very well in recent years, as it did during the years when the company was growing the business at a faster rate and generating higher ROEs.[6]

In the March 27, 2000, issue of *BusinessWeek,* where the ROEs of the S&P 500 companies were reported, we can see how Wal-Mart's ROE stacks up against the ROEs of other highly visible companies. Relative to the market, we can begin to ask whether an ROE of 20.8% is good or bad. Is Wal-Mart among the leaders or back in the middle of the pack? Selected ROEs of other firms included in the 1999 Discount and Fashion Retailing Industry are presented in the following table. Given this information, we can begin to get a sense of how well Wal-Mart stacks up against other top firms and competitors in the retail business.[7]

Company	ROE
Industry Average	17.8%
GAP	58.8%
Dollar General	23.6%
Wal-Mart	21.6%[8]
Target	21.2%
Home Depot	18.8%
Kohl's	16.5%
Staples	15.8%
Costco	14.6%
Lowe's	14.3%

As we can see, Wal-Mart is generating an ROE somewhat above the 17.8% average ROE for the industry but substantially below competitors such as GAP (58.8%) and Dollar General (23.6%).

In Part Two, we will look *outward* and compare Wal-Mart's financial performance with other publicly traded companies. We will look at the relationship between a firm's ROE and its stock price. For the remainder of Part One, we will look *internally* to see how the concept of ROE can be used to develop a comprehensive understanding of a firm's business operations. In Part Two, we will extend our analysis to develop a comprehensive understanding of a firm's long-term financing and investment activities.

In keeping with our optical illusion analogy, using a simple calculation of ROE (net income ÷ shareholders' equity) might be equivalent to describing the location of the cow's ears. Describing the location of the ears is a step in the right direction, but it does not provide a complete outline of the cow's head and body.

The Strategic Profit Model (SPM) is the communications tool we use to help managers see how all of the firm's economic activity may be interrelated through the concept of ROE. If ROE represents the firm as a whole, then the SPM helps everyone to see the whole in terms of its component parts. We use the quick overview of the SPM (discussed in the following section) to flesh out a complete outline of a firm's financial (cash?) cow.

By breaking ROE into its component parts, managers can begin to see how they can influence the overall profitability of their firms. They begin to see where they can make immediate contributions in their areas of responsibility. They also begin to see how they can have a greater impact by coordinating their efforts with managers in other functional areas or other lines of business.

STRATEGIC PROFIT MODEL: QUICK OVERVIEW

Throughout this book, we will use terms such as *quick overview, insight, visualize,* and *as we shall see* to describe the process of understanding the business through financial information. Our emphasis on seeing and visualizing can be traced back to the early years of the twentieth century and is captured by the management philosophy underlying DuPont's executive charting system:

Since 1919, the DuPont Company has used a chart system for appraising performance. The charts are designed to present, in readily

15

understandable *visual* form the financial results of each of the company's industrial departments and of the company as a whole.

In the use of this formula to bring results before the Executive Committee, the presentation is not based on a step-by-step build up to the ultimate objective of Return on Investment. Instead, the end result is presented first and thereafter the important elements that contribute to it. By doing so, as the chart presentation unfolds, the viewers' attention may be focused clearly on those underlying factors that are responsible for any fluctuation in this end result.

The charts themselves *do not* utilize narrative explanation. There is no opportunity for one reviewing the figures to be bogged down under the weight of particular words or phrases that might be chosen to explain a given development.

It is comparatively easy *to hold the attention* of an entire group to one item at the same moment.

A given format is adhered to until it becomes clear that a change would make a substantial improvement. *Frequent changes are avoided.*[9]

As we shall see, the SPM is the charting tool we use to show how all of the elements found in the balance sheet and income statement contribute to the ROE. We always begin with the whole and then break down that whole into its component parts. If the whole is ROE, then its component parts consist of

- Profit margin
- Asset turnover
- Return on assets
- Financial leverage

We can begin to see how the parts fit into an integrated whole using just four elements taken from the income statement and balance sheet:

1. Net sales
2. Net income
3. Total assets
4. Shareholders' equity

In combination, these four elements will allow us to complete an outline of Wal-Mart's financial performance for 1990 and 2000 centered on the concept of ROE. The four elements we will use to prepare a quick overview of Wal-Mart's financial performance are

Net sales. The amount of customer financing generated through the sales of the firm's goods and services.

Net income. The amount of net assets generated by management on behalf of the shareholders after covering all expenses incurred during the year.

Total assets. The amount of resources under management control at year-end used to generate a return on the shareholders' behalf.

Shareholders' equity. The amount of money paid-in by the shareholders and the amount earned by management on the shareholders' behalf and retained in the business.

The net sales and net income amounts (in millions) presented in the following table come from Wal-Mart's 1990 and 2000 income statements (Figure 1.3), and the total asset and shareholders' equity amounts (in millions) come from Wal-Mart's 1990 and 2000 balance sheets (Figure 1.2). Taken together, these four elements provide the foundation for taking a more in-depth look at how a firm's business strategy is linked to shareholder accountability through the financial statements.

Elements	1990	2000
Net Sales	$25,985	$166,809
Net Income	$1,075	$5,377
Total Assets	$8,198	$70,349
Shareholders' Equity	$3,965	$25,834

Figure 1.4 presents a quick overview of Wal-Mart's SPM for 1990 and 2000 based on the net sales, net income, total assets, and shareholders' equity reported in the financial statements for those years. After anchoring our discussion with the ROE percentages reported on the left side of the model, we will work our way through the SPM, beginning in the upper right-hand corner.

Figure 1.4 Wal-Mart Strategic Profit Model: Quick Overview (for the Fiscal Years Ended January 31, 1990 and 2000—Amounts in Millions)

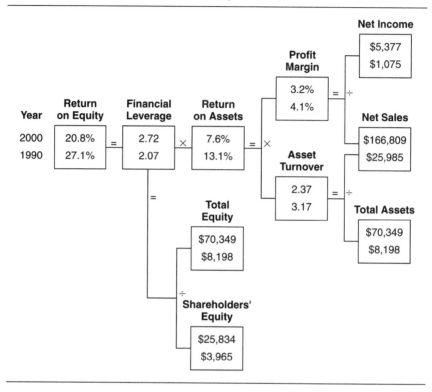

As stated previously, in dollars ($) and cents (¢) terms,

In 1990, Wal-Mart generated 27.1¢ in profit on every $1 of shareholders' equity; in 2000, Wal-Mart generated 20.8¢.

In the process of growing the business over this ten-year period, Wal-Mart experienced a 6.3¢ drop in ROE. With the quick overview provided by the SPM, we can now take a more in-depth look at the individual components contributing to Wal-Mart's ROE in 1990 and 2000 and the 6.3¢ drop.

Profit Margin

The concept of profit margin establishes the relationship between customers (the principal source of financing for any firm) and the net income (net earned assets) remaining after all expenses and other charges for the period have been taken into consideration.

As we can see from Figure 1.4, the profit margin is calculated by dividing net income by the net sales for the period.

▶

In 1990, Wal-Mart earned 4.1¢ in profit for every $1 of net sales; in 2000, Wal-Mart earned 3.2¢ in profit.

◀

Between 1990 and 2000, Wal-Mart experienced pressure on its margins. In other words, in pursuing its overall business strategy, Wal-Mart was not able to maintain the 4.1¢ of profit margin on every $1 of net sales.

▶

The 0.9¢ decline in profit margin translates into $1.501 billion of net income (0.9¢ × $166.809 billion in net sales).

◀

In Chapter 2, we will expand the profit margin component of the SPM to see how margin management fits into Wal-Mart's overall business strategy. For the time being, we will leave you with one of Sam Walton's ten rules for running a successful company.

RULE 9: CONTROL your expenses better than your competition. This is where you can always find the competitive advantage. For twenty-five years running—long before Wal-Mart was known as the nation's largest retailer—we ranked number one in our industry for the lowest ratio of expenses to sales. You can make a lot of different mistakes and still recover if you run an efficient operation. Or you can be brilliant and still go out of business if you're too inefficient.[10]

If Wal-Mart is still the most efficient retailer in the business, why has their profit margin fallen over the past ten years?

Asset Turnover

The concept of asset turnover establishes the relationship between the customer as the principal source of financing (net sales) and the economic resources (assets) utilized to run the business.

As we can see from Figure 1.4, asset turnover is calculated by dividing net sales by total assets.

▶──

In 1990, Wal-Mart generated $3.17 in revenue for every $1 of total assets; in 2000, Wal-Mart generated $2.37.

──◀

All things considered, management (and shareholders) would prefer to generate more dollars in net sales per $1 of assets than less. The greater the asset turnover, the greater the amount of customer financing management has generated with a given amount of assets. Effective managers are constantly attempting to get the most bang for their investment buck, to do more with less, to increase their turns. Within the context of the SPM, the asset turnover ratio is just one way of visualizing what doing more with less might mean.

In Wal-Mart's case, the asset turnover actually decreased between 1990 and 2000. For every $1 of assets, Wal-Mart generated 80¢ less in net sales in 2000 than it generated in 1990. The 80¢ decline in asset turnover translates into $56.297 billion in net sales on the 2000 asset base of $70.349 billion (80¢ × $70.349B in assets). Stated differently, if Wal-Mart had maintained a $3.17 asset turnover in 2000, it would have required only $52.621 billion in assets ($166.809B ÷ $3.17). The difference of $17.278 billion ($70.349B − $52.621B = $17.728B) represents money that shareholders would not have had to tie up in the business if management had been able to maintain the $3.17 turnover.

In Chapter 3, we will expand the asset turnover component of the SPM to see how asset management fits into Wal-Mart's overall business strategy. As we shall see, Wal-Mart's overall business strategy differs with respect to the utilization of current assets and productive assets. Wal-Mart's business strategy (as reflected in the financial performance measures) represents a combination of efficient operations and global expansion.

Return on Assets

The concept of return on assets (ROA) establishes the relationship between the net income earned by management and the total assets under management control. If we were only concerned with making the ROA calculation as efficient as possible, we would divide net income by total assets and omit any intermediate steps.

▶

$$ROA = Net\ Income \div Total\ Assets$$

◀

The trouble with efficient calculations is that they can get in the way of effective communications. In Figure 1.4, we can see how ROA is the product of the combination of profit margin and asset turnover.

▶

In 1990, Wal-Mart earned 13.1¢ in profit for every $1 of total assets; in 2000, Wal-Mart earned 7.6¢.

◀

In terms of the imagery presented in Figure 1.4, management can increase ROA by taking a "northern route" and improving its profit margin and/or by taking a "southern route" by increasing asset turnover and utilizing assets more efficiently. A comprehensive management strategy would focus on the most effective way to increase net sales while keeping expenses down and controlling the growth of the asset base.

In Wal-Mart's case, with both profit margin and asset turnover declining between 1990 and 2000, ROA had nowhere to go but down. As management was growing the business, ROA suffered a 5.5¢ decline. If management could have maintained the 13.1% ROA achieved in 1990, Wal-Mart would have generated an additional $3.869 billion in net income on the $70.349 billion asset base under management control in 2000 (5.5¢ × $70.349B).[11]

At this point in our journey toward using the SPM to understand the business, it might be a little more enjoyable if we learn to sing the Strategic Profit Model song. The first three verses of Wal-Mart's 2000 song go like this:

For every $1 of assets, Wal-Mart generated $2.37 in net sales.

For every $1 of net sales, Wal-Mart earned 3.2¢ in profit.

By multiplying the profit margin by the asset turnover, we know that for every $1 of assets, Wal-Mart generated 7.6¢ in profit in 2000.

The 1990 version of Wal-Mart's SPM song was somewhat more joyous and may provide a battle cry for management to improve future versions of the SPM song. The 1990 versions goes like this:

For every $1 of assets, Wal-Mart generated $3.17 in net sales.

For every $1 of net sales, Wal-Mart earned 4.1¢ in profit.

By multiplying the profit margin by the asset turnover, we know that for every $1 of assets, Wal-Mart generated 13.1¢ in profit in 1990.

In Chapter 4, we will return to a discussion of ROA after we have blown up the margin-management and asset-management components of the SPM.

Financial Leverage

The concept of financial leverage establishes the relationship between the total equity (liabilities + shareholders' equity) of the firm and the amount provided by (and earned by management on behalf of) the shareholders.

As we can see from Figure 1.4, financial leverage is calculated by dividing total equity by shareholders' equity.

In 1990, Wal-Mart utilized $2.07 in total equity for every $1 of shareholders' equity; in 2000, Wal-Mart utilized $2.72.

The $1.07 difference between total equity and shareholders' equity in 1990 ($1.72 in 2000) represents Wal-Mart's total liabilities.

Since total equity equals total assets, you could think of financial leverage as the total amount of assets under the control of management relative to the amount of the shareholders' investment in the company.

In 1990, management was responsible for controlling $2.07 in total assets for every $1 of shareholders' equity; in 2000, management was responsible for $2.72.

The "lever" in financial leverage refers to the impact of using someone else's (creditors') money to run the business. In 1990, the $2.07 financial lever turned a 13.1¢ ROA into a 27.1¢ ROE (2.07 × 13.1%). In 2000, a $2.72 lever turned a 7.6¢ ROA into a 20.8¢ ROE. If management had maintained the 1990 level of financial leverage in 2000, Wal-Mart's ROE would have been 15.7¢ (2.07 × 7.6%). By increasing financial leverage, management limited the decline in ROE by 4.1¢ per $1 of shareholders' equity.

In Chapter 5, we will expand the financial-leverage component of the SPM to see how financial management fits into Wal-Mart's overall business strategy. As we shall see, Wal-Mart has been growing the business through a combination of long-term debt and retained earnings. Between 1990 and 2000, Wal-Mart issued very few shares of additional common stock.

Return on Equity: Closing the Loop

After walking through a quick overview of Wal-Mart's SPM, anyone can begin to see the cow hidden in Wal-Mart's financial statements. The quick overview is equivalent to taking a half-day Berlitz course in understanding the business through financial information. We can now order simple meals from the menu and ask for directions to the restroom. "*Donde está el baño?*" Taking care of the basics makes it a lot easier to sit through the afternoon session and feel good about coming back to class the next day.

With a little help, managers are now able to sing (or at least hum to themselves) all of the verses to the SPM song. The 1990 version goes like this:

For every $1 of assets, Wal-Mart generated $3.17 in net sales.

For every $1 of revenue, Wal-Mart earned 4.1¢ in profit.

By multiplying the profit margin by the asset turnover, we know that for every $1 of assets, Wal-Mart generated 13.1¢ in profit.

When we multiply ROA by the $2.07 in total assets management controlled for every $1 of shareholders' equity, we see that Wal-Mart generated 27.1¢ in profit for every $1 of shareholders' equity invested in the business.

The 2000 version of Wal-Mart's SPM song is not quite as joyful, but it goes like this:

For every $1 of assets, Wal-Mart generated $2.37 in net sales.

For every $1 of net sales, Wal-Mart earned 3.2¢ in profit.

By multiplying the profit margin by the asset turnover, we know that for every $1 of assets, Wal-Mart generated 7.6¢ in profit.

When we multiply ROA by the $2.72 in total assets management controlled for every $1 of shareholders' equity, we see that Wal-Mart generated 20.8¢ in profit for every $1 of shareholders' equity invested in the business.

We believe that the summary version of the SPM helps managers begin to see the benefits of opening up the communications process within their own firms. To our way of thinking, the SPM (which helps visualize and humanize the financial communications process) is a key component of a

Business Advocate Model of financial management. If firms want to make everyone aware of the financial implications of their decisions and actions, introducing the SPM throughout the firm would be a good place to start.

When used within a Business Advocate environment, the SPM helps senior management balance the need for individual autonomy and effective control within the firm. Sam Walton quote captures this thought quite nicely:

> We decided a long time ago to share so much information about the company with our associates, rather than keep everything secretive.
>
> We share everything with them: the cost of their goods, the freight costs, the profit margins. We let them see how their store ranks with every other store in the company on a constant, running basis, and we give them incentives to want to win.
>
> We're always trying for that fine balance between autonomy and control.[12]

In the next four chapters, we will take a closer look at the margin management, asset management, ROA, and financial management components of the SPM.

NOTES

1. We have included the financial statements of other major U.S. corporations as case studies in the appendices. The concepts developed in each chapter may be applied to these financial statements to reinforce the learning experience. However, as mentioned in the Introduction, one of the best ways to learn how to understand a business is to apply the concepts to (1) your own firm's financial statements and/or (2) the financial statements of a firm you might be thinking of investing in. Nothing reinforces the learning experience more than self-interest.

2. A number of accounts shown in the balance sheets have been collapsed together to simplify the discussion of key concepts. The operating expenses shown on the income statements include operating, selling, general, and administrative expenses.

3. We refer to the statement of income and retained earnings as simply the income statement to simplify the discussion of key concepts. From a practical perspective, the statement of income and retained earnings provides us with two important pieces of financial information: (1) the amount of dividends

that were declared during the year and (2) the amounts of any charges or credits that were made to retained earnings that bypassed the income statement.

4. Even though some financial advisory services (Standard & Poor's, Moody's, Dun and Bradstreet, etc.) and some business periodicals (*Business Week, Fortune, Forbes,* etc.) exclude some elements of net income in reporting on particular aspects of the business, *each* of these users provides an explanation for making these adjustments. In assessing the profitability of a firm, everyone begins with the amount reported as net income.

5. For these compound growth rates, other income has been and should be excluded from total revenue and included as an offset to the total costs and expenses. More on this point will appear later in the chapter.

6. The market valuation process is discussed more fully in Part Two of this book. For the current discussion, all we want to do is generate interest in learning more about how ROE can help us in understanding the business through financial information.

7. The rankings are based on the total market value of the firm's common stock.

8. The *Business Week* calculations are based on Wal-Mart's financial performance through Fiscal Year 1999.

9. "Executive Committee Control Charts: A Description of the DuPont Chart System for Appraising Operating Performance, " AMA no. 6, 1950.

10. Sam Walton and John Huey, *Sam Walton, Made in America: My Story* (New York: Doubleday, 1992), 248–49.

11. In Wal-Mart's 1996 annual report to shareholders, CEO David Glass stated that ROA was going to play a more significant role in the company's overall business strategy. During 1997 through 2000, Wal-Mart completed a series of major acquisitions.

12. Sam Walton and John Huey, *Sam Walton, Made in America: My Story* (New York: Doubleday, 1992), 227.

APPENDIX 1A: COMPOUND ANNUAL GROWTH RATES

When the current year's financial information is compared with that of the previous year, the percentage increase (or decrease) for the year is determined by dividing the change from one year to the next by the amount reported for the earlier year. For example, Wal-Mart's total assets increased from $49.996 billion at January 31, 1999, to $70.349 billion at January 31, 2000, an increase of $20.353 billion, or 40.7% ($20.353B ÷ $49.996B).

Appendix 1A: Compound Annual Growth Rates

Over the ten-year period January 31, 1990, through January 31, 2000, total assets increased from $8.198 billion to $70.349 billion, an increase of $62.151 billion, or 758%. While this is an accurate description of the total percentage increase, most managers and investors have a hard time relating to a number such as 758%. The increase or decrease in total assets over two or more years is much easier to understand when it is expressed as an annual percentage change or compound annual growth rate (CAGR).

Wal-Mart's 758% increase in total assets translates into a 24.0% CAGR. Expressed in this manner, it becomes quite easy for managers to compare the growth in assets with the growth in other measures of company performance—that is, liabilities, shareholders' equity, sales, net income, and so on. Compound annual growth rates also provide a convenient way for managers to compare themselves against the competition and against other investment opportunities.

Most software spreadsheet packages (i.e., Excel) contain the mathematical formula for computing CAGRs. For example, in Microsoft Excel™, using the "RATE" function, enter the starting amount ($8.198 billion in total assets), the ending amount ($70.349 billion), and the number of periods or years (ten years), and the computer calculates the rate needed to grow the starting amount to equal the ending amount.

The actual year-to-year increase in total assets is compared with the hypothetical increase if total assets increased at a uniform 24.0% per year.

Wal-Mart Total Assets (Amounts in Millions)

Year	Actual	24.0% CAGR*
1990	$8,198	$8,198
1991	$11,389	$10,164
1992	$15,443	$12,601
1993	$20,565	$15,623
1994	$26,441	$19,370
1995	$32,819	$24,015
1996	$37,541	$29,774
1997	$39,604	$36,914
1998	$45,384	$45,767
1999	$49,996	$56,742
2000	$70,349	$70,349

*Compound annual growth rate

In Part One of this book, CAGR calculations will be used to help explain various aspects of Wal-Mart's business strategy. In Part Two, CAGRs will be used to help explain how investors and financial analysts evaluate companies from a capital market perspective.

CHAPTER 2

Strategic Profit Model: Margin Management

The quick overview of the Strategic Profit Model (SPM) presented in Chapter 1 showed how return on shareholders' equity (ROE) can be visualized in terms of its component parts: profit margin, asset turnover, return on assets (ROA), and financial leverage. By exploring the interrelationships among the parts, we can begin to see how each of the components of the SPM must be managed in order for the firm to be a success. As we shall see, success begins with the customer and ends with the shareholders.

The concept of profit margin (net income ÷ net sales) can be brought to life for most managers by talking about what they are doing currently to increase or maintain their firm's profit margin. Or if their firm's profit margin has declined in recent years (like Wal-Mart's), managers can be asked to describe what they are doing to get the profit margin back to past performance levels, or how the new reduced profit margin fits into their firm's current business strategy. In either case, we ask managers to think of the financial numbers in terms of their *actions*. From an action perspective, profit margin becomes the performance indicator that links the customer to the firm's ongoing operations that must be managed on a day-to-day basis.

Firms must meet the customers' needs at a cost that allows them to generate a profit. Customers provide the money the firm needs to cover current expenses and generate a profit on behalf of the owners. How to pursue customer dollars at a profit is where business strategy starts. According to Sam Walton,

Everything we've done since we started Wal-Mart has been devoted to this idea that the customer is our boss. The controversies it has led us into have surprised me, but they've been easy to live with because we have never doubted our philosophy that the customer comes ahead of everything else.[1]

A blow-up of the margin management component of the SPM allows us to see how this emphasis on the customer (net sales) is related to the costs, expenses, and net income reported in the income statement. The income statement is where we go to see if the firm has operated at a profit in the pursuit of customer satisfaction.

Wal-Mart's statements of income and retained earnings for the fiscal years ended January 31, 1990 and 2000, presented in Chapter 1, are represented in Figure 2.1.[2] We will be exploring the interrelationships among the elements found in these income statements with the knowledge that Wal-Mart generated a profit margin (net income ÷ net sales) of 4.1% in 1990 and 3.2% in 2000. **Please note that all numbers in this text have been rounded to one decimal place. Any minor differences in calculations are due to rounding and should not affect any interpretations.**

In 1990, Wal-Mart earned 4.1¢ in profit for every $1 of net sales; in 2000, Wal-Mart earned 3.2¢ in profit.

Given this prior knowledge, we will want to use the margin management component of the SPM to develop a better understanding of Wal-Mart's business operations than are captured in an income statement.

Before taking a more in-depth look at the margin management component of the SPM, we would like to reinforce the substantive meaning of the term *net income*.

Net income equals the increase in net assets (assets – liabilities) earned by management on behalf of the shareholders during the year.

In 1990, management earned $1.075 billion on behalf of the shareholders; in 2000, management earned $5.377 billion.

Figure 2.1 Wal-Mart Statements of Income and Retained Earnings (for the Fiscal Years Ended January 31, 1990 and 2000—Amounts in Millions)

	1990	2000
Net Sales	$25,985	$166,809
Total Revenue	$25,985	$166,809
Costs and Expenses		
Cost of Sales	$20,070	$129,664
Operating Expenses	$4,070	$27,040
Interest Expense	$138	$1,022
Other Expense (Income)	$0	$368
Total Costs and Expenses	$24,278	$158,904
Income before Income Taxes	$1,707	$8,715
Provision for Income Taxes		
Current Portion	$609	$3,476
Deferred Portion	$23	($138)
Total Provision	$632	$3,338
Net Income	$1,075	$5,377
Dividends	($124)	($890)
Adjustments to Retained Earnings	$0	($99)
Retained Earnings, Beginning Balance	$2,777	$20,741
Retained Earnings, Ending Balance	$3,728	$25,129

Between 1990 and 2000, Wal-Mart increased net assets through the earnings process at a 17.5% compound annual growth rate (CAGR).[3]

By taking a closer look at the income statement through the lens of the SPM, we can develop a better understanding of what Wal-Mart actually did to generate those results. The margin management component of the SPM brings the numbers to life in a visual format that makes sense to managers.

Figure 2.2 presents the margin management component of Wal-Mart's SPM using the amounts taken from the 1990 and 2000 income statements.

Figure 2.2   Wal-Mart Strategic Profit Model: Margin Management (For the Fiscal Years Ended January 31, 1990 and 2000—Amounts in Millions)

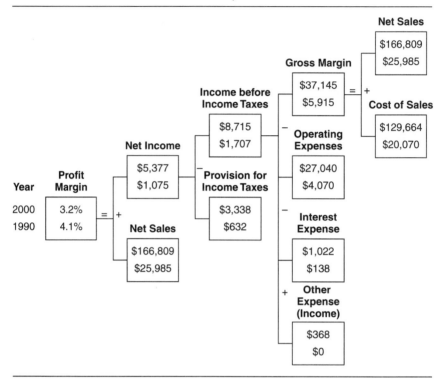

Figure 2.3 helps us make the transition from seeing how each of the components of the SPM affects the firm's overall profitability to thinking about how to improve Wal-Mart's financial performance in the future. Figure 2.3(a) converts the income statement from dollars to a percentage of net sales. The percentages for each line item on the income statement will allow us to talk about management's performance in dollars and cents terms.

Figure 2.3(b) converts the changes between 1990 and 2000 into CAGRs. We will use these CAGRs to talk about how management grew the business between 1990 and 2000.

We begin the discussion of the margin management component of the SPM with net sales (the customer financing for the period) and end with net income and the profit margin. In between net sales and net income, we will find all of the costs, expenses, and other income that have to be managed in order for Wal-Mart to be a success.

Figure 2.3   Wal-Mart Strategic Profit Model: Margin Management

(a) Percentage of Net Sales

	1990	2000	Change
Net Sales	100.0%	100.0%	0.0%
Cost of Sales	77.2%	77.7%	0.5%
Gross Margin	22.8%	22.3%	−0.5%
Operating Expenses	15.7%	16.2%	0.5%
Interest Expense	0.5%	0.6%	0.1%
Other Expense (Income)	0.0%	0.2%	0.2%
Income before Income Taxes	6.5%	5.2%	−1.3%
Income Taxes	2.4%	2.0%	−0.4%
Net Income	4.1%	3.2%	−0.9%

(b) Compound Annual Growth Rates (1990–2000)

Net Sales	20.4%
Cost of Sales	20.5%
Gross Margin	20.2%
Operating Expenses	20.8%
Other Expense (Income)	NM*
Interest Expense	22.2%
Income before Income Taxes	17.7%
Income Taxes	18.1%
Net Income	17.5%

*Not meaningful.

NET SALES

Net sales represents the sale of goods and services to customers in exchange for money and/or promises of money.

Since customers are the primary source of financing for any firm, we anchor the discussion of the margin management component of the SPM to net sales. Net sales equals price (P) times quantity (Q). No matter how you cut it, any firm's business strategy can be understood in terms of price and quantity. Firms such as Wal-Mart grow the business and increase market share by keeping prices below the competition while increasing volume.

COST OF SALES

As the name implies, cost of sales represents the dollar cost of the goods sold to customers. The cost of all goods on hand at the beginning of the period plus all purchases made during the period is either recovered through operations (cost of sales) or remains to be recovered and is reported as inventory on the balance sheet.[4]

Like sales, cost of sales equals price times quantity. In fact, the "Q" for both net sales and cost of sales is the same quantity. As a sale is made to a customer, money flows in and goods and services flow out of the business. As the goods and services flow out the door, the cost of those sales is matched to the revenue generated.

GROSS MARGIN

A firm's gross margin represents the amount of money remaining after recovering the cost of sales made during the period. Gross margin is one of the first performance measures that managers use to monitor the financial health of their firm. If a firm cannot generate an adequate gross margin, it cannot begin to cover its other operating expenses, interest charges, and income taxes, let alone pay dividends and reinvest earnings into the business.

In 1990, Wal-Mart generated a gross margin of $5.915 billion; in 2000, Wal-Mart generated a gross margin of $37.145 billion.

In 1990, Wal-Mart earned a 22.8¢ gross margin for every $1 of net sales; in 2000, Wal-Mart earned a 22.3¢ gross margin.

During that decade, gross margin dollars increased at a 20.2% compound annual growth rate. Over this same period, net sales grew at a 20.4% compound rate, and cost of sales grew at a 20.5% compound rate.

The following statement about Wal-Mart's gross margin provides an interesting beginning for trying to understand a firm's business strategy.

When net sales grows at a different rate than the cost of sales, that difference will be reflected in gross margin dollars.

In Wal-Mart's case, a difference of 0.1 percentage points in the compound growth rates of net sales and cost of sales (20.4% − 20.5%) resulted in a lower growth in gross margin dollars (20.2%). Even though total gross margin dollars have increased, they have not increased as fast as they could have if Wal-Mart had been able to maintain its historical relationship between sales and cost of sales.

The difference in growth rates for net sales and cost of sales is captured in the gross margin percentage. In 1990, Wal-Mart was generating 22.8¢ in gross margin for every $1 of net sales. In 2000, the gross margin had fallen by 0.5¢ for every $1 of net sales (22.8¢ − 22.3¢).

For a firm such as Wal-Mart, a drop in gross margin of 0.5¢ per $1 of net sales translates into $826 million gross margin dollars on sales of $166.8 billion. One half-cent means a lot to Wal-Mart! Even though management is growing the business through increased sales, the current business is nowhere near as profitable as it was in 1990.

Question: Is a decline in gross margin as a percentage of net sales dollars necessarily bad for the shareholders?

Answer: It depends.

At first glance, a 0.5¢ decline would appear to be bad. On the one hand, the 0.5¢ decline translates into $826 million in lower gross margin dollars. On the other hand, it is not clear that net sales would have reached $166.8 billion if Wal-Mart had attempted to maintain a higher gross margin percentage. Wal-Mart's strategy of using low gross margins to generate additional sales started very early in the company's history.

Here's the simple lesson we learned . . . say I bought an item for 80 cents. I found that by pricing it at $1.00 I could sell three times more of it than by pricing it at $1.20. I might make only half the profit (gross margin) per item, but because I was selling three times as many, the overall profit was much greater. Simple enough. But this is really the essence of discounting: by cutting your price, you can boost sales to the point where you earn far more at a cheaper retail price than you would by selling the item at the higher price. In retailer language, you can lower your markup but earn more because you increased volume.[5]

From a management perspective, there might be some benefit to being able to claim that you are the world's largest retailer. However, from the shareholders' perspective, increased size without increased profits is of dubious value. For a decline in gross profit to have no effect on the shareholders, it must be offset by savings or productivity increases in other parts of the business operations. To explore these possibilities, it is necessary to continue our journey toward Wal-Mart's profit margin.

OPERATING EXPENSES

Operating expenses represent all of the costs incurred to operate the distribution centers, sell the goods and services, and run those parts of the business not captured within the gross margin calculation.

In 1990, operating expenses accounted for 15.7¢ of every $1 of net sales; in 2000, operating expenses accounted for 16.2¢ of net sales.

Between 1990 and 2000, operating expenses increased at a 20.8% compound annual growth rate.

Although many people look to Wal-Mart as the exemplar of superior management performance, operating expenses have increased at a faster rate (20.8% CAGR) than net sales (20.4% CAGR). The difference in compound annual growth rates resulted in a 0.5¢ increase in operating expenses as a percentage of net sales.

A major part of Wal-Mart's ability to control operating expenses can be traced directly to Wal-Mart's decision to invest in telecommunications technology to support interactive communications with each store and distribution center. After implementing the new computer-based information system, managers and associates (employees) had low-cost, direct access to the information they needed to run the business more efficiently.

When operating expenses increase at a faster rate than net sales, the difference will be reflected in income before income taxes (operating income).

INTEREST EXPENSE

This expense represents the "charge" Wal-Mart incurs for the use of creditors' money to run the business. Wal-Mart incurs interest charges on its short- and long-term borrowings and capital lease obligations.

In 1990, Wal-Mart incurred an interest expense of 0.5¢ for every $1 of net sales; in 2000, Wal-Mart incurred an interest expense of 0.6¢.

Even though Wal-Mart finances a large part of the growth of the business through debt, interest charges have always remained below 1.0¢ for every $1 of net sales since Wal-Mart went public in 1970.

As discussed more fully under the financial management component of the SPM, Wal-Mart has required a substantial amount of debt to grow the business. However, interest charges do not use up a significant portion of every sales dollar. Sears Roebuck, on the other hand, was spending between 3.0¢ and 4.0¢ per sales dollar on interest expense during the late 1980s and early 1990s. The high interest costs and related high debt levels contributed, in part, to the "downsizing" of Sears that occurred in the mid-1990s.

OTHER EXPENSES (INCOME)

Other expense (income) represent the amount of expenses (income) that Wal-Mart incurs (generates) from nonroutine business transactions. For example, the sale of property or equipment may result in a gain or loss, but this gain or loss is not directly related to Wal-Mart's primary business of selling merchandise to customers. In 1990, no other expenses were reported.

INCOME BEFORE INCOME TAXES

Income before income taxes represents the amount of customer financing remaining after covering all of the costs matched against net sales for the period, other than income taxes. In dollars-and-cents terms, the $1.707 billion in income before income taxes Wal-Mart generated in 1990 represented 6.5¢ of net sales. The $8.715 billion generated in 2000 represented 5.2¢ of net sales.

Every time we create a subtotal for the margin management component of the SPM, we can consolidate our understanding of the firm's basic business strategy. For Wal-Mart, we have been able to make the following observations. Between 1990 and 2000,

- Net sales increased from $25.985 billion to $166.809 billion, a 20.4% CAGR.
- Cost of sales increased from $20.070 billion to $129.664 billion, a 20.5% CAGR. Cost of sales increased from 77.2¢ to 77.7¢ of every dollar of net sales.
- Gross margin dollars increased from $5.915 billion to $37.145 billion, a 20.2% compound annual growth rate. In terms of dollars of net sales, the gross margin declined by 0.5¢, resulting in $826 million less in gross margin dollars on net sales of $166.809 billion.
- Operating expenses increased from $4.070 billion to $27.040 billion, a 20.8% CAGR. In terms of dollars of net sales, operating expenses increased by 0.5¢, resulting in $826 in less income.
- Interest expense remained roughly the same over the ten-year period (a 0.1¢ increase from 0.5¢ to 0.6¢).

PROVISION FOR INCOME TAXES

This expense represents the income tax expense associated with the firm's performance for a given year. The total provision consists of a current portion and a deferred portion. The income taxes actually due and payable as a result of operating during the year represent the current portion. The income tax effects of timing differences between tax reporting and financial reporting represent the deferred portion.[6]

Stated in terms of sales dollars, the impact of tax savings can be quite dramatic.

▶

In 1990, income taxes accounted for 2.4¢ for every $1 of sales; in 2000, income taxes accounted for 2.0¢—a reduction of 0.4¢.

◀

When a change in the law provides a corporation with income tax benefits, management has two basic choices on what to do with the savings: (1) pass the savings along to the shareholders in the form of a higher net income or (2) pass the savings along to the customer in the form of lower prices. Based on our analysis up to this point, we would argue that Wal-Mart chose to pass the tax savings along to its customers as part of its overall strategy to grow the business through increased sales and, in the long run, generate even more net income. The decrease in the effective tax rate of 0.4¢ per $1 of net sales translates into $719 million on $166.809 billion in net sales. It would appear that this 0.4¢ tax savings went a long way toward minimizing the effects of the 0.5¢ decline in gross margin and a 0.5¢ increase in operating expenses.

NET INCOME

Net income summarizes the results of all of the economic activity that resulted in a change in the net assets (assets − liabilities) earned by management on behalf of shareholders during the year.

▶

In 1990, management earned $1.075 billion on behalf of the shareholders; in 2000, management earned $5.377 billion.

◀

After discussing each of the elements making up net income within a margin management perspective, we should have developed a better understanding of Wal-Mart's basic business strategy. At this point, all we need to do is bring the profit margin calculation back into the picture and recouple this analysis to the full SPM.

PROFIT MARGIN

Profit margin represents the amount of each dollar of net sales left over after covering all operating expenses, interest charges, and income taxes for the year.

In 1990, Wal-Mart earned 4.1¢ in profit for every $1 of net sales; in 2000, Wal-Mart earned 3.2¢ in profit.

In Chapter 1, we began the process of understanding the whole (ROE) in terms of its component parts (profit margin, asset turnover, ROA, and financial leverage). In this chapter, we set the whole equal to the profit margin and looked at how each of the parts (sales, cost of sales, etc.) contributed to our understanding of the business.

In Chapter 3, we will set the whole equal to asset turnover to discover how knowledge of each of the parts (cash, receivables, inventory, property, plant and equipment, etc.) adds to our understanding of the business as a whole.

NOTES

1. Sam Walton and John Huey, *Sam Walton, Made in America: My Story* (New York: Doubleday, 1992), 188.
2. The statement of income and change in retained earnings (hereafter, income statement) allows the reader to see all of the elements that have affected the change in retained earnings during the year. Net income increases retained earnings and shareholder dividends decrease retained earnings. In recent years, firms have been showing other adjustments (increases and decreases) to retained earnings that result from the regulatory reporting requirements in force at the time the financial statements are prepared.

3. Growing the firm's asset base by issuing long-term debt and common stock will be explored in Chapters 7 and 8, when we take a look at the firm's long-term *investment* and *financing* activities.

4. In practice, a number of accounting techniques have been devised for determining the amounts to report as cost of sales (recovered cost) and inventory (unrecovered cost). From a management communications perspective, we are more concerned with the relationship among selling prices, unit costs, and sales volume than with the choice of a particular accounting technique.

5. Sam Walton and John Huey, *Sam Walton, Made in America: My Story* (New York: Doubleday, 1992), 25.

6. For a firm such as Wal-Mart, the majority of the timing differences relate to depreciation. Firms write down (depreciate) property, plant, and equipment at a faster rate for tax purposes than they do for financial reporting purposes in order to minimize current income tax payments. The depreciation included in the income statement is based on an asset's useful economic life. The timing differences are reflected in the deferred income tax computation.

CHAPTER 3

Strategic Profit Model: Asset Management

In Chapter 2, we emphasized how the margin management component of the Strategic Profit Model (SPM) helps us see how expenses are related to net sales through the concept of profit margin. In this chapter, we are going to emphasize how the asset management component of the SPM helps us focus on how assets are related to net sales through the concept of asset turnover.

In the quick overview of the SPM presented in Chapter 1, we used the concept of asset turnover to visualize the relationship between the firm's net sales for the year (customer financing) and the total assets under management control at year-end. By visualizing the relationship in this manner, we can begin to think about how assets are deployed to generate a return on the shareholders' investment. Within the context of the quick overview provided by Wal-Mart's SPM, we could see the following:

▶

In 1990, management controlled $8.198 billion in total assets; in 2000, management controlled $70.349 billion.

In 1990, management generated $3.17 in net sales for every $1 of assets; in 2000, management generated $2.37.

◀

Initial reaction: even though Wal-Mart's asset base grew, management generated 80¢ less in net sales for every $1 of assets in 2000 than it did in

1990. On the surface, it would appear that management has become less effective in utilizing the resources under its control.

Has Wal-Mart really become less efficient, or is there some other explanation for the decline? The facts (a 80¢ decline in asset turnover) appear to be inconsistent with Wal-Mart's reputation for operational efficiency. If the asset management component of the SPM is going to be of any value to us, it should help us understand why asset turnover declined by 80¢ per $1 of assets.

As we shall see, the power of any turnover ratio lies in its ability to help us explore the relationship between *time* and *money*.

▶

For every $1 invested in assets during the year, how fast has management been able to convert those dollars invested in assets into dollars of customer financing?

Management can increase the speed (efficiency) by either generating more net sales dollars from a given asset base or reducing the assets needed to generate a given level of net sales.

◀

In a competitive business environment, all firms are facing the same efficiency imperative. Managers are constantly being required to do more with less. And when a firm such as Wal-Mart starts doing less with more, everyone who follows the company wants to know why this is happening and what the implications are for future performance.

Figure 3.1 presents the asset section of Wal-Mart's balance sheets for 1990 and 2000, which we will use to help us understand the business through the asset management component of the SPM. As we can see, total assets consist of current assets, productive assets, and other assets.[1] Each of these categories in turn consists of specific types of assets.

Taken at face value, Figure 3.1 fulfills management's responsibility for reporting on the total assets under its control. Unfortunately, as reported in the balance sheets, the information provides us with virtually no understanding of Wal-Mart's business strategy. A context for understanding the business through financial information is missing.

Figure 3.2 presents that missing context in the form of the asset management component of Wal-Mart's SPM. As we can see, the amounts taken from Wal-Mart's 1990 and 2000 balance sheets have been supplemented

Figure 3.1   Wal-Mart Balance Sheets: Asset Section (for the Fiscal Years Ended January 31, 1990 and 2000—Amounts in Millions)

	1990	2000
Assets		
Current Assets		
Cash and Equivalents	$13	$1,856
Receivables	$156	$1,341
Inventory	$4,428	$19,793
Other	$116	$1,366
Total Current Assets	$4,713	$24,356
Productive Assets		
Property, Plant, and Equipment	$4,402	$45,348
Accumulated Depreciation	($972)	($9,379)
Net Productive Assets	$3,430	$35,969
Other Assets	$55	$10,024
Total	$8,198	$70,349

with the net sales of $25.985 billion for 1990 and $166.809 billion for 2000, taken from Wal-Mart's income statements. Figure 3.2 shows how the elements found in the asset section of the balance sheet are interrelated and linked to net sales through the concept of asset turnover. Asset turnover is an indicator of how well management is using the resources under its control to grow the business.

Figure 3.3(a) presents an analysis of the asset section of both balance sheets in terms of days net sales, and Figure 3.3(b) presents the compound annual growth rates (CAGRs) over this ten-year period. The days net sales analysis and compound annual growth rates will be used to help tell a story about Wal-Mart's asset management strategy.

The discussion of asset management is divided into three parts before returning to a discussion of asset turnover:

1. Current assets
2. Productive assets
3. Other assets

Figure 3.2 **Wal-Mart Strategic Profit Model: Asset Management (for the Fiscal Years Ended January 31, 1990 and 2000— Amounts in Millions)**

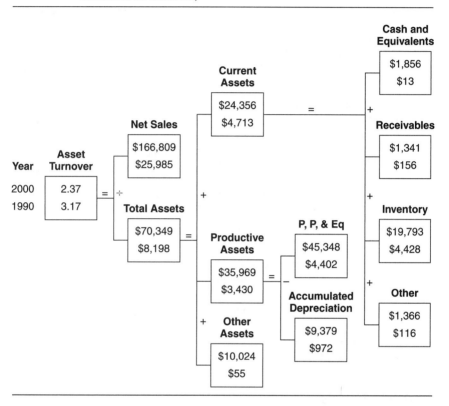

CURRENT ASSETS

Current assets represent resources that will be converted into cash within the firm's operating cycle (usually one year or less). This category includes four financial elements:

1. Cash and equivalents
2. Receivables
3. Inventory
4. Other current assets

Figure 3.3   Wal-Mart Strategic Profit Model: Asset Management

(a) Days Net Sales

	1990	2000	Change
Cash and Equivalent	0.2	4.1	3.9
Receivables	2.2	2.9	0.7
Inventory	62.2	43.3	−18.9
Other Current Assets	1.6	3.0	1.4
Current Assets	66.2	53.3	−12.9
Productive Assets	48.2	78.7	30.5
Other Assets	0.8	21.9	21.2
Days Total Assets	115.2	153.9	38.8

(b) Compound Annual Growth Rates CAGR (1990–2000)

Cash and Equivalents	NM*
Receivables	24.0%
Inventory	16.2%
Other Current Assets	28.0%
Current Assets	17.9%
Productive Assets	26.5%
Other Assets	NM*
Total Assets	24.0%

*Not meaningful. The starting base was effectively zero.

Cash and Equivalents

Cash and equivalents represent money and short-term investments maturing in ninety days or less. Virtually all firms monitor their cash balances and short-term financial investments on a daily basis. On the one hand, all firms want to have enough cash on hand to cover current obligations, to pay for investments in productive assets, and to acquire other businesses. On the other hand, firms do not want to have too much cash on hand. Cash in the bank and cash sitting in a money market fund do not earn a very high return. Firms walk a fine line between holding enough cash to meet normal business needs and not tying up too much cash in noninterest bearing investments.

Firms such as Wal-Mart generate a high level of cash flow from the business but do not let the money sit around in a bank account after it has been generated. Rather than leave the money in the bank, Wal-Mart would prefer to invest in other parts of the business.

In 1990, Wal-Mart had $13 million invested in cash and equivalents; in 2000, Wal-Mart had $1.856 billion invested in cash and equivalents.

Management held more cash to run the business in 2000 than it did in 1990 relative to the net sales being generated each year. Wal-Mart had more days sales tied up in cash in 2000 than it did in 1990.

In 1990, Wal-Mart had 0.2 days net sales tied up in cash and equivalents; in 2000, Wal-Mart had 4.1 days net sales tied up in cash and equivalents.

The days net sales calculations for cash and equivalents (and each of the other current assets) provide a convenient way of seeing how efficiently management is utilizing the resources under its control.

Days net sales for cash and equivalents is computed using the following formula:

Days Net Sales = Cash and ÷ Net Sales × 365 Days
(Cash)   Equivalents

Wal-Mart's days net sales tied up in cash and equivalents for 1990 and 2000 are as follows:

1990: 3.1 Days = $13M ÷ $25.985 × 365 Days
2000: 4.1 Days = $1.856B ÷ $166.809B × 365 Days
Between 1990 and 2000, Wal-Mart increased its investment in cash and equivalents by 3.9 days net sales.

Any time a firm can reduce its investment in a particular asset without having a negative impact on other parts of the business, it becomes more efficient. Of course, firms are willing to accept increases in cash and equivalents. The increase of 3.9 days net sales invested in cash and equivalents translates into a decline in efficiency of $1.782 billion. The decline in efficiency was calculated as described next.

In 2000, one day of sales equaled $457.0 million.

One Day of Sales = Net Sales ÷ 365 Days
2000: $457.0M = $166.809B ÷ 365 Days

By operating the business with 4.1 days net sales invested in cash and equivalents versus the 0.2 days invested in 1990, the 3.9-day increase translates into the decline in efficiency of $1.782 billion.

Efficiency Decrease = Sales per Day × Days Increased
2000: $1.782B = $457.0 Million per Day × 3.9 Days

Between 1990 and 2000, it would appear that Wal-Mart held more cash on a relative basis.

Receivables

Receivables represent the amount of money owed to the business by customers. Since most of Wal-Mart's sales are made for cash, customer receivables do not represent a large part of the ongoing operations of the business. Receivables do, however, represent a significant portion of current assets.

In 1990, Wal-Mart had $156 million invested in receivables; in 2000, Wal-Mart had $1.341 billion invested in receivables.

Since most of Wal-Mart's sales are for cash, the number of days net sales tied up in receivables remained relatively stable (2.2 days in 1990 and 2.9 days in 2000). From an overall asset management perspective, the increase in days net sales tied up in receivables (from 2.2 days to 2.9 days) equates to a $319.6 million efficiency decline. Wal-Mart is extending more credit on a relative and absolute basis.

As the old saying goes, "A bird in the hand is worth two in the bush." Firms extend credit to customers to get their business and to develop long-term relationships. However, once credit is extended, customers are expected to pay within the terms of the agreement. Delays in collecting receivables from customers can translate into delays in paying suppliers and creditors.

Inventory

Inventory represents the unrecovered cost of goods purchased and held for resale. Until sold, all product costs are included in inventory. As discussed in Chapter 2, the cost of sales represents the inventory costs that were recovered through sales during the year.

Like cash management, inventory management plays a big role in Wal-Mart's overall business strategy. As mentioned in Chapter 2, Wal-Mart likes to keep selling prices low and generate more gross margin dollars by keeping inventory turnover high. The more Wal-Mart turns its inventory, the more sales it generates relative to its investment in inventory.

> To a certain extent, the concept of asset turnover is nothing more than an extension of the logic of inventory turnover to all of the assets under management control.

Between 1990 and 2000, Wal-Mart experienced a decrease in its investment in inventory relative to net sales. Wal-Mart invested 43.3 days net sales in inventory to support its retail operations in 2000. In 1990, Wal-Mart was investing 62.2 days net sales in inventory.

Days Net Sales (Inventory) = Inventory ÷ Net Sales × 365 Days
2000: 43.3 Days = \$19.793B ÷ \$166.809B × 365 Days
1990: 62.2 Days = \$4.428B ÷ \$25.985B × 365 Days

If we had chosen to use 1971 instead of 1990 as the base year to compare with 2000, we would have seen an even more dramatic decrease in days net sales tied up in inventory. In 1971, Wal-Mart invested 87.1 days of net sales in inventory. Compared with 1971, Wal-Mart has decreased the days net sales invested in inventory by over a full month (43.8 days, to be more exact).

Although Wal-Mart has increased actual inventories by over \$15.3 billion, the efficiency gains of 18.9 days means that Wal-Mart carried \$8.6 billion less of inventory than if it had continued to perform at 1990 levels. Thus, while Wal-Mart has grown the business over the past three decades, inventory management has been one of Wal-Mart's greatest strengths, providing it with a competitive edge over other retailers.

1990: \$8.632B = \$457.0M per Day × 18.9 Days

Other Current Assets

Other current assets represent prepaid expenses (primarily pre-opening costs for new stores) that will be charged against earnings during the first full month of operations at the new store.

As with cash and equivalents and inventory, Wal-Mart has dramatically reduced its investment in the prepaid expenses associated with opening new stores. Due to the continued expansion, the number of days net sales rose from 1.6 days to 3.0 days, requiring management to restrict an additional \$639.8 million from being used in other parts of the business.

2000: \$639.8M = \$457.0M per Day × 1.4 Days

If more information were provided about other current assets, we could probably be more specific about the source of those savings. If the number of days net sales invested in other current assets had changed by a significant amount, we would probably have been more interested in probing a little deeper into the cause of the change.

Total current assets represent the aggregate investment in cash and equivalents, receivables, inventory, and other current assets. Cash and equivalents, receivables, and inventory are closely identified with the firm's operating cycle and the firm's ongoing business operations.

If we compare Wal-Mart's investment in current assets from 1990 with that of 2000, we can see a net savings of 12.9 days net sales (66.2 days—53.3 days). And at $457.0 million per day, management was running the business with $5.9 billion less of an investment in current assets in 2000, as compared with 1990 performance levels.

2000: $5.899B = $457.0M per Day × 12.9 Days

As Wal-Mart has been growing the business, it has become much more efficient in utilizing the current assets under management control. Compared with 1990, Wal-Mart invested relatively less money in current assets in 2000 than it invested in productive and other assets. In 1990, current assets represented 57.5% of total assets; in 2000, current assets represented 34.6% of total assets.

% Current Asset = Current Assets ÷ Total Assets
2000: 34.6% = $24.356B ÷ $70.349B
1990: 57.5% = $4.713B ÷ $8.198B

The change in the relative mix of current assets, productive assets, and other assets is also reflected in the difference in CAGRs. Between 1990 and 2000, Wal-Mart's investment in current assets increased at a 17.9% CAGR versus the 24.0% growth rate for total assets. This tells us that the growth in Wal-Mart's asset base can be attributed primarily to the net investment in productive assets due to expansion and acquisitions.

If we include only current assets in Wal-Mart's turnover calculation, we can see management's increased efficiency from another angle.

Current Asset Turnover = Net Sales ÷ Current Assets
2000: 6.85 = $166.809B ÷ $24.356B
1990: 5.51 = $ 25.985B ÷ $ 4.713B

In 1990, Wal-Mart generated $5.51 in net sales for every $1 invested in current assets; in 2000, Wal-Mart generated $6.85 for every $1 invested in current assets.

Between 1990 and 2000, management grew the business and increased current asset efficiency by $1.34 per $1 of investment in current assets. Simply stated, Wal-Mart is getting more "bang for the buck" for its investment in current assets. Since we know that overall asset turnover has declined, we can say that Wal-Mart has yet to achieve similar sales levels from its new stores and acquisitions.

PRODUCTIVE ASSETS

Productive assets represent the resources held for the long-term support of business operations. This category includes two financial elements, which are netted out against each other to create a third element:

1. Property, plant, and equipment
2. Accumulated depreciation
3. Net productive assets

Property, Plant, and Equipment

Property, plant, and equipment represent the productive assets under management control.

In the early 1970s, the basis for reporting productive assets in the balance sheet shifted from ownership to control. Under the present financial reporting rules, all assets owned or controlled through capital leases are included on a firm's balance sheet.

Accumulated Depreciation

Accumulated depreciation represents the cost of plant and equipment that has been recovered through charges against net income in past years. The accumulated depreciation shown for Wal-Mart includes the amortization associated with the property, plant, and equipment controlled through capital leases.

Net Productive Assets

From a management perspective, the net productive assets represent the cost of productive assets to be recovered through future business operations.[2]

▶

$$\text{Property, Plant,} \atop \text{and Equipment} - {\text{Accumulated} \atop \text{Depreciation}} = {\text{Net Productive} \atop \text{Assets}}$$

In 1990, Wal-Mart's net investment in productive assets equaled $3.430 billion; in 2000, Wal-Mart's net investment equaled $35.969 billion.

◀

Between 1990 and 2000, the investment in net productive assets grew at a 26.5% compound annual rate. The growth in net productive assets is out of line when compared with the growth in net sales (20.4%), current assets (17.9%), and total assets (24.0%).

In 1990, net productive assets represented 41.8% of total assets versus 51.1% of total assets in 2000.

▶

% Net Productive Assets = Net Productive Assets ÷ Total Assets
2000: 51.1% = $35.969B ÷ $70.349B
1990: 41.8% = $3.430B ÷ $8.198B

◀

53

Since turnover is the name of the asset management game, it might be interesting to see what would happen if we were to include only net productive assets in our turnover calculation. Just how efficiently is management using its investment in net productive assets?

▶────────────────────────────────────

Productive Asset Turnover = Net Sales ÷ Net Productive Assets
2000: 4.64 = $166.809B ÷ $35.969B
1990: 7.58 = $ 25.985B ÷ $3.430B

In 1990, for every $1 invested in net productive assets, Wal-Mart generated $7.58 in net sales; in 2000, Wal-Mart generated $4.64.

────────────────────────────────────◀

For every $1 of investment in net productive assets, Wal-Mart generated $2.94 less in net sales in 2000 than it generated in 1990.

OTHER ASSETS

Other assets represent the resources, other than productive assets, that are held for the long-term support of the business operations.

▶────────────────────────────────────

In 1990, Wal-Mart's investment in other assets equaled $55 million; in 2000, Wal-Mart's investment in other assets equaled $10.024 billion.

────────────────────────────────────◀

Between 1990 and 2000, investment in other assets grew considerably due to a great number of acquisitions, which occurred during 1997 through 2000. Other or intangible assets arise when a firm pays more than the fair market value of assets to acquire another firm. This asset is called goodwill.

In 1990, other assets represented 0.01% of total assets versus 14.2% of total assets in 2000.[3]

% Other Assets = Other Assets ÷ Total Assets
2000: 14.2% = $10.024B ÷ $70.349B
1990: 0.01% = $55M ÷ $8.198B

The increase from 0.01% to 14.2% will have a negative effect on the overall asset turnover ratio.

If we combine the discussion of other assets with net productive assets, it would appear that Wal-Mart is doing one of three things, two of which are not good. Wal-Mart is:

1. paying too much money for the long-term investments it is making,
2. picking locations that are not generating the anticipated sales levels, and
3. building a foundation for future growth that will not turn into net sales until some time in the future.

TOTAL ASSETS

Total assets represent all of the resources under management control. As mentioned previously, the total assets under management control at Wal-Mart grew at a 24.0% compound annual rate between 1990 and 2000.

Based on the discussion of each of the elements making up total assets, we should be more aware of the different issues surrounding the management of current assets, productive assets, and other assets. The overall growth rate for total assets (24.0%) represents a combination of three growth rates.

1. Current assets (17.9%)
2. Productive assets (26.5%)
3. Other assets (NM)

When compared with the growth in net sales (20.4%), Wal-Mart appears to be becoming *more* efficient in managing its current assets while becoming *less* efficient in managing its productive assets and other assets.

▶ ──

Bottom line: The increase in current asset efficiency has not been large enough to offset the decreases in productive and other asset efficiency.

── ◀

Net sales represents all of those dollars of customer financing generated during the year that we have used as a benchmark for trying to understand how Wal-Mart manages its assets. By dividing net sales by the total assets under management control, we have created a powerful tool for helping us understand a major part of any firm's business operations.

Since the customer is the primary source of financing for any firm, it only seems natural to use net sales as a basis for trying to understand the business. On the one hand, Wal-Mart does a good job of turning inventory and receivables into cash and then moving that money out into other parts of the business. On the other hand, Wal-Mart has not been as successful in deploying its productive and other asset dollars to support the overall level of sales on a relative basis.

ASSET TURNOVER

In the quick overview of the Strategic Profit Model, we showed that asset turnover equals net sales divided by total assets. We also saw that Wal-Mart's asset turnover declined from 3.17 in 1990 to 2.37 in 2000. By taking a closer look at the asset management component of the SPM, we have now seen that current assets, productive assets, and total assets have all been growing at different rates.

In making the transition to the return on asset component of the SPM, we would like to summarize the two trends that we see when we take a closer look at the assets underlying the turnover calculation.

▶ ──

Current assets: Between 1990 and 2000, Wal-Mart actually increased its effectiveness in managing current assets. The number of days sales tied up in current assets dropped from 66.2 days to 53.3 days. In 2000, management ran the business with $5.9 billion less of an investment in current assets as compared with 1990 performance levels.

Productive assets: Between 1990 and 2000, Wal-Mart generated substantially fewer dollars of net sales per $1 invested in productive assets. The number of days sales tied up in productive assets increased from 48.2 days to 78.7 days. In 2000, management ran the business with $13.95 billion more of an investment in productive assets as compared with 1990 performance levels.

Total assets: Taken in total, the efficiencies that management achieved in the area of current asset management were more than offset by the decline in net sales per dollar of investment in productive (and other) assets.

For those among us who are new to understanding the business through financial information, Wal-Mart's management team is aware of the need to improve the yield from its productive and other asset management practices. Financial analysts and investors who track the performance of Wal-Mart's common stock are quick to remind management of the problems it is facing. The real trick is to come up with a strategy that will correct the situation.

In Chapter 4, we will broaden the lens, so to speak, by looking at how asset management and margin management issues are integrated through the concept of return on assets (ROA). In order to generate a profit on behalf of the shareholders, management must turn the assets under its control and make sure that every $1 of assets turned includes an adequate margin of profit. Turns and margins represent the financial heart of the business.

As mentioned in Chapter 1, Wal-Mart's former CEO, David Glass, indicated in the mid-1990s that ROA would be playing a more significant role in Wal-Mart's overall business strategy. As we shall see, the concept of ROA provides us with an additional opportunity to understand the business through financial information.

NOTES

1. We have followed the convention used in the *Value Line Investment Survey* of subdividing current assets into cash and equivalents, receivables, inventory, and other current assets. Productive assets include property, plant, and equipment and capital leases. The combination of the elements making up productive assets will have no material effect on the analysis in this chapter.

2. Within the context of the asset management component of the SPM, the distinctions between gross productive assets and accumulated depreciation do not add much to our understanding of the business. As we shall see, these distinctions play a much larger role in looking at the business through the lens of the Strategic Financing Model, to be discussed in Chapters 7 and 8.

3. For Wal-Mart, other assets represent goodwill and other acquired intangible assets. These assets arise from Wal-Mart's global expansion and acquisitions, which occurred in the late 1990s. For companies that have acquired other firms, other assets may represent a material portion of total assets.

CHAPTER 4

Strategic Profit Model: Return on Assets

In this chapter, we use the concept of return on assets (ROA) to integrate our understanding of the margin management and asset management issues discussed in Chapters 2 and 3.

As mentioned in Chapter 1, our approach to understanding the business through financial information is grounded in the management philosophy underlying the DuPont executive charting system developed in the early years of the twentieth century. In the American Management Association (AMA) monograph describing the DuPont system, all of the parts of the model were integrated through the concept of ROA. Within the context of the Strategic Profit Model (SPM), these same parts are integrated through the concept of ROA.[1]

Since the DuPont management philosophy underlies our approach to understanding the business through financial information, it seems appropriate to restate the principles presented in the original AMA monograph:

1. The charts are designed to present in readily understandable visual form the financial results of each of the company's industrial departments and of the company as a whole.

2. The presentation is not based on a step-by-step buildup to the ultimate objective of return on investment. Instead, the end result is presented first and thereafter the important elements that contribute to it.

3. The charts themselves do not utilize narrative explanation.

4. It is comparatively easy to hold the attention of an entire group to one item at the same moment.[2]

Converting financial information into management action is where the SPM comes into play. The ROA component of the model helps managers see how profit margins and asset turnovers interact to produce the firm's ROA. By combining what they see with what they know (from experience), they can begin to think in terms of what they will have to do to increase ROA.

Figure 4.1 presents the ROA component of Wal-Mart's SPM using the amounts taken from the 1990 and 2000 income statements and balance sheets presented in the previous two chapters. As we can see from this figure, ROA is presented as the combined result of Wal-Mart's margin

**Figure 4.1 Wal-Mart Strategic Profit Model: Return on Assets
(for the Fiscal Years Ended January 31, 1990 and 2000—
Amounts in Millions)**

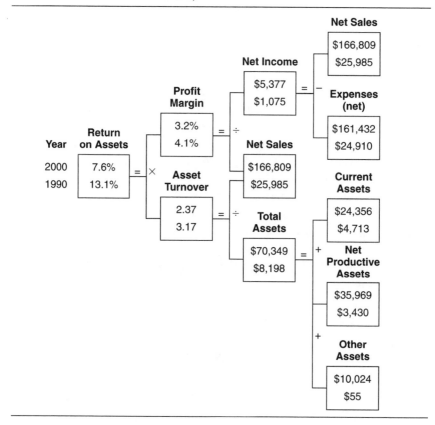

management and asset management strategies discussed in the previous two chapters. By combining margin management and asset management through the concept of ROA, we can summarize our observations about both aspects of Wal-Mart's business operations and look for additional insights into the business that result from widening the lens we use to understand the business.

Up through the ROA component of the SPM, we are trying to use financial information to understand a firm's basic business operations (industrial departments, in the DuPont case). The financial results are visualized and contain no narrative explanations. Once the financial results are visualized, through the SPM, we try to understand what the numbers mean from a business strategy perspective.

In 1990, management earned $1.075 billion on total assets of $8.198 billion; in 2000, management earned $5.377 billion on total assets of $70.349 billion.

In 1990, Wal-Mart earned 13.1¢ on every $1 of assets invested in the business; in 2000, Wal-Mart earned 7.6¢.

Even though net income increased in absolute terms, Wal-Mart generated 5.5¢ less profit per $1 of assets in 2000 than it did in 1990.

On the one hand, managers and investors need to know that ROA has fallen by 5.5¢ for every $1 of assets invested in the business. On the other hand, this knowledge is not of much use if it cannot be converted into actions that will result in improved performance in the future.

Figure 4.2(a) presents the percentage change in profit margin, asset turnover, and ROA between 1990 and 2000 and Figure 4.2(b) presents the compound annual growth rates (CAGRs) over this ten-year period. The percentage changes and CAGRs will be used to help tell a story about Wal-Mart's combined margin management and asset management strategy. By looking at ROA in terms of its component parts, we can see that the 5.5¢ decline from 1990 to 2000 resulted from a decline in both the profit margin and asset turnover.

Figure 4.2   Wal-Mart Strategic Profit Model: Return on Assets

(a) Percentage Change (1990–2000)

Profit Margin	−22.0%
Asset Turnover	−25.2%
Return on Assets	−42.0%

(b) Compound Annual Growth Rates (1990–2000)

Net Sales	20.4%
Expenses (Net)	20.5%
Net Income	17.5%
Current Assets	17.9%
Productive Assets	26.5%
Other Assets	NM*
Total Assets	24.0%

*Not meaningful

▶──

In 1990, Wal-Mart generated 4.1¢ in net income for every $1 of net sales; in 2000, Wal-Mart generated 3.2¢.

In 1990, Wal-Mart generated $3.17 in net sales for every $1 of assets; in 2000, Wal-Mart generated $2.37.

──◀

At first glance, a 0.9¢ decline in profit margin and an 80¢ decline in asset turnover may not appear to be very high. However, when the decline in profit margin is *combined* with the decline in asset turnover, the effects on ROA are magnified.

▶──

In 1990, Wal-Mart earned 13.1¢ on every $1 of assets invested in the business; in 2000, Wal-Mart earned 7.6¢.

A 5.5¢ decline in ROA translates into $3.9 billion less net income being earned on a $70.3 billion asset base.

──◀

Stated in a slightly different way,

▶
___

Between 1990 and 2000, Wal-Mart's profit margin decreased by 22.0%, and asset turnover decreased by 25.2%. The combined effect of a decrease in profit margin and asset turnover resulted in a 42.0% decrease in ROA.

A 42.0% decline in ROA translates into $3.9 billion less net income being earned on a $70.3 billion asset base.

___
◀

As we can see from the ROA component of the SPM, the key performance measures (profit margin, asset turnover, and ROA) provide a convenient way to help us understand Wal-Mart's business.

RETURN ON ASSETS

In using ROA to help us understand the business,

- We start by summarizing what we know about the growth in Wal-Mart's net sales.
- We then take a "northern route" (as visualized in Figure 4.1) to summarize what we know about Wal-Mart's margin management strategy.
- We then take a "southern route" to summarize what we know about Wal-Mart's asset management strategy.
- We can then begin to look at the interactive effects of combining margin management and asset management strategies to increase Wal-Mart's ROA.

Net Sales: Growing the Business

As mentioned in the previous three chapters, any story we tell about Wal-Mart has to be built on a foundation of growing the business. Between 1990 and 2000, total revenue increased at a 20.4% CAGR. In 1990, Sam Walton set a goal of becoming a $125 billion company (as measured in terms of net sales) by the year 2000. That goal probably seemed to be very ambitious when Wal-Mart had $25.9 billion in sales in 1990. As we can see, by 2000 Wal-Mart exceeded its target by nearly one-third. Given this commitment to continue growing the business from the shareholders' perspective, the question becomes one of growing the business at a profit.

Profit Margin: The Northern Route

Since 1990, Wal-Mart has been experiencing pressure on its profit margins. "Experiencing pressure" is a nice way of saying that Wal-Mart has not been able to maintain its historical spread between net sales and net expenses. As was shown in Figure 4.2(b), net sales grew at a 20.4% compound annual rate between 1990 and 2000, as compared with 20.5% compound annual growth rate for net expenses. This seemingly small difference between the growth in net sales and net expenses (20.4% − 20.5% = −0.1%), compounded over ten years, translates into a substantially slower compound growth rate in net income (17.5%) and a correspondingly lower profit margin (3.2% versus 4.1%).

At $166.809 billion net sales, a 0.1% difference in CAGRs for sales and expenses translates into a 0.9¢ decline in profit margin over the ten-year period, and a 0.9¢ decline in profit margin translates into $1.5 billion less net income.

Unless that reduction can be offset by improved performance in other parts of Wal-Mart's operations, the effects of a lower profit margin will flow all the way through to a reduction in ROA and ROE.

As discussed in Chapter 2, low prices (P) relative to the competition translate into more gross margin dollars when a firm can increase quantity (Q). Unfortunately, this pricing strategy does not work when competitors match your low prices. When you multiply a lower price (P) times the same quantity (Q), you end up with fewer gross margin dollars and no additional market share. As far as the customers are concerned, they are more than happy to reap the benefit of lower prices. In a highly competitive environment, customers may win and the shareholders may lose if the lost gross margin dollars are not offset by reductions in total expenses.

As discussed more fully in Chapter 2, Wal-Mart's gross margin fell from 22.8¢ to 22.3¢ from 1990 to 2000. This 0.5¢ decline was compounded by a 0.5¢ increase in operating expenses and was partially offset by a 0.4¢ decrease in income taxes per dollar of net sales.

Asset Turnover: The Southern Route

When successful, taking the southern route may be characterized as getting more bang for each buck invested in total assets.

Wal-Mart's southern route strategy has focused on utilizing current assets more efficiently while expanding the productive and other asset base to support future sales growth. As discussed in Chapter 3, the decline in asset turnover from $3.17 in 1990 to $2.37 in 2000 reflects the effects of focusing on efficiency and expansion.

The efficiency aspect of Wal-Mart business strategy is captured by the difference in compound growth rates between net sales (20.4%) and current assets (17.9%). Between 1990 and 2000, Wal-Mart grew the business while reducing its investment in current assets relative to net sales. If shareholders were to use only the relationship between current assets and net sales to evaluate management, Wal-Mart's management team would receive high marks. Current asset turnover increased from $5.51 per $1 of current assets in 1990 to $6.85 per $1 of current assets in 2000 (see discussion in Chapter 3). For the current asset management aspects of the business, Wal-Mart receives high marks.

Unfortunately, these high marks cannot be extended (at least at the present time) to management's productive and other asset management practices. Compared with the growth in total revenue (20.4%) and in total assets (24.0%), the growth in productive and other assets is out of line.

Since we know that the composition of other assets is primarily the intangible asset called goodwill, we will focus on Wal-Mart's productive asset strategy. In 1990, Wal-Mart was generating $7.58 in net sales per $1 of productive assets. By 2000, productive asset turnover had fallen to $4.64, or $2.94 fewer net sales per $1 of productive assets in 2000 versus 1990.

Based on these observations about Wal-Mart's asset management practices, any change in business strategy would appear to have to be targeted at Wal-Mart's productive asset management practices.

Return on Assets: Going Both Routes

In keeping with the management philosophy underlying the DuPont executive charting system, ask yourself the following questions:

1. If you had to explain the decline in Wal-Mart's ROA between 1990 and 2000 in three sentences, what would you say?
2. In devising a five-year plan to take Wal-Mart forward from its 2000 performance, what would you say in three sentences?

In other words, given all of the financial information we have reviewed, how would you go about providing a concise answer that is consistent with the facts that we see right before our eyes?

We have found that making a connection between what we see and what we say is an integral part of understanding any business through financial information. The old adage "those that do not learn from the past are bound to repeat it" captures the essence of the practice of saying what we see.

The following discussion is our attempt to say what we thought we saw and to speculate about the future.

EXPLAINING PAST PERFORMANCE

- Between 1990 and 2000, Wal-Mart was able to grow the business but was not able to maintain its profit margin and asset turnover, compared with past performance.
- The decline in gross margin per $1 of net sales was compounded by increases in operating expenses and only partially offset by reductions in income taxes.
- The efficiency gains related to the increase in net sales generated per $1 invested in current assets more than offset by the expansionary effects related to declines in net sales generated per $1 invested in productive (and other) assets.

SPECULATING ABOUT THE FUTURE

- Profitable growth cannot occur through reducing prices, since competitors will match price reductions to avoid losing market share.

- Increases in cost of sales and operating expenses will result in lower profit margins if selling prices remain the same.
- Management needs to focus on growing the productive assets base in locations that will generate higher levels of net sales per $1 of investment in total assets.

If asked to justify our position, we would return to the more detailed discussion of the margin management and asset management components of the SPM.

If you have been applying our approach to understanding the business through financial information to your own company, we suggest you try to describe your firm's past performance and possible future performance in six questions or less. After you have come up with your own assessment, we suggest that you compare your assessment with those of your co-workers. The ensuing conversations are likely to prove very stimulating.

In the words of Warren Buffett, there are only five ways of increasing a firm's return on equity (or, in our case, explain a decrease). A firm can

1. Increase asset turnover
2. Widen operating margins
3. Pay lower taxes
4. Increase leverage
5. Use cheaper leverage[3]

Of the five ways to increase return on equity, four ways are captured by the concept of ROA:

1. Increasing asset turnover
2. Widening operating margins
3. Paying lower taxes
4. Using cheaper leverage (i.e., paying lower interest rates)

With four of the five ways of increasing profitability captured through ROA, we have 80% of the information we need to explain increases and decreases in ROE. The remaining 20% of the information we need is captured by increasing (or decreasing) financial leverage.

In Chapter 5, we will blow up the financial management component of the SPM and see how financial leverage fits into Wal-Mart's overall business strategy.

NOTES

1. The SPM is more comprehensive in the sense that it goes beyond the DuPont charting system by including the financial management aspects of the business that are needed to reach ROE, but, up to the ROA presentation, the model is virtually identical to the DuPont model.
2. "Executive Committee Control Charts: A Description of the DuPont Chart System for Appraising Operating Performance," *AMA* no. 6, 1950.
3. Robert G. Hagstrom, Jr., *The Warren Buffett Way* (New York: John Wiley & Sons, 1994), 58.

CHAPTER 5

Strategic Profit Model: Financial Management

In this chapter, we use the concept of financial leverage to show how a firm's relationships with its creditors and shareholders are linked to the management issues captured by the concept of return on assets (ROA).

In the quick overview of the Strategic Profit Model (SPM) presented in Chapter 1, we used the concept of financial leverage to link return on equity (ROE) back to the return on the total assets under management control. As we could see from the quick overview, financial leverage had a positive effect on Wal-Mart's ROE in both 1990 and 2000. As discussed more fully in this chapter, the total liabilities included in the firm's capital structure provided the lever that increased the shareholders' return.

Figure 5.1 presents the liabilities and shareholders' equity section of Wal-Mart's balance sheets for the fiscal years ended January 31, 1990 and 2000, which will be used to explore the concept of financial leverage in more depth. As we can see from Figure 5.1, current liabilities and long-term liabilities equal total liabilities. Shareholders' equity consists of common stock, retained earnings, and other equity adjustments.[1]

In setting the stage for looking at the financial management aspects of a firm's business strategy, we often refer to the liability and shareholders' equity (total equity) section of the balance sheet as the "invisible" side of the business. There are no *things,* such as inventory and productive assets, in this section of the balance sheet. All we find under liabilities and shareholders' equity are *promises*—promises made by management to pay suppliers and employees for goods and services received in the past, promises to repay lenders principal and interest on money borrowed in the past, and promises made to shareholders to earn a return on their investment.

69

**Figure 5.1 Wal-Mart Balance Sheets, Liabilities and Shareholders'
Equity Section (for the Fiscal Years Ended January 31,
1990 and 2000—Amounts in Millions)**

	1990	2000
Liabilities and Shareholders' Equity		
Liabilities		
Current Liabilities		
Accounts Payable	$1,827	$13,105
Current Debt Due	$24	$2,085
Accrued Liabilities	$995	$10,613
Total Current Liabilities	$2,846	$25,803
Long-Term Liabilities		
Long-Term Debt	$185	$13,672
Long-Term Lease Obligations	$1,087	$3,002
Deferred Income Taxes and Other	$115	$759
Minority Interest	$0	$1,279
Total Long-Term Liabilities	$1,387	$18,712
Total Liabilities	$4,233	$44,515
Shareholders' Equity		
Common Stock	$237	$1,160
Retained Earnings	$3,728	$25,129
Other Equity Adjustments	$0	($455)
Total Shareholders' Equity	$3,965	$25,834
Total	$8,198	$70,349

Like other concepts embedded within the concept of ROE (i.e., profit margin, asset turnover, and ROA), the concept of financial leverage is useful because it allows us to see important aspects of managing the business that might otherwise go unnoticed. As discussed under the quick overview of the SPM, the concept of financial leverage allows us to shift gears and move from management's responsibilities to all parties who have a financial interest in the firm to its specific responsibilities to shareholders.

Figure 5.2 presents the financial leverage component of the SPM using the amounts taken from the 1990 and 2000 liabilities and shareholders' equity sections of Wal-Mart's balance sheets.

**Figure 5.2   Wal-Mart Strategic Profit Model: Financial Leverage
(for the Fiscal Years Ended January 31, 1990 and 2000—
Amounts in Millions)**

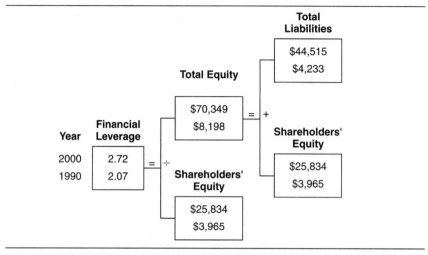

Figure 5.3(a) presents the percentage breakdown of total liabilities and shareholders' equity in 1990 and 2000, and Figure 5.3(b) presents the compound annual growth rates (CAGRs) over this ten-year period. The percentage breakdowns and CAGRs will be used to help tell a story about Wal-Mart's financial management strategy. (The CAGR for net sales has been included for comparison purposes.)

The material presented in this chapter will unfold in the following manner:

- We begin by discussing how the concept of financial leverage allows us to move from looking at the firm as a whole to looking at the firm from the shareholders' perspective.
- We then take a closer look at the composition of Wal-Mart's total liabilities and total shareholders' equity.
- We then summarize the key financial management issues from a business strategy perspective.

FINANCIAL LEVERAGE

As shown in Figure 5.2, the financial leverage component of the SPM provides us with an opportunity to see how management's responsibilities to

Figure 5.3   Wal-Mart Strategic Profit Model: Financial Leverage

(a) Percent of Total Liabilities and Shareholders' Equity

	1990	2000
Total Liabilities	51.6%	63.3%
Shareholders' Equity	48.4%	36.7%
Total Liabilities and Shareholders' Equity	100.0%	100.0%

(b) Compound Annual Growth Rates (1990–2000)

Net Sales	20.4%
Total Liabilities	26.5%
Shareholders' Equity	20.6%
Total Liabilities and Shareholders' Equity	24.0%

all creditors and shareholders is transformed into management's *specific* responsibilities to shareholders.

In 1990, Wal-Mart utilized $2.07 in total equity for every $1 of shareholders' equity in running the business; in 2000, Wal-Mart utilized $2.72.

In 1990, total liabilities accounted for 51.6% of total equity; in 2000, total liabilities accounted for 63.3% of total equity.

The increasing role played by total liabilities relative to shareholders' equity is also reflected in the difference in compound growth rates. Total liabilities grew at a 26.5% compound rate between 1990 and 2000, versus a 20.6% compound rate for shareholders' equity.

In terms of overall business strategy, a change or difference in financial leverage can be measured in terms of its impact on ROE, as discussed in Chapter 1.

The 2.07 in financial leverage increased the 13.1¢ ROA to a 27.1¢ ROE in 1990. The 2.72 in financial leverage increased the 7.6¢ ROA to a 20.8¢ ROE in 2000.

Relative to 1990 performance levels, the increase in financial leverage had a positive impact on the 2000 ROE. If management had maintained a financial leverage of 2.07 in 2000, ROE would have been 5.1% lower (2.07 × 7.6% = 15.7%; 20.8% − 15.7% = 5.1%).

On a shareholders' equity base of $25.834 billion, 5.1¢ translates into $1.3 billion in lower returns to shareholders from using less debt to run the business. Thus, increased leverage limited the overall decline in ROE.

To a certain extent, borrowing money to finance the business seems somewhat at odds with Sam Walton's underlying business philosophy.

From the time I took out my first bank loan—the $1,800 to buy that ice cream machine for the Ben Franklin down in Newport—I was never really comfortable with debt. But I recognized it as a necessity of doing business, and I had gotten pretty good at accumulating it.[2]

Debt has its advantages and disadvantages. Firms such as Wal-Mart are no different from the rest of us. If we have a goal or an objective we want to realize (e.g., own our own home) and we do not have the money, paying 20% up front and borrowing the remaining 80% looks pretty good. However, if we lose our job, those principal and interest payments can wipe out our life's savings or force us into bankruptcy.

The same type of thinking holds for Wal-Mart. If Wal-Mart needs more money to grow than it can generate through the business, borrowing money provides the fuel for growth. However, there is always the danger (or risk) that Wal-Mart might not be able to meet its principal and interest payments in the future.

As we shall see, Sam Walton and his successor, former CEO David Glass, have become "pretty good" at accumulating debt over the years. As we shall also see beginning in Chapter 9, Wal-Mart has an excellent credit rating and can borrow money at very favorable interest rates, compared with its competitors.

Within the context of the SPM, our primary objective is to see how management maintains a balance between liabilities and shareholders' equity, as well as how the elements making up liabilities and shareholders' equity change in response to management's overall business strategy.

We will begin our discussion with total liabilities and then move on to shareholders' equity. Total liabilities will be discussed in terms of current liabilities and long-term liabilities. Shareholders' equity will be discussed in terms of common stock, retained earnings, and translation adjustments.

TOTAL LIABILITIES: A CLOSER LOOK

Figure 5.4 presents an expansion of Wal-Mart's total liabilities for 1990 and 2000. As we can see from Figure 5.4, the distinctions between current and long-term liabilities will be used to help us understand the financial management aspects of running the business.[3]

Figure 5.5(a) presents an analysis of current liabilities in terms of days net sales, and Figure 5.5(b) presents the CAGRs over this ten-year period. The days net sales analysis and CAGRs will be used to help tell a story about the liability component of Wal-Mart's financial management strategy.

Current Liabilities

Current liabilities represent obligations or management responsibilities to creditors that must be satisfied within the year or within the firm's normal operating cycle, whichever is longer. This category includes three financial elements: (1) accounts payable, (2) accrued liabilities, and (3) current debt due.

Accounts Payable. Accounts payable represent the outstanding promises to pay suppliers for goods and services received. Since accounts payable

**Figure 5.4   Wal-Mart Strategic Profit Model: Financial Management
Liabilities (for the Fiscal Years Ended January 31, 1990
and 2000—Amounts in Millions)**

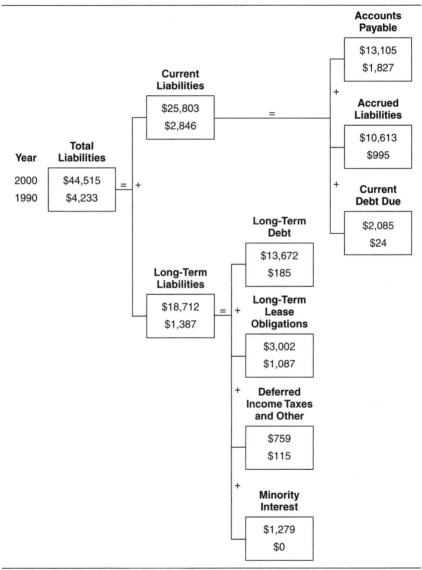

are directly related to the firm's ongoing business activities, the days' net
sales calculations provide a convenient way of seeing how the firm is
managing its relationships with suppliers.

Figure 5.5   Wal-Mart Strategic Profit Model: Financial Management Liabilities

(a) Days Net Sales

	1990	2000	Change
Accounts Payable	25.7	28.7	3.0
Accrued Liabilities	14.0	23.2	9.2
Current Debt Due	0.3	4.6	4.3
Current Liabilities	40.0	56.5	16.5

(b) Compound Annual Growth Rates (1990–2000)

Net Sales	20.4%
Current Liabilities	24.7%
Long-Term Liabilities	29.7%
Total Liabilities	26.5%

In 1990, accounts payable represented 25.7 days net sales; in 2000, the number of days net sales associated with accounts payable was 28.7 days, an increase of 3.0 days between 1990 and 2000.

2000: 28.7 Days = $13.105B ÷ $166.809B × 365 Days
1990: 25.7 Days = $ 1.827B ÷ $ 25.985B × 365 Days

Part of the conventional wisdom in running a business is to collect your accounts receivable as soon as possible and pay your accounts payable as late as possible; in that way, a firm can maximize the amount of cash it has to use in other parts of the business. The only trouble with conventional wisdom is that firms can get into trouble if everyone plays the same game.

In a broader business context, one firm's accounts payable are another firm's accounts receivable. By paying as late as possible, customers are creating asset management problems for their suppliers. At a 2000 rate of $457.0 million in net sales per day, paying suppliers 3.0 days slower resulted in a $1.377 billion benefit from Wal-Mart's suppliers. Nonetheless, Wal-Mart paid its accounts off in less than one month—the sign of a solid borrower.

▶

2000: $1.371B = $457.0 Million per Day × 3.0 Days

◀

Building relationships with suppliers is a key element in Wal-Mart's over-all business strategy. The "people" side of Wal-Mart's business strategy includes suppliers along with customers and associates.

Accrued Liabilities. Accrued liabilities represent all other short-term obligations that will have to be met in the coming year.

▶

In 1990, accrued liabilities represented 14.0 days net sales; in 2000, the number of days net sales associated with accrued liabilities was 23.2 days, an increase of 9.2 days over 1990.

2000: 23.2 Days = $10.613B ÷ $166.809B × 365 Days
1990: 14.0 Days = $ 995M ÷ $ 25.984B × 365 Days

◀

The 9.2-days increase in accrued liabilities equals $4.226 billion of additional short-term financing relative to the 1990 level of short-term financing.

▶

2000: $4.204B = $457.0 Million per Day × 9.2 Days

◀

Current Debt Due. Current debt due represents the current portion of long-term debt coming due within the next year. Between 1990 and 2000, Wal-Mart's current debt due increased by 4.3 days net sales.

▶

2000: 4.6 Days = $2.085B ÷ $166.809B × 365 Days
1990: 0.3 Days = $ 24M ÷ $ 25.985B × 365 Days

◀

The long-term debt a firm incurs must eventually be repaid. When the original long-term debt is due to be repaid within the year, it is reclassified as a current liability.

Current Liabilities: Summary. Overall, Wal-Mart's current obligations increased by 16.5 days between 1990 and 2000. The increase resulted from three management practices. Wal-Mart increased the time it takes to pay regular suppliers, employees (i.e., salaries and wages), and the government (accrued income taxes). Between 1990 and 2000, accounts payable and accrued liabilities increased by 12.2 days. Further, the amount of long-term debt coming due within 2000 increased by 4.3 days.

The 16.5-day increase in current liabilities is also reflected by the difference in compound growth rates between net sales (20.4%) and current liabilities (24.7%). Unlike current assets (17.9% CAGR), management was unable to keep the growth in current liabilities below the growth in net sales.

Long-Term Liabilities

Long-term liabilities represent management's obligations to creditors and scorekeeping differences between financial reporting and income tax reporting that extend beyond the year or normal business operating cycle. This category includes four financial elements:

1. Long-term debt
2. Long-term lease obligations
3. Deferred income taxes and other long-term liabilities
4. Minority interest

At this stage of trying to understanding the business through financial information, our discussion of long-term liabilities will be somewhat brief. We will return to a more in-depth analysis of these financial elements when we begin our discussion of financing the business beginning in Chapter 7.

Long-Term Debt. Long-term debt represents the amounts owed to lenders that will come due beyond one year. Between 1990 and 2000, Wal-Mart's long-term debt increased from $185 million to $13.7 billion.

Capital Lease Obligations. Long-term lease obligations are similar to long-term debt in that they represent amounts owed to lessors that will come due beyond one year. They differ in that the lease obligations are directly related to the productive assets controlled by management through capital lease agreements. Between 1990 and 2000, Wal-Mart's capital leases increased from $1.087 billion to $3.002 billion.

Deferred Income Taxes and Other Long-Term Liabilities.   Deferred income taxes and other long-term liabilities represent a firm's long-term obligations not included in long-term debt and long-term lease obligations. Deferred income taxes represent the cumulative effects of timing differences that occur in computing the firm's actual income tax obligation and the hypothetical calculation used for financial reporting to shareholders. Although deferred income taxes typically appear with other long-term liabilities on the balance sheet, some users of financial statements reclassify deferred income taxes as part of shareholders' equity.[4] Wal-Mart's deferred income taxes and other long-term liabilities increased from $115 million in 1990 to $759 million in 2000.

Minority Interest.   For 2000, Wal-Mart's long-term liabilities included minority interest of $1.279 billion. Minority interest represents the ownership interest of Wal-Mart's joint venture partners.

Long-Term Liabilities: Summary.   Since the discussion of long-term liabilities will receive more attention beginning in Chapter 7, the primary concern at this point is to understand how total long-term liabilities have changed relative to current liabilities.

Between 1990 and 2000, Wal-Mart's long-term liabilities increased at a 29.7% CAGR versus the 24.7% growth rate for current liabilities.

The increasing role played by long-term debt in Wal-Mart's overall business strategy is also reflected in the percentage of total liabilities represented by long-term liabilities. In 1990, long-term liabilities represented 32.8% of total liabilities; in 2000, long-term liabilities represented 42.0%.

After discussing the elements making up shareholders' equity, we will see how long-term liabilities fit into Wal-Mart's overall business strategy.

SHAREHOLDERS' EQUITY

Figure 5.6 presents a blow-up of Wal-Mart's shareholders' equity for 1990 and 2000. As we can see, shareholders' equity consists of three financial elements:

1. Common stock
2. Retained earnings
3. Other equity adjustments

Figure 5.7 presents the percentage breakdown of the elements making up shareholders' equity in 1990 and 2000 and the CAGRs over this ten-year period. The percentage breakdowns and CAGRs will be used to help tell a story about the shareholders' equity component of Wal-Mart's finan-

Figure 5.6   Wal-Mart Strategic Profit Model: Financial Management—Shareholders' Equity (for the Fiscal Years ended January 31, 1990 and 2000—Amounts in Millions)

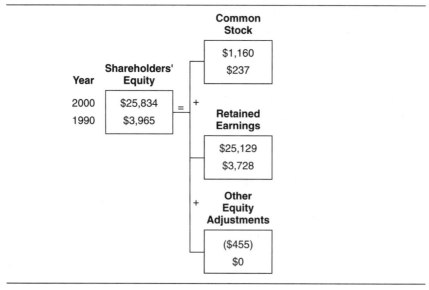

cial management strategy. (The CAGR for net sales has been included for comparison purposes.)

Common Stock

Common stock represents the money received by management from issuing common stock to shareholders. In effect, management promises to be held accountable by the shareholders in exchange for the right to control the future of the firm.

In 1990, Wal-Mart had $237 million in common stock outstanding; in 2000, common stock outstanding equaled $1.160 billion.

Between 1990 and 2000, common stock grew at a 17.2% compound annual rate.

Compared with all of the other compound growth rates we have been discussing throughout this book, the 17.2% compound annual growth rate for common stock is relatively low. This low growth rate is also reflected in the declining percentage of total shareholders' equity.

In 1990, Wal-Mart's common stock represented 6.0% of total shareholders' equity; in 2000, common stock represented 4.5%.

As we can see, issuing additional shares of common stock has not been a big part of Wal-Mart's business strategy since 1990.

Retained Earnings

These earnings represent management's cumulative contribution to growing the business on the shareholders' behalf. Aside from some minor charges to retained earnings for the repurchase of some shares of common stock outstanding, the year-end balances represent Wal-Mart's cumulative net income less dividends paid to shareholders.

In 1990, Wal-Mart had $3.728 billion in retained earnings; in 2000, retained earnings equaled $25.129 billion. Management grew retained earnings at a 21.0% compound rate over this ten-year period.

In 1990, retained earnings equaled 94.0% of total shareholders' equity; in 2000, retained earnings equaled 97.3%.

We typically refer to firms with such a high percentage of shareholders' equity accounted for by retained earnings as a business that has been "financed by management." That is, management relies primarily on its own efforts to grow the business through shareholders' equity.

Other Equity Adjustments

These adjustments represent the cumulative effects of translating foreign operations into U.S. dollars and other minor accounting adjustments that have not been included in the determination of net income.

In 1990, Wal-Mart was not involved in international operations to any great extent. By 2000, global expansion had become part of Wal-Mart's overall business strategy. Based on changes in global exchange rates, the $455 million equity adjustment is likely to fluctuate up and down in the future.

Shareholders' Equity: Summary

Keeping our analysis to within total shareholders' equity, the difference in compound growth rates between common stock (17.2%) and retained earnings (21.0%) speaks for itself. Between 1990 and 2000, Wal-Mart's management continued to increase its contribution (through retained earnings) to growing the business on the shareholders' behalf rather than asking the shareholders for additional funds.

In the early 1970s, after Wal-Mart had just gone public, retained earnings accounted for only 40% of shareholders' equity, with common stock accounting for the other 60%. Between 1970 and 2000, management truly financed the growth in the business through retained earnings.[5]

Figure 5.7   Wal-Mart Strategic Profit Model: Financial Management—Shareholders' Equity

(a) Percent Shareholders' Equity

	1990	2000
Common Stock	6.0%	4.5%
Retained Earnings	94.0%	97.3%
Other Equity Adjustments	0.0%	−1.8%
Shareholders' Equity	100.0%	100.0%

(b) Compound Annual Growth Rates (1990–2000)

Net Sales	20.4%
Common Stock	17.2%
Retained Earnings	21.0%
Other Equity Adjustments	NM*
Total Shareholders' Equity	20.6%

*Not meaningful

FINANCIAL MANAGEMENT PERSPECTIVE

As discussed at the beginning of the chapter (and seen in Figure 5.2), Wal-Mart's financial leverage increased from 2.07 in 1990 to 2.72 in 2000. Based on a comparison of the compound growth rates in total liabilities and shareholders' equity, we could see that total liabilities were growing at a much faster rate than shareholders' equity. However, at that point in our discussion, we could not see the dynamics occurring within those two categories.

Figure 5.8 presents a broader view of the financial leverage component of Wal-Mart's SPM. This extended view allows us to see the dynamics occurring with total liabilities and shareholders' equity.

Figure 5.9 presents an extended version of the percentage breakdown of total equity (liabilities and shareholders' equity) in 1990 and 2000, and Figure 5.9 presents the CAGRs over this ten-year period. The percentage breakdowns and CAGRs will be used to help tell a story about Wal-Mart's overall financial management strategy.

Based on our current understanding of the elements making up total liabilities and shareholders' equity, we can make the following observations

Figure 5.8 Wal-Mart Strategic Profit Model: Financial Leverage—
Extended View (for the Fiscal Years Ended January 31, 1990
and 2000—Amounts in Millions)

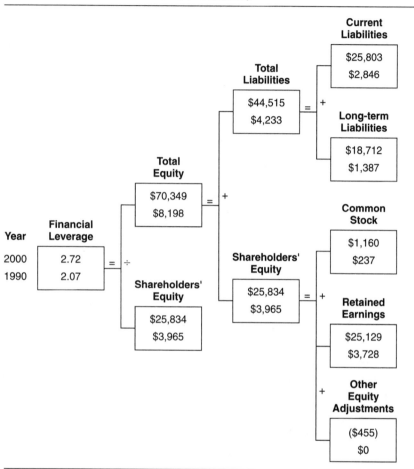

about how Wal-Mart's financial management practices fit into management's overall business strategy:

- Between 1990 and 2000, financial leverage increased from 2.07 to
  2.72. This increase resulted from total liabilities growing at a much
  faster CAGR than total shareholders' equity (26.5% versus 20.6%).
- Within total liabilities, current liabilities grew at a slower rate (24.7%)
  than long-term liabilities (29.7%). In addition, current liabilities grew

faster than net sales (20.4%). This faster growth rate is reflected in the fact that current liabilities represented 56.5 days net sales in 2000 versus 40.0 days net sales in 1990.

- Between 1990 and 2000, long-term liabilities grew to represent a greater percentage of total equity. In 1990, long-term liabilities represented 16.9% of total equity versus 26.6% in 2000. Long-term debt financing (to be discussed more fully in Chapter 7) represents a significant part of Wal-Mart's overall business strategy.
- Between 1990 and 2000, Wal-Mart did not issue significant amounts of common stock to grow the business (17.2% CAGR). At the end of 1990, common stock represented 2.9% of total equity. By the end of 2000, common stock represented only 1.6% of total equity.
- Between 1990 and 2000, retained earnings increased at a 21.0% compound annual rate. Although it decreased from 45.5% to 35.7% of total equity between 1990 and 2000, retained earnings represents a large source of financing for the business.

Figure 5.9   Wal-Mart Strategic Profit Model: Financial Leverage

	1990	2000
(a) Percent Total Equity		
Current Liabilities	34.7%	36.7%
Long-Term Liabilities	16.9%	26.6%
Common Stock	2.9%	1.6%
Retained Earnings	45.5%	35.7%
Other Equity Adjustments	0.0%	−0.6%
Total Equity	100.0%	100.0%
(b) Compound Annual Growth Rates (1990–2000)		
Net Sales	20.4%	
Current Liabilities	24.7%	
Long-Term Liabilities	29.7%	
Common Stock	17.2%	
Retained Earnings	21.0%	
Other Equity Adjustments	NM*	
Total Equity	24.0%	

*Not meaningful

- In summary, from 1990 to 2000, management grew the business through its own contribution (retained earnings) and the contribution from long-term and short-term creditors (long-term and current liabilities). The increase in financial leverage from 2.07 to 2.72 is due to the fact that the liabilities have been increasing at a faster rate than shareholders' equity.

As we can see from this summary, by working our way through the financial management component of the SPM, we have added to our list of insights into Wal-Mart's overall business strategy.

In Chapter 6, we will put all of the individual pieces (of insight) we have been accumulating back together in our attempt to develop a more comprehensive understanding of the profitability aspects of Wal-Mart's overall business strategy.

NOTES

1. We have followed the convention used in the *Value Line Investment Survey* of subdividing current liabilities into accounts payable, current debt due, and other accrued liabilities. Long-term liabilities include long-term debt, long-term lease obligations, and deferred income taxes. The combination of the elements making up current liabilities and long-term liabilities will have no material effect on the discussion in this chapter.

2. Sam Walton and John Huey, *Sam Walton, Made in America: My Story* (New York: Doubleday, 1992), 92.

3. In Chapter 7, when we introduce our second business strategy model, the Strategic Financing Model, the distinction between current liabilities and long-term liabilities will help us develop the concept of "working capital" (current assets − current liabilities) needed to talk about a firm's long-term financing and investment activities.

4. We will return to the issue of how to treat deferred income taxes in Chapter 7.

5. Beginning in Chapter 7, we will focus more specifically on how management finances the business from internal and external sources of funds. At that time, we will return to the role retained earnings plays in growing the business.

CHAPTER 6

Strategic Profit Model: Comprehensive Management

In taking the amounts reported in Wal-Mart's income statements and balance sheets and recasting them within the framework of the Strategic Profit Model (SPM), we have been engaging in a process of "double description." We have taken exactly the same information used to describe the firm in income statement and balance sheet terms and described the firm in a second way, through the visual framework provided by the SPM.

The term *double description* comes from the work of Gregory Bateson.[1] According to Bateson, "an increment of insight is provided by a second language of description without the addition of any extra so-called objective information.[2] The financial statements provide a way of looking at the firm that emphasizes management's stewardship responsibility for safeguarding assets and the fair presentation of financial information. The SPM emphasizes management's responsibility for generating a return on the shareholders' investment in the firm. The two ways of describing the firm's business activities complement each other. The financial statements emphasize formal accountability to shareholders; the SPM emphasizes substantive accountability. The combination of formal and substantive accountability provides a strong foundation for understanding any business through financial information.

Before returning to Wal-Mart's SPM to summarize what we have learned about the business, we would like to reemphasize the importance of working from the financial statements to understand the firm's overall business strategy.

INTEGRITY OF FINANCIAL STATEMENTS

Our approach to understanding the business through financial information is based on two principles:

1. Charity
2. Due diligence

Our ability to rely on the first principle in trying to understand any business is based on the assertions, made by both management and the firm's external auditors, that are included in the annual report to shareholders. In those few instances where we have had to fall back on the principle of due diligence, we have not felt comfortable in accepting the assertions made by either party.

SHAREHOLDER ACCOUNTABILITY

The annual reports to shareholders of public companies typically include a statement of management's responsibility for financial statements. The wording of these statements has become standardized over the years. The statement of responsibility includes four assurances on behalf of the company:

1. Management is responsible for the integrity and objectivity of the financial statements and information included in the annual report.
2. The financial statements have been prepared in conformity with generally accepted accounting principles and include certain estimates and judgments made by management in light of current conditions and circumstances.
3. Management maintains a system of accounting and controls that is designed to protect assets from being used improperly and to create accounting records that provide a reliable basis for the preparation of financial statements.
4. The board of directors, through the activities of its audit committee consisting solely of outside directors, participates in the process of reporting financial information.

From our perspective, these assurances provide the basis for moving from the financial statements to the quick overview version of the SPM. Then in the process of trying to understand the business in more depth, we can tack back and forth between each component of the SPM and particular elements of financial information found in the income statements and balance sheets.

If anyone feels uncomfortable relying on the assurances of management, the report of the independent auditors provides additional assurances to establish the foundation for thinking about how shareholder accountability may be linked to business strategy through financial information.

REPORT OF INDEPENDENT AUDITORS

To further assure investors about the integrity of the financial statements, public firms' annual reports include a report from the independent auditors. Over the years, the independent auditors have also standardized the wording of their report to the board of directors and shareholders. The audit report includes the following assertions about the firm's financial statements:

1. The financial statements are the responsibility of management. The responsibility of the independent auditors is to express an opinion on these statements based on their auditor performance in accordance with generally accepted auditing standards.

2. The standards require the auditors to plan and perform the audit to obtain reasonable assurance that the financial statements are free of material misstatement.

3. In the auditors' opinion, the financial statements present fairly, in all material respects, the financial position (balance sheet) of the company for the past two years and the consolidated results of operations for the previous three years.

If you have already begun the process of trying to understand the business operations of your own firm, take a moment to assure yourself of the integrity of senior management and the independent auditors. Management's statement of responsibilities and the report of the independent auditors are typically found at the end of the notes to the financial statements.

FROM FORMAL TO SUBSTANTIVE ACCOUNTABILITY

Even though all annual reports of publicly traded companies must include assurances about the integrity of the information found in the financial statements, not all firms have been equally successful in creating value on behalf of the shareholders.

If we had used the financial statements for Kmart or Sears to illustrate the process of understanding the business through financial information, our discussion of management's business strategy would be quite different. Over the past decade, Kmart sold off noncore businesses and closed down underperforming stores. Sears has sold off or spun off Caldwell Banker (real estate), Dean Witter (brokerage), and Allstate (insurance) as management has attempted to refocus on its core business (retailing). A second description of a Kmart or a Sears using the SPM would provide a binocular view of what would be different in terms of management's success in creating value for the shareholders.

STRATEGIC PROFIT MODEL REVISITED

Figure 6.1 presents the same SPM for Wal-Mart that was presented in Figure 1.5 as the quick overview.

Figure 6.2 presents the compound annual growth rates (CAGRs) associated with each of the elements of the summary version of the SPM.

After working our way through the material presented in Chapters 2 through 5, this summary version of the SPM should trigger a much deeper understanding of Wal-Mart's business than we had when we began this journey to understanding the business through financial information. The information contained in Figures 6.1 and 6.2 can be used to pull together everything we have learned about Wal-Mart's business up to this point.

We have organized our summary under two headings: return on assets (ROA) and return on equity (ROE). Under the ROA heading, we summarize what we know about Wal-Mart's margin management and asset management strategies. Under the ROE heading, we summarize what we know about Wal-Mart's financial management practices. We would not have been in a position to prepare this summary without working our way through the materials presented in Chapters 2 through 5.

**Figure 6.1   Wal-Mart Strategic Profit Model: Summary Version
(for the Fiscal Years Ended January 31, 1990 and 2000—
Amounts in Millions)**

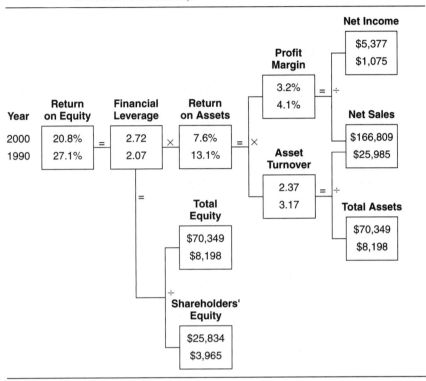

**Figure 6.2   Wal-Mart Strategic Profit Model: Summary Version
(for the Fiscal Years Ended January 31, 1990 and 2000)**

Compound Annual Growth Rates (1990–2000)

Income Statement	
Net Sales	20.4%
Expenses (Net)	20.5%
Net Income	17.5%
Balance Sheet	
Assets	24.0%
Liabilities	26.5%
Shareholders' Equity	20.6%

RETURN ON ASSETS

Margin Management

Between 1990 and 2000, Wal-Mart experienced pressure on its margins. The 0.9¢ decline in profit margin resulted from management's inability to offset the decrease in gross margin and increase in operating expenses. The 0.5¢ decline in gross margin per $1 of net sales and 0.5¢ increase in operating expense could not be completely offset by the 0.4¢ decline in income taxes.

The 0.9¢ decline in profit margin translates into $1.5 billion less net income on net sales of $166.809 billion in 2000.

Asset Management

Between 1990 and 2000, Wal-Mart became "more efficient" and "less efficient" in utilizing the total assets under management's control. By reducing the number of days net sales tied up in current assets (53.3 days in 2000 versus 66.2 days in 1990), management was able to generate more net sales per $1 of investment in current assets in 2000 than it did in 1990. The overall decline in asset turnover of 80¢ from 1990 to 2000 can be attributed to the growth in productive and other assets. Over this ten-year period, productive assets increased as a percentage of total assets, and the net sales generated per $1 of productive assets decreased substantially.

The 80¢ decline in asset turnover translates into $17.728 billion in additional assets in 2000 needed to generate $166.809 billion in net sales.

Combined Effects

Given the pressure from competitors, it is unlikely that Wal-Mart will be able to increase market share by lowering prices. If Wal-Mart is to improve its profit margin, management will have to create operating efficiencies that result in higher net income.

Since Wal-Mart increased the efficiency of its current asset management practices between 1990 and 2000, any improvement in asset turnover will likely have to come from improved productive asset management. Whether management is paying too much for new properties or it is overestimating the revenue that can be generated from these properties, some action must be taken to reverse the decline in revenue per dollar of productive assets.

▶──────────────────────────────────────

If management could have maintained the 13.1% ROA achieved in 1990 versus the actual ROA of 7.6%, Wal-Mart would have generated an additional $3.9 billion in net income on the $70.349 billion asset base under management control in 2000.

──────────────────────────────────────◀

In recent years, and in situations where firms cannot grow the business as fast as they have in the past, many companies have increased their emphasis on increasing ROA.

RETURN ON EQUITY

Financial Management

Between 1990 and 2000, management increased the amount of debt it used to run the business. The increase of 65¢ per $1 of shareholders' equity invested in the business reflects changes in both total liabilities and shareholders' equity.

Liabilities

Between 1990 and 2000, current liabilities expressed in terms of days net sales increased by 16.5 days. That increase reflects a 3.0-day increase in accounts payable (28.7 days in 2000 versus 25.7 days in 1990), a 9.2-day increase in accrued liabilities, and a 4.3-day increase in current debt coming due within the year.

Like the relationship between current assets and productive assets, Wal-Mart's long-term liabilities (29.7% CAGR) have been growing at a faster rate than current liabilities (24.7%). Long-term liabilities have accounted for the largest increase in Wal-Mart's total liabilities.

Shareholders' Equity

Between 1990 and 2000, shareholders' equity grew primarily through increasing retained earnings (21.0% CAGR), with only a small amount of the growth coming from the issuance of additional common stock (17.2% CAGR). As of January 31, 2000, retained earnings accounted for 97.3% of shareholders' equity and 35.7% of total equity.

Combined Effects

The increase in Wal-Mart's financial leverage from 2.07 to 2.72 (a 31.4% increase), combined with the 5.5 percentage point decrease in ROA (7.6% − 13.1%) contributed to the overall decrease in ROE from 27.1% to 20.8%. However, even if Wal-Mart had maintained a financial leverage of $2.07, ROE would have declined to 15.7%.

Given management's future emphasis on increasing ROA as part of Wal-Mart's overall business strategy, we would not expect financial leverage to change dramatically over the next several years. Based on the insights developed by using the SPM to help us understand Wal-Mart's business, we would suspect that management will be taking a close look at how it can increase its gross margin on sales while growing the business and managing the productive assets under its control.

DRAWING YOUR OWN CONCLUSIONS

In this summary of our understanding of Wal-Mart's business through the SPM, we have ventured a little further away from explanation and more toward speculation than we have done in the past. We have done so in the hopes of stimulating you to engage in the same sort of speculation process as you attempt to understand more about your own business through use of the SPM.

Hopefully, by developing a better understanding of the business, you will become a more effective manager and/or investor. Understanding is nice, but the rewards flow to those who take action.

Throughout the remainder of this book, we will follow the same approach that we have followed in developing the full-blown SPM. Translating understanding into action is a three-step process:

1. We have to *see,* or visualize, the numbers to make them meaningful to us.

2. We have to *say* what we *see* in order to make sure we know what we are talking about.

3. We have to translate what we *see* and what we *say* into action (*do* it).

In Chapter 7, we will introduce a second business strategy model—the Strategic Financing Model (SFM)—to help us develop a better understanding of how management builds the firm's long-term financing and investment base. In Chapter 8, we shall see how management factors its commitment to grow the business on behalf of the shareholders into the firm's overall business strategy.

NOTES

1. Gregory Bateson is the author of *Mind and Nature* (Bantam Books, 1979) and *Steps to an Ecology of Mind* (Chandler Press, 1972). Trained in cultural anthropology, Bateson provides an approach to biological, psychological, and social systems that emphasizes the "pattern which connects" all of the elements of those systems together into a unified whole.

2. Gregory Bateson, *Mind and Nature* (Bantam Books, 1979), 82.

CHAPTER 7

Strategic Financing Model: Long-Term Investment and Financing

Income statements and balance sheets provide a wealth of information for helping users of financial information understand the business. When we view the information included in those statements through the lens of the Strategic Profit Model (SPM), we are able to see profitability relationships that otherwise might go unnoticed by most people.

If we were limited to just one model in helping managers understand the business, there is no doubt that we would stick with the SPM. The SPM helps everyone see how profitable a firm has been in the past, and it provides a framework for speculating about how the firm might perform in the future. If Wal-Mart earned 20.8¢ on every $1 of shareholders' equity in 2000, what is management likely to earn in 2002, in the year 2004, 2010, or 2025?

As useful as the SPM is in helping us understand how profitable a firm has been in a particular year, it falls a little short in two areas:

1. Understanding how long-term investment and financing decisions fit into the firm's overall business strategy
2. Understanding the relationship between the firm's financial performance as reflected in the financial statements and the market valuation of the firm's common stock

In order to correct for the first shortfall, we restructure the balance sheet and visualize the long-term investment and long-term financing aspects of the business through a second business strategy model, the Strategic Financing Model (SFM). The restructured balance sheet focuses on the firm's long-term capital commitments (to working capital and gross productive/other assets) and on who provided the long-term money to finance those commitments (creditors, shareholders, and management). The SFM then allows us to see how these capital commitments and sources of financing fit together in a manner that makes sense to managers.

This chapter is organized into two parts. In the first part of the chapter, we restructure the balance sheet in order to focus on the long-term investment and long-term financing aspects of the firm's overall business strategy. By taking managers through the process of restructuring the balance sheet, we introduce the additional financial concepts senior executives use when planning for the future.

In the second part of the chapter, we introduce our second business strategy model, the SFM. Like the SPM, the SFM helps managers see how long-term investment and long-term financing decisions fit into the firm's overall business strategy.

RESTRUCTURING THE BALANCE SHEET

Virtually all of us know of someone who has lost his or her job as management has restructured the business to become more competitive. To these people, the term *restructuring* conjures up all sorts of unpleasant images.

When we restructure the balance sheet, we have a much more constructive use in mind. We want to see how firms such as Wal-Mart have built the long-term investment and long-term financing foundation that supports all of their business operations.[1]

We base our approach to the restructuring process on the guidance provided by Gregory Bateson:

> The division of the perceived universe into parts and wholes is convenient and may be necessary, but no necessity determines how it shall be done.[2]

Since we want to understand the long-term investment and financing aspects of the firm's business strategy, we need to restructure the balance sheet to provide a foundation for visualizing the firm from a long-term perspective.

Figure 7.1 presents Wal-Mart's balance sheets for 1990 and 2000, which were first presented in Chapter 1. As discussed more fully in that chapter, we indicated that the basic financial control equation underlying the balance sheet is

Assets = Liabilities + Shareholders' Equity

For the fiscal years ended January 31, 1990 and 2000, Wal-Mart's balance sheet equations appear as

Assets = Liabilities + Shareholders' Equity
2000: $70.349B = $44.515B + $25.834B
1990: $8.198B = $ 4.233B + $3.965B

We used that financial control equation to anchor our understanding of all of the information found in a balance sheet.

For example, we saw that total assets equaled current assets plus productive and other assets. We also saw that current assets consisted of cash and equivalents, receivables, inventory, and other current assets. Any mystery or possible misunderstanding surrounding the meaning of any of the elements making up the balance sheet (and the income statement) was eliminated as we looked at each of these elements within the context of the SPM.

When we move to a restructured balance sheet, the financial control equation shifts from

Assets = Liabilities + Shareholders' Equity

Figure 7.1   Wal-Mart Balance Sheets (for the Fiscal Years Ended January 31, 1990 and 2000—Amounts in Millions)

	1990	2000
Assets		
Current Assets		
Cash and Equivalents	$13	$1,856
Receivables	$156	$1,341
Inventory	$4,428	$19,793
Other	116	$1,366
Total Current Assets	$4,713	$24,356
Productive Assets		
Property, Plant, and Equipment	$4,402	$45,348
Accumulated Depreciation	($972)	($9,379)
Net Productive Assets	$3,430	$35,969
Other Assets	$55	$10,024
Total	$8,198	$70,349
Liabilities and Shareholders' Equity		
Liabilities		
Current Liabilities		
Accounts Payable	$1,827	$13,105
Current Debt Due	$24	$2,085
Accrued Liabilities	$995	$10,613
Total Current Liabilities	$2,846	$25,803
Long-Term Liabilities		
Long-Term Debt	$185	$13,672
Long-Term Lease Obligations	$1,087	$3,002
Deferred Income Taxes and Other	$115	$759
Minority Interest	$0	$1,279
Total Long-Term Liabilities	$1,387	$18,712
Total Liabilities	$4,233	$44,515
Shareholders' Equity		
Common Stock	$237	$1,160
Retained Earnings	$3,728	$25,129
Other Equity Adjustments	$0	($455)
Total Shareholders' Equity	$3,965	$25,834
Total	$8,198	$70,349

to the following equation:

Total Long-Term Investment = Total Long-Term Financing

A restructured balance sheet differs from a regular balance sheet in three ways:

1. The long-term investment section of the restructured balance sheet is made up of *working capital, gross productive assets,* and *gross other assets.*
2. The long-term financing section is made up of *external debt financing, external equity financing,* and *internal equity financing.*
3. *Internal equity financing* equals retained earnings plus several score-keeping adjustments that have been added back to retained earnings.

The process of learning how long-term investment and financing activities fit into the firm's overall business strategy begins with understanding the reasons for restructuring the balance sheet to promote long-term thinking.

Figure 7.2 presents the same information found in Wal-Mart's balance sheets for 1990 and 2000, only restructured to account for the three differences previously mentioned. The amounts shown in italics represent the changes that occurred between 1990 and 2000.

The new financial control equation underlying the restructured balance sheet emphasizes the relationship between Wal-Mart's cumulative long-term investment and long-term financing decisions.

Total Long-Term Investment = Total Long-Term Financing
2000: $53.925B = $53.925B
1990: $6.324B = $6.324B

As we can see from a comparison of the 1990 and 2000 control equations, Wal-Mart increased its long-term investment from $6.3 billion to $53.9 billion. On the financing side of the equation, we see the mirror image of the investment side of the equation. Over this ten-year period, Wal-Mart increased its long-term financing and long-term investment by $47.6 billion.

Figure 7.2 Wal-Mart Restructured Balance Sheets (for the Fiscal Years Ended January 31, 1990 and 2000—Amounts in Millions)

	1990	*Change*	2000
Long-Term Investment			
Current Assets			
Cash and Equivalents	$13	*$1,843*	$1,856
Receivables	$156	*$1,185*	$1,341
Inventory	$4,428	*$15,365*	$19,793
Other	116	*$1,250*	$1,366
Total Current Assets	$4,713	*$19,643*	$24,356
Current Liabilities			
Accounts Payable	$1,827	*$11,278*	$13,105
Accrued Liabilities	$995	*$9,618*	$10,613
Current Debt Due	$24	*$2,061*	$2,085
Total Current Liabilities	$2,846	*$22,957*	$25,803
Working Capital	$1,867	*($3,314)*	($1,447)
Gross Productive Assets			
Property, Plant, and Equipment	$4,402	*$40,946*	$45,348
Gross Other Assets			
Other Assets	$55	*$9,969*	$10,024
Total Long-Term Investment	$6,324	*$47,601*	$53,925
Long-Term Financing			
External Debt Financing			
Long-Term Debt	$185	*$13,487*	$13,672
Long-Term Lease Obligations	$1,087	*$1,915*	$3,002
Minority Interest	$0	*$1,279*	$1,279
Total External Debt	$1,272	*$16,681*	*$17,953*
External Equity Financing			
Common Stock	$237	*$923*	$1,160
Stock Repurchases	$0	*($3,105)*	($3,105)
Total External Equity	$237	*($2,182)*	($1,945)
Internal Equity Financing			
Retained Earnings	$3,728	*$21,401*	$25,129
Accumulated Depreciation	$972	*$8,407*	$9,379
Deferred Income Taxes and Other	$115	*$644*	$759
Stock Repurchases	$0	*$3,105*	$3,105
Other Equity Adjustments	$0	*($455)*	($455)
Total Internal Equity	$4,815	*$33,102*	$37,917
Total Long-Term Financing	$6,324	*$47,601*	$53,925

Even though we might not be able to provide a detailed description of Wal-Mart's long-term investment and financing strategy at this time, we do know that it invested $47.6 billion for the long term, and management had to come up with $47.6 billion of long-term financing to match that investment. Given this start, we can begin to develop a more in-depth understanding of the long-term aspects of Wal-Mart's overall business strategy.

We will explain the differences between a regular balance sheet and a restructured balance sheet in the process of describing Wal-Mart's restructured balance sheets, which were presented in Figure 7.2.

Long-Term Investment

Working Capital. Current liabilities are subtracted from current assets to arrive at Wal-Mart's working capital for the fiscal years ended January 31, 1990 and 2000. Working capital represents the long-term investment in the business that must be maintained in order to run the day-to-day operations of the business.

When we shift gears and move from the regular balance sheet to the restructured balance sheet, current assets and current liabilities become part of the firm's long-term investment base. Using the language of investing and financing, current assets represent short-term investments related to the firm's operating cycle (cash, receivables, inventory, etc.), while current liabilities represent short-term financing provided by suppliers and other short-term creditors (accounts payable, current debt due to creditors, and other accrued liabilities).

When the amount of short-term financing provided by current liabilities is subtracted from the short-term investment in current assets, any balance must be financed from long-term sources of funds. As discussed more fully within the context of the SFM, most firms cannot survive without some level of long-term investment in working capital.

▶──────────────────────────────────

In 1990, Wal-Mart had $1.867 billion invested in working capital; in 2000, Wal-Mart had $1.447 billion deficit in working capital.

Over the ten-year period, Wal-Mart decreased its long-term investment in working capital by $3.314 billion.

──────────────────────────────◀

The language of investment and financing that underlies the restructured balance sheet helps us develop a different frame of reference for understanding the business. While current assets and current liabilities have both increased, current liabilities now exceed current assets. This deficit is likely a timing difference at year-end 2000.

Gross Productive Assets.   When we want to see how much money has been invested in new stores, distribution centers, and other long-term commitments, we look at the firm's gross productive assets.

When we compare the restructured balance sheet with the regular balance sheet, we see that accumulated depreciation has not been subtracted from property, plant, and equipment. Accumulated depreciation has been added back to retained earnings (to be discussed more fully in a later section).

▶ ──

In 1990, Wal-Mart had $4.402 billion invested in gross productive assets; in 2000, that investment equaled $45.348 billion.

Over the ten-year period, Wal-Mart increased its long-term investment in gross productive assets by $40.946 billion.

─── ◀

As discussed in Chapter 4 under the asset management component of the SPM, the growth in net productive assets (property, plant, and equipment less accumulated depreciation) was out of line, compared with the growth in current assets. Within the context of a restructured balance sheet, we can see that the investment in gross productive assets represented 84.1% of the total long-term investing base in 2000 compared to only 69.6% in 1990.

Gross Other Assets.   For a firm such as Wal-Mart, the *gross other assets* shown on the restructured balance sheets are the same as the *other assets* reported on the regular balance sheet. However, for some companies, the difference can be quite large.[3]

▶ ──

In 1990, Wal-Mart had $55 million invested in gross other assets; in 2000, that investment equaled $10.024 billion.

Over the ten-year period, Wal-Mart increased its long-term investment in gross other assets by $9.969 billion.

Total Long-Term Investment.   As we can see from Figure 7.2, Wal-Mart has only three places to put its long-term investment dollars: (1) working capital, (2) gross productive assets, and (3) gross other assets.

In 1990, Wal-Mart had $6.324 billion invested for the long term; in 2000, the total long-term investment equaled $53.925 billion.

Based on the logic of the financial-control equation underlying the restructured balance sheets, if Wal-Mart had $47.601 billion invested for the long term as of January 31, 2000, it had to have come up with an equivalent amount of long-term financing.[4]

Long-Term Financing

When it comes to financing the long-term future of the business, the money can come from only one of three sources: external debt financing (creditors), external equity financing (shareholders), or internal equity financing (management).

External Debt Financing.   In Wal-Mart's case, external debt financing comes from long-term notes, bonds, capital lease obligations, and minority interests.

In 1990, Wal-Mart employed $1.272 billion of external debt financing for the long term; in 2000, external debt financing equaled $17.953 billion.

Over the ten-year period, external debt financing increased by $16.681 billion.

When we compare the restructured balance sheet with the regular balance sheet, we see that deferred income taxes have been added back to retained earnings and are not included as a part of external debt financing. Deferred income taxes, like depreciation charges, represent scorekeeping adjustments that reflect the timing differences between financial reporting and income tax reporting. Until the income taxes are actually due and payable, the deferred income taxes are part of management's (internal) contribution to financing the future of the business.

External Equity Financing.   Since Wal-Mart has only common stock outstanding, its external equity financing consists solely of the money received for the common stock issued and outstanding.

▶

Over the ten-year period, external equity financing decreased from \$237 million to a net \$1.945 billion deficit.

◀

As discussed more fully within the context of the SFM, we see that the issuance of common stock was not a major factor in financing the business during this ten-year period. During 1990 through 2000, Wal-Mart repurchased \$3.1 billion of common stock. These repurchases were recorded through retained earnings. We reclassify these amounts to more appropriately reflect management's contribution to growing the business. We add back these amounts to Retained Earnings and deduct them from External Equity Financing

Wal-Mart uses this repurchased stock to complete its acquisitions and to meet obligations to employees who exercised stock options.

Internal Equity Financing.   Internal equity financing can be defined either passively as a residual amount or actively as management's positive contribution to financing the future of the firm.

Defined passively, internal equity financing equals retained earnings plus amounts added back for accumulated depreciation, deferred income taxes, stock repurchases, and other equity adjustments. As we saw from the amounts reported for 2000 (in Figure 7.1), \$9.379 billion was added back to retained earnings for accumulated depreciation, \$759 million added back for deferred income taxes, \$3.105 billion added back for stock repurchases, and \$455 million subtracted for other equity adjustments.

In 1990, Wal-Mart employed $4.815 billion of internal equity financing for the long term; in 2000, internal equity financing equaled $37.917 billion.

Within the context of the SFM, we will emphasize a more active and positive definition of internal equity financing. We will assume that, if we were working within the firm, we could monitor the level of internal equity financing generated by management without having to make all of these scorekeeping adjustments to retained earnings.

Between 1990 and 2000, the internal equity financing contributed by management increased by $33.102 billion.

Total Long-Term Financing. When it comes time to finance the business for the long term, management has only three places to go to get the money: (1) long-term creditors (external debt financing), (2) shareholders (external equity financing), or (3) itself (internal equity financing).

External Debt Financing + External Equity Financing + Internal Equity Financing = Total Long-Term Financing

Since Wal-Mart had $53.925 billion invested for the long term, we know that the total long-term financing had to equal that amount, which it did, as shown in Figure 7.2.

As mentioned previously, a restructured balance sheet differs from a regular balance sheet in three ways:

1. The long-term investment section of the restructured balance sheet is made up of *working capital, gross productive assets,* and *gross other assets.* As of January 31, 1990, Wal-Mart had $6.3 billion invested

for the long term. By January 31, 2000, that long-term investment had increased to $53.9 billion.

2. The long-term financing section is made up of *external debt financing, external equity financing,* and *internal equity financing.* Between January 31, 1990, and January 31, 2000, Wal-Mart's long-term financing increased from $6.3 billion to $53.9 billion, exactly equaling the increase in long-term investment.

3. *Internal equity financing* equals retained earnings plus several score-keeping adjustments that have been added back to retained earnings. As of January 31, 1990, Wal-Mart's internal equity financing equaled $4.8 billion. By January 31, 2000, internal equity financing had increased to $37.9 billion.

Even though managers need to understand the language of long-term investment and long-term financing, they are really more interested in knowing how long-term investment and financing decisions affect their lives. That is where the SFM comes into play. The SFM helps managers see what senior management is doing to structure the firm's finances in order to be successful in the future.

STRATEGIC FINANCING MODEL

If the SPM helped us see the profitability "cow" in Wal-Mart's income statements and balance sheets, then the SFM should help us see the financing and investment "bull" in Wal-Mart's restructured balance sheets. As we all know, it takes both cows and bulls to make a herd. Without a well-thought-out long-term investment and financing strategy, even highly profitable firms can get themselves into financial difficulty.

We use the SFM to help managers develop a better understanding of how a firm matches a long-term financing strategy with its long-term investment plan, as well as how the long-term financing and investment strategy is driven, in part, by the amount of internal equity financing generated by management on the shareholders' behalf.

Long-term investing and financing activities do not just happen. Senior management must decide on how fast to grow the business (including whether growth is even a realistic possibility) and how to finance that growth. The first component of the SFM shows how the long-term financing aspects of the business are matched to the firm's long-term investment strategy. The second component of the SFM looks at the firm's long-term business strategy from the internal perspective of the managers responsible for generating a return on the shareholders' behalf.

Figure 7.3 presents the long-term financing and long-term investment foundation for Wal-Mart's SFM, using the amounts taken from the 1990 and 2000 restructured balance sheets.

Figure 7.4(a) presents a percentage breakdown of Wal-Mart's long-term financing and long-term investment base, and Figure 7.4(b) presents the related compound annual growth rates (CAGRs) for the ten-year period. The percentage breakdowns and CAGRs will be used to help us understand the long-term financing and investment aspects of Wal-Mart's overall business strategy.

As we did with the SPM, the narrative explanation of Wal-Mart's business strategy follows the visual representation of the business.

Long-Term Financing = Long-Term Investment (LTF = LTI)

Figure 7.3   Wal-Mart Strategic Financing Model: Long-Term Financing = Long-Term Investment (for the Fiscal Years Ended January 31, 1990 and 2000—Amounts in Millions)

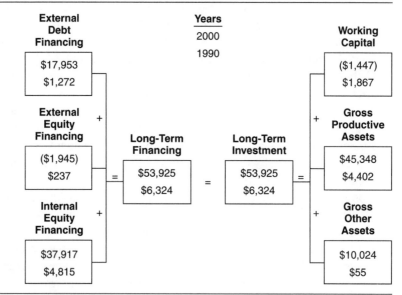

Figure 7.4   Wal-Mart Strategic Financing Model: Long-Term Financing = Long-Term Investment

(a) Percent Total Financing and Total Investment

	1990	2000
External Debt Financing	20.1%	33.3%
External Equity Financing	3.7%	−3.6%
Internal Equity Financing	76.2%	70.3%
Total Long-Term Financing	100.0%	100.0%

	1990	2000
Working Capital	29.5%	−2.7%
Gross Productive Assets	69.6%	84.1%
Gross Other Assets	0.9%	18.6%
Total Long-Term Investment	100.0%	100.0%

(b) Compound Annual Growth Rates (1990–2000)

External Debt Financing	30.3%
External Equity Financing	NM*
Internal Equity Financing	22.9%
Total Long-Term Financing	23.9%
Working Capital	NM*
Gross Productive Assets	26.3%
Gross Other Assets	NM*
Total Long-Term Investment	23.9%

*Not Meaningful

No matter how much a firm's long-term investment base increases or decreases, it will always have to be matched by an equivalent increase or decrease in long-term financing.

In 1990, Wal-Mart's long-term financing and investment base equaled $6.324 billion; in 2000, the long-term base equaled $53.925 billion.

Between 1990 and 2000, Wal-Mart's long-term financing and investment foundation increased by $47.601 billion, a 23.9% CAGR.

As previously mentioned, the logic of financial control underlying the restructured balance sheet requires the long-term financing to equal the long-term investment. However, logic does not require Wal-Mart to grow at a 23.9% compound annual rate. The decision on how fast to grow the business resides with senior management in consultation with the board of directors.

In looking back over Wal-Mart's past performance, the SFM should help us see how management has matched its long-term investment needs with the three sources of long-term financing as part of the firm's overall business strategy.

In discussing the long-term aspects of a firm's business strategy, we begin with Wal-Mart's working capital.

Long-Term Investment

Working Capital. Working capital represents Wal-Mart's long-term investment in the day-to-day operations of the business, which must be financed from long-term sources.

In 1990, Wal-Mart's investment in working capital equaled $1.867 billion; in 2000, the working capital deficit equaled $1.447 billion.

Between 1990 and 2000, the investment in working capital decreased, significantly compared with the 26.3% growth rate for gross productive assets.

To a certain extent, the fact that working capital decreased while gross productive assets increased should come as no surprise. As discussed in Chapter 3, the days net sales tied up in current assets decreased from 66.2 days in 1990 to 53.3 days in 2000. From the discussion in Chapter 5, we know that the days net sales tied up in current liabilities increased from 40.0 days in 1990 to 56.5 days in 2000.

When current liabilities are subtracted from current assets, we can see that Wal-Mart's long-term investment in working capital decreased from 26.2 days net sales in 1990 to -3.2 days in 2000.

	Days Net Sales	
	1990	2000
Current Assets	66.2	53.3
Current Liabilities	40.0	56.5
Working Capital	26.2	(3.2)

Between 1990 and 2000, Wal-Mart was able to reduce its long-term investment in working capital by 29.4 days net sales. At $457.0 million of net sales per day (see Chapters 3 and 5 for a more complete discussion of days net sales), Wal-Mart reduced the working capital portion of its total long-term investment by $13.436 billion in 2000 when compared with 1990 performance levels.

In 1990, working capital equaled 29.5% of the total long-term investment. By 2000, the investment in working capital had dropped to -2.7%. No matter how you measure Wal-Mart's long-term investment in working capital (the percentage decline, days net sales invested in working capital, and percentage of total long-term investment), Wal-Mart reduced its working capital over the ten years between 1990 and 2000, resulting in a $13.436 billion reduction in long-term investment.

Gross Productive Assets. Gross productive assets represent Wal-Mart's cumulative long-term investment in property, plant, and equipment owned by the firm or controlled through capital lease arrangements.

Between 1990 and 2000, Wal-Mart's investment in gross productive assets increased from $4.402 billion to $45.348 billion, a CAGR of 26.3%.

Since the investment in gross productive assets grew while working capital declined, we should modify our explanation of what Wal-Mart is doing with part of its "savings" from reductions in the number of days net sales invested in working capital.

► _____

It appears that, between 1990 and 2000, Wal-Mart was able to at least partially redirect the $13.436 billion in working capital savings to accelerate the growth of its investment in gross productive assets.

_____ ◄

Compared with 1990 performance levels, Wal-Mart had made a significant increase in its investment in property, plant, and equipment by 2000.

With the decrease in net sales per $1 of investment in productive assets (discussed in Chapters 3 and 4), we can see that Wal-Mart's long-term investments in productive assets were not delivering the same bang for the buck in 2000 that they delivered back in 1990.

Gross Other Assets. As previously mentioned, the investment in gross other assets increased by $9.969 billion on a base of $55 million in 1990. Given the lack of details about the composition of other assets, about all we can say is that they constituted 18.6% of the long-term investment base in 2000 versus 0.9% in 1990. This change reflects the considerable number of acquisitions Wal-Mart completed in the late 1990s.

Long-Term Investment. Between 1990 and 2000, Wal-Mart reduced its investment in working capital while increasing its investment in gross productive and other assets.

When firms such as Wal-Mart allow the ratio of gross productive and other assets to increase at a disproportionate rate, we can speculate that management has fallen victim to a common business affliction—growing productive assets faster than sales.

If we recall the discussion in Chapters 3 and 4 about asset turnover and return on assets (ROA), we can come to the same conclusion within the context of the SFM. Growing the business through increasing sales is of no benefit to the shareholders if the growth requires a disproportionate growth in long-term investment. However, to turn around and overinvest in gross productive and other assets does not produce benefits to shareholders.

Long-Term Financing

External Debt Financing. External debt financing represents the amount of money raised from long-term creditors that is used to finance the total long-term investment in the business.

In 1990, Wal-Mart utilized $1.272 billion of external debt financing to run the business; in 2000, Wal-Mart utilized $17.953 billion.

Between 1990 and 2000, external debt financing increased at a 30.3% CAGR.

In 1990, external debt financing represented 20.1% of total long-term financing; in 2000, external debt financing represented 33.3%.

As discussed more fully in Chapter 10, Standard & Poor's and Moody's give Wal-Mart their highest credit rating relative to risk-free government bonds. With a strong credit rating, firms such as Wal-Mart can take advantage of the leverage effects of debt financing (see Chapter 5). However, like any other firm that finances its business with long-term debt, Wal-Mart is subject to interest rate risk (changes in interest rates). If interest rates go up, the interest costs associated with issuing new debt and/or refinancing old debt will also go up. If that happens, Wal-Mart will experience additional pressure on its margins, with interest charges consuming a greater portion of every net sales dollar (see Chapter 3).

External Equity Financing. External equity financing represents the amount of money raised by issuing common stock to shareholders, less any amounts paid out to reacquire outstanding shares.

In 1990, Wal-Mart utilized $237 million of external equity financing to run the business; in 2000, Wal-Mart had a net $1.945 billion deficit.

Between 1990 and 2000, Wal-Mart repurchased more common stock than it issued.

In 1990, external equity financing represented 3.7% of total long-term financing; in 2000, external equity financing represented −3.6%.

Aside from minor amounts of common stock issued through the exercise of stock options, external equity financing has not been a major source of long-term financing for Wal-Mart. In fact, in recent years, Wal-Mart has been reacquiring shares on the open market to meet its obligations to employees who are exercising their options to acquire common stock and to fund acquisitions.

Internal Equity Financing.   Internal equity financing represents management's contribution to financing the long-term future of the firm.

In 1990, Wal-Mart utilized $4.815 billion of internal equity financing in the business; in 2000, Wal-Mart utilized $37.917 billion.

Between 1990 and 2000, internal equity financing increased at a 22.9% CAGR.

In 1990, internal equity financing represented 76.2% of total long-term financing; in 2000, internal equity financing represented 70.3%.

As discussed more fully in Chapter 8, a significant part of management's overall business strategy must focus on how the future of the firm is to be financed from internal sources. In Wal-Mart's case, management generates high ROEs, pays low dividends, and finances a substantial portion of the firm's growth through internal equity financing.

Long-Term Financing.   Between 1990 and 2000, Wal-Mart increased its reliance on long-term creditors (external debt financing), decreased its shareholders (external equity financing) in growing the business, and decreased its reliance on internal equity financing.

| | Percent Long-Term Financing | | |
	1990	2000	Change
External Debt Financing	20.1%	33.3%	13.2%
External Equity Financing	3.7%	-3.6%	-7.3%
Internal Equity Financing	76.2%	70.3%	-5.9%

The 5.9 percentage point decrease in internal equity financing has been off-set by the 13.2 percentage point increase in external debt financing and the 7.3 percentage point decrease in external equity financing.

As we can see from the 1990 and 2000 percentages of total long-term financing, despite the changes, internal equity financing has been and continues to be the primary driver for financing the future of the firm. This internal equity financing has been and continues to be supplemented by a significant amount of external debt financing.

Even though our discussion in this chapter has focused on what happened at Wal-Mart between 1990 and 2000, we hope that you would agree that we now have a pretty good foundation for speculating about Wal-Mart's future performance. Firms cannot change their culture overnight, and we are firm believers that knowledge of past performance is a good place to start in assessing possible future performance.

In Chapter 8, we are going to extend our analysis of the long-term investment and long-term financing aspects of Wal-Mart's overall business strategy by bringing the customer into play and focusing on the primary role played by internal equity financing in growing the business.

NOTES

1. Restructuring information found in a firm's financial statements is a practice followed by virtually every investment advisory service (Standard & Poor's, Moody's, Dun and Bradstreet, etc.) and management consulting firm (McKinsey & Company, Inc.; Stern, Stewart and Co.; Ernst & Young; Marakon Associates; Alcar; etc.). For whatever reason, these users of financial information believe that they can gain additional insights into the business by restructuring the information found in the financial statements. In this respect, we are no different than these other financial advisors. We believe there are additional insights to be gained through the restructuring process. The restructured balance sheets discussed in this chapter reflect the most common adjustments made by the advisory services and consulting firms mentioned above. The investment advisory services typically provide a multi-year summary of selected information. In effect, they provide the reader with a partial balance sheet. The management consulting firms typically ignore scorekeeping adjustments for depreciation, amortization, deferred income taxes, and changes in accounting methods in their restructuring of the financial statements. As you become more comfortable with the process of restructuring the balance sheet, please feel free to experiment with other types of restructurings.

2. Gregory Bateson, *Mind and Nature* (New York, NY, Bantam Books, 1979), 39.

3. If one company buys another company and incurred "goodwill" (i.e., pays more for the company than the fair market value of its assets and liabilities), the goodwill is typically included in the balance sheet under other assets. Over time, the goodwill is amortized, and the accumulated amortization is treated the same as accumulated depreciation. If Wal-Mart had reported its accumulated amortization, the accumulated amortization would have been added back to retained earnings on the restructured balance sheet.

4. In making the transition from *total assets* to *total long-term investment*, we subtracted current liabilities from current assets to focus on the long-term investment in working capital, and we added back the accumulated depreciation.

CHAPTER 8

Strategic Financing Model: Financing the Business

In using the Strategic Financing Model (SFM) to develop a better understanding of the long-term aspects of a firm's business strategy, we get an opportunity to practice using the language of financing and investing. Even though we may not yet be fluent speakers, the discussion of the restructured balance sheet in Chapter 7 provided us with the basic vocabulary of long-term investing and financing. We know that the firm's long-term investment base consists of working capital, gross productive assets, and gross other assets. We also know that the long-term investment can only be financed from one of three long-term sources: (1) external debt financing (creditors), (2) external equity financing (shareholders), and (3) internal equity financing (management).

In this chapter, we are going to add an "action" component to the SFM and link the long-term aspects of the firm's business strategy directly back to the customer, the primary source of financing for any firm. In order to see a firm's long-term business strategy in action, we will focus on the *changes* between the restructured balance sheets for the fiscal years ended January 31, 1990 and 2000.

In order to focus on the strategic implications of the changes in the components of the restructured balance sheets between the fiscal years ended January 31, 1990 and 2000, we create one additional financial statement. The financial flow statement:

1. Includes only the amounts reported for each of the major categories reported for the two restructured balance sheets;

2. Presents the long-term financing information before the long-term investment information, and

3. Includes a history and summation of the net sales made during the years 1991 through 2000.

With this information in hand, we can begin to understand how Wal-Mart built and financed its long-term investment base between 1990 and 2000.

Figure 8.1 presents Wal-Mart's financial flow statement for the ten-year period ended January 31, 2000. The financial flow statement includes two sections. The top section of the statement provides a summary, by major category, of the information found in Wal-Mart's restructured balance sheets, discussed in Chapter 7 (see Figure 7.2). As previously mentioned, the one notable difference is that the information about Wal-Mart's long-term financing activities is presented above the information about Wal-Mart's long-term investment activities. The lower section of Figure 8.1 presents Wal-Mart's net sales for the fiscal years ended January 31, 1990 through 2000.

In Chapter 7, we discussed the reasoning behind restructuring the balance sheet. Now we can concentrate on how management actually financed the increase in long-term investment. As we can see from Figure 8.1, the "change" column, which extends down to include Wal-Mart's net sales for the years 1990 through 2000, has been presented in italics. By focusing on the changes that have occurred over this ten-year period, we are able to increase our understanding of the long-term financing and investment aspects of Wal-Mart's overall business strategy.

The logic of financial control underlying the financial flow statement is represented as a self-balancing equation similar to the self-balancing equations underlying the balance sheet, the income statement, and the restructured balance sheet.

Total Long-Term Financing = Total Long-Term Investment

LTF = LTI

From Figure 8.1, we can see that, between January 31, 1990, and January 31, 2000, Wal-Mart increased its long-term financing by $47.6 billion. That increase in long-term financing was used to meet Wal-Mart's long-term investment needs, which equal $47.6 billion. However, like all of the

Figure 8.1   Wal-Mart Financial Flow Statement (for Ten Years Ended January 31, 2000—Amounts in Millions)

Long-Term Financing	1990	Change	2000
External Debt Financing	$1,272	$16,681	$17,953
External Equity Financing	$237	($2,182)	($1,945)
Internal Equity Financing	$4,815	$33,102	$37,917
Total Long-Term Financing	$6,324	$47,601	$53,925

Long-Term Investment	1990	Change	2000
Working Capital	$1,867	($3,314)	($1,447)
Gross Productive Assets	$4,402	$40,946	$45,348
Gross Other Assets	$55	$9,969	$10,024
Total Long-Term Investment	$6,324	$47,601	$53,925

Year	Net Sales (in Millions)
1991	$32,863
1992	$44,290
1993	$55,984
1994	$67,985
1995	$83,412
1996	$94,773
1997	$106,178
1998	$119,299
1999	$139,208
2000	$166,809
Ten-Year Total	$910,801

other financial statements we have looked at in Chapters 1 through 7, it is not easy to tell a story about how management went about growing the business. That is where the "financing the business" component of the SFM comes into play. Sales totaled $910.8 billion over the period. With nearly $1 trillion in sales, we would naturally expect some growth in long-term investing.

The financing the business component of the SFM allows us to see how management has combined its external debt and equity financing and internal equity financing to grow the business. As discussed more fully in the following section, a firm has only three sources of long-term financing: external debt financing, external equity financing, and internal equity financing.

The total long-term financing, no matter what source it came from, can be invested only in one of the three components of long-term investment—working capital, gross productive assets, and gross other assets. From a communications perspective, the question becomes one of arranging the information found in Figure 8.1 in a way that makes sense to managers.

In order to increase our understanding of how Wal-Mart management financed the business between 1990 and 2000, we follow a three-step process:

1. Align the net sales provided by customers over the ten-year period with the internal equity financing generated by management.
2. Relate the internal equity financing generated by management to the change in long term investing over the ten-year period.
3. Determine the additional external debt and equity financing, if any, that was needed to meet Wal-Mart's strategic business objectives.

Figure 8.2 presents our way of helping managers make sense out of the long-term financing and investment information found in Figure 8.1. The percentages shown below the dollar amounts are based on the total net sales for the ten-year period. For example, internal equity financing represented 3.6% of the total net sales from 1990 through 2000.

MANAGEMENT'S CONTRIBUTION TO FINANCING THE BUSINESS

The primary purpose of business operations is to grow shareholder wealth through profitable operations. Management's contribution to growing a company's investment base provides a good starting point for looking at Wal-Mart's long-term financing and investment activity over the 1990–2000 period. Before we focus on management's contribution, we need to take one step back and take a look at net sales, the primary source of financing for any business.

Net Sales

One way of trying to understand the long-term aspects of a firm's business strategy is to anchor all of the financial relationships back to the customer. Since the customer is the primary source of financing, it would only seem

Figure 8.2 **Wal-Mart Strategic Financing Model: Financing the Business (for the Period January 31, 1990 through 2000—Amounts in Millions)**

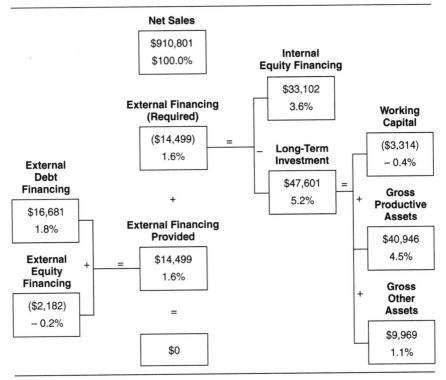

logical to keep the customer in mind when we think about positioning the firm for success in the future.

Between 1990 and 2000, Wal-Mart generated $910.801 billion in customer financing through the sale of merchandise to customers.

Since we are emphasizing the long-term aspects of a firm's business strategy, it only seems natural to use a time horizon that is consistent with taking a longer-term perspective. Even though Wal-Mart's net sales of

$166.809 billion in 2000 are quite impressive, the fact that Wal-Mart generated $910.801 billion in net sales between 1990 and 2000 reinforces the need to keep the customer in the forefront of thinking about the firm's future.

Given that Wal-Mart has demonstrated the ability to generate almost one trillion dollars through sales to customers, the question now becomes one of understanding how Wal-Mart has used these dollars of customer financing to run the business and grow the company over this ten-year period.

If we look at the elements presented in the SFM in terms of total net sales for the ten-year period, we can ask the following question:

For every $1 of net sales generated from customers, what did management do with the money?

Internal Equity Financing

Internal equity financing represents management's contribution to growing the business. It consists of the money "left over" after covering all operating costs, interest, income taxes, and shareholder dividends.

Between 1990 and 2000, management generated $33.102 billion of internal equity financing.

The $33.102 billion represented 3.6¢ of every $1 of net sales generated by management.[1]

Since we have to account for every cent of every dollar of net sales received from customers, it might be nice to know what happened to the other 96.4¢ of customer financing. Between 1990 and 2000, management spent $877.699 billion to cover operating costs, interest, income taxes, and shareholder dividends.

If any firm wants to increase the money generated from internal operations to finance the future of the business, it must reduce the amount of money spent on running the day-to-day operations of the firm.

If Wal-Mart could have generated an additional 1.0¢ of internal equity financing from the business over the period between 1990 and 2000, management would have had an additional $9.108 billion to invest in the business for the long term.

Even before we look at the remainder of the action component of the SFM, we know that we have three options for using the internal equity financing generated by management. The money can be used to

1. Grow the business by increasing the long-term investment in working capital, gross productive assets, and gross other assets
2. Reduce the level of external debt financing
3. Reduce the level of external equity financing

As we work through the remainder of the action component of the SFM, the number of possibilities decreases as management makes specific, strategic commitments to financing the future of the firm.

LONG-TERM INVESTMENT

As we can see from Figure 8.2, Wal-Mart increased its long-term investment base by $47.601 billion. The increase in long-term investment represents the total net change in working capital, gross productive assets, and gross other assets. In discussing each element of Wal-Mart's long-term investment, we will develop a better understanding of how management has grown Wal-Mart's long-term investment base.

Working Capital

The investment in working capital represents the money spent to support the ongoing operations of the firm.

> Between 1990 and 2000, Wal-Mart decreased the investment in working capital by $3.314 billion.
>
> For every $1 of net sales, management generated 0.4¢ through its decrease in working capital.

As discussed in Chapter 7, Wal-Mart has decreased working capital while growing its gross productive assets and gross other assets. Overall, Wal-Mart was at a deficit position at the end of 2000.

Investment in Gross Productive Assets

This investment represents the money spent to expand the business and modernize operations.

> Between 1990 and 2000, Wal-Mart spent $40.946 billion to increase the investment in gross productive assets.
>
> For every $1 of net sales, management spent 4.5¢ to increase its investment in productive assets.

Between 1990 and 2000, 123.7% of internal equity financing generated by management was invested in gross productive assets (123.7% = $40.946B ÷ $33.102B).

Investment in Gross Other Assets

This investment represents the money spent on unspecified long-term commitments.

> Between 1990 and 2000, Wal-Mart spent $9.969 billion to increase the investment in gross other assets.

For every $1 of net sales, management spent 1.1¢ to increase its investment in other assets.

Between 1990 and 2000, 153.8% of internal equity financing generated by management was invested in gross productive assets and gross other assets (153.8% = [$40.946B + $9.969B] ÷ $33.102B).

Even without considering the long-term investment in working capital, Wal-Mart seems to be running into a bit of a problem. Any time you spend more money than you generate from internal operations, management must go outside the firm to raise money from creditors and shareholders.

Total Long-Term Investment

When we combine the long-term requirements for working capital with the requirements for gross productive assets and gross other assets, we see that management has more than exhausted all of the internal equity financing generated between 1990 and 2000.

Between 1990 and 2000, Wal-Mart spent $47.601 billion to increase the total long-term investment in the firm.

For every $1 of net sales, management spent 5.2¢ to increase the total long-term investment.

Given this information about Wal-Mart's long-term investment expenditures, we can make the following observations about the long-term aspects of Wal-Mart's business strategy:

- If Wal-Mart is spending 5.2¢ of every $1 of net sales on building the long-term investment base, management is obviously putting all of the internal equity financing it is generating (3.6¢) back into the business.
- The total long-term investment equals 143.8% of the internal equity financing generated between 1990 and 2000. That 143.8% represents the decrease in working capital and the investment in gross productive assets and gross other assets.

- When a firm's long-term investment needs cannot be met from money generated internally, management has to go outside the business to raise the additional money.

Based on these three observations, we have information that reinforces some of the insights gained from looking at the business through the Strategic Profit Model (SPM) and provides a somewhat different perspective on the business.

The difference between the 5.6¢ being spent on gross productive assets and gross other assets is only partially offset by the 0.4¢ reduction in working capital. Wal-Mart is not getting the same number of net sales dollars out of its investment in gross productive assets and gross other assets as in previous years.

The new insight provided by this action component of the SFM is that, no matter where Wal-Mart is putting its long-term investment dollars, management cannot finance the increased investment entirely from internally generated funds. Between 1990 and 2000, the shortfall equaled $14.5 billion. From the logic of the financial-control equation underlying the financial flow statement, we know that management must have gone outside the business to raise the additional money from external sources (creditors and shareholders).

EXTERNAL FINANCING

External Financing (Required)

External financing required represents the shortfall, or gap, between what management has been able to provide from internal sources to grow the business and the total long-term investment.

Between 1990 and 2000, Wal-Mart generated $33.102 billion in internal equity financing and invested $47.601 billion to increase the firm's long-term investment base.

For every $1 of net sales, the 3.6¢ in internal equity financing fell short of the 5.2¢ invested in the business for the long term.

The shortfall of $14.499 billion equaled 1.6¢ of every $1 of net sales generated over the period between 1990 and 2000.

Since Wal-Mart has been, and still is, committed to growing the business, it is not surprising that additional external financing has been required. If we had used this component of the SFM to understand a firm with little or no growth possibilities, it is quite possible that management would be generating more money than it was reinvesting in the business and actually reducing the amount of external debt and equity financing employed in the business.

Depending on whether the external financing is required (a negative amount) or not required (a positive amount), management is faced with different choices:

1. If external financing is required, management must decide whether to borrow more money and/or issue additional common stock.

2. If external financing is not required, management must decide whether to pay down the debt financing or repurchase some of the outstanding common stock and thereby pay down the external equity financing.

Since the long-term financing reported in the financial flow statement equals the long-term investment (see Figure 8.1), we know that the shortfall was covered. The question that remains is one of seeing how management used a combination of debt and equity financing to cover the shortfall.

External Financing (Required) = External Financing Provided

Aside from monitoring the level of return on equity (ROE) within the context of the firm's overall business strategy, senior management is responsible for deciding whether to grow the business and how to finance that growth. When management goes outside the firm to raise additional money, it must consider if the firm can meet the expectations of the creditors and shareholders who are providing the additional money.

Between 1990 and 2000, Wal-Mart required an additional $14.499 billion to meet its long-term investment needs. That long-term need was met by raising $14.499 billion in external financing.

The shortfall of 1.6¢ of internal equity financing was made up by a net increase of 1.6¢ of external financing being provided by creditors and shareholders.

Whether we are talking about $1, $1 million, or $14.5 billion, the logic of financial control dictates that the amount of external financing required must equal the amount provided.

External Financing Required = External Financing Provided
$14.499B = $14.499B

or, as visualized through Figure 8.2,

External Financing (Required) + External Financing Provided = $0
($14.499B) + $14.499B = $0

If we had to identify one responsibility that senior management cannot delegate to other managers, it would be determining the amount of external financing that will be needed to run the business and decide on the amounts to be raised from creditors and shareholders.

By the time we work our way to the "external financing provided" part of the SFM, a number of strategic choices have already been made. Management has

- Committed all of the internal equity financing it has generated to grow the business
- Decided to grow the business at a faster rate than could be supported by the amount of internal equity financing provided
- Chosen to go outside the firm to raise the additional money needed to grow the business

The only choice left for management to make is deciding how much money to raise from creditors and how much to raise from shareholders.

External Debt Financing

This source of external financing represents the amount of money raised from creditors to grow the business.

Between 1990 and 2000, Wal-Mart raised $16.681 billion in external debt financing. The external debt financing represented 115% of the total financing raised from external sources during this ten-year period.

For every $1 of net sales, Wal-Mart raised an additional 1.8¢ from long-term creditors.

Since we have already considered the effects of internal equity financing on growing the business, the importance of Wal-Mart's debt financing strategy in growing the business becomes even more evident. As we can see, external debt financing (115%) offset the net reduction in external equity financing and covered the overall financing requirement.

Since we know that Wal-Mart raised 1.8¢ of its external financing needs through debt financing, the additional −0.2¢ had to be offset by an external equity financing reduction.

External Equity Financing

This source of financing represents the amount of money raised from shareholders through the issuance of common stock.

Between 1990 and 2000, Wal-Mart reduced external equity financing by $2.182 billion.

For every $1 of net sales, Wal-Mart paid 0.2¢ to shareholders.

The stock repurchases in 1990 through 2000 account for the decrease in external equity financing. Like any number of other firms committed to increasing the value of the shareholders' investment in the firm, external equity financing has not been a prime source of funds for large firms. Since large firms like Wal-Mart attract the attention of numerous financial analysts, any decrease in external equity financing not accompanied by a proportional increase in earnings or cash flow per share (earnings plus depreciation and other noncash adjustments) will likely have a negative impact on the firm's stock price (more on this issue in Chapters 11 and 12).

THE SFM AND UNDERSTANDING THE BUSINESS

As mentioned in Chapter 7, the SFM supplements the SPM by focusing on the long-term financing and investment aspects of the firm's overall business strategy. In restructuring the balance sheet, we make two basic adjustments that support taking a long-term view of the firm. First, we subtract current liabilities from current assets to arrive at the long-term investment in working capital. Second, we add back the scorekeeping adjustments for depreciation, deferred income taxes, and translation adjustments to retained earnings to create a long-term financing and investment perspective.

By focusing on the changes in each of the major categories in the restructured balance sheet, we can create a financial flow statement that allows us to build an action component for the SFM.

In visualizing these restructured balance sheets and the financial flow statement through the lens of the SFM, we can gain additional insights into the long-term aspects of the firm's overall business strategy. In Wal-Mart's case, we were able to make the following observations about the long-term aspects of management's overall business strategy.

Long-Term Financing = Long-Term Investment

- Between 1990 and 2000, Wal-Mart's long-term investments were heavily weighted toward gross productive and other assets versus working capital. Consistent with the insights we gained through the SPM during this ten-year period, Wal-Mart reduced its working capital and appeared to have become less efficient in managing its investment in gross productive assets.
- Between 1990 and 2000, external debt financing played a prominent role in Wal-Mart's overall business strategy, while external equity financing played a less important role. External debt financing to represented 115% of the total external financing required.
- Between 1990 and 2000, the bulk of Wal-Mart's long-term financing came from internal equity financing and external debt financing.
- Between 1990 and 2000, the $33.102 billion of internal equity financing generated by management equaled 3.6¢ of every $1 of net sales.

- All of the internal equity financing (and then some) was used to grow the long-term investment base—$14.499 billion of the increase in long-term investment of $47.601 billion could not be financed from internal sources. The 5.2¢ increase in long-term investment per $1 of net sales resulted in a 1.6¢ shortfall, which had to be financed from external sources.
- The $14.499 billion needed to cover the shortfall from internal equity financing came primarily from long-term creditors. Long-term creditors provided $16.681 billion, or 1.8¢ of long-term financing for every $1 of net sales. External debt financing accounted for over 115% of the external financing raised between 1990 and 2000. External debt financing offset the decrease in external equity financing.
- The role played by external equity financing in the period between 1990 and 2000 was interesting. The $2.182 billion decrease in external equity financing increased the total external financing needed to grow the business. Wal-Mart repurchased more common stock than it issued.

In Part Two of the book, beginning in Chapter 9, we will attempt to increase our understanding of the business a bit further by adding market information into our thinking about business strategy. We will cross the boundaries of the firm (as represented by the information found in the financial statements) and add information about interest rates, inflation rates, stock prices, and risk measures to the framework we have been developing throughout Part One. We will consider how the market value of debt and equity securities fit into the firm's overall business strategy.

NOTES

1. If we were to restructure Wal-Mart's income statements to determine the amount of internal equity financing included in Figure 8.2, we would make the following adjustments to net income:

   Net Income + Depreciation + Change in Deferred Income Taxes + Other Equity Adjustments − Shareholder Dividends = Internal Equity Financing

   Based on our experiences working with managers in executive education programs, restructuring the income statement creates more problems than it solves. Instead of trying to understand the business, we typically end up trying to understand how the reconciliation process works. It is much easier to talk our way through the reconciliation process. Internal equity financing equals net income less shareholder dividends plus or minus adjustments for depreciation stock repurchases in retained earnings, deferred income taxes, and other equity adjustments.

PART TWO

Market Valuation and Business Strategy

CHAPTER 9

Market Valuation: Market Performance Measures

In Part One (Chapters 1 through 8), we concentrated on the relationship between business strategy and the information found in the firm's financial statements. As we saw, the Strategic Profit Model (SPM) and the Strategic Financing Model (SFM) provide a systematic framework for seeing how all of the parts of the business fit into an integrated whole. Within the boundaries provided by the financial statements, the SPM and the SFM have proven to be powerful tools for helping managers understand the business through financial information.

But what happens when we have to cross the boundaries provided by the financial statements and start to factor additional market information into the firm's business strategy?

▶

If we want to understand the business through financial information, we cannot stop at the boundaries of the firm. We must also incorporate market information into the management communications process.

◀

As soon as we acknowledge that we must factor market information into our understanding of the business, the firm becomes part of a greater whole known as the global capital marketplace. In global capital markets, firms are evaluated in terms of the value they create for their shareholders.

Many managers of publicly traded companies own shares of their firm's common stock directly or indirectly through their company's pension plan and individual 401(k) plan. The same managers, along with millions of other investors, typically invest in the common stock of other companies individually or through mutual fund investments. As investors, these managers have a personal interest in seeing the value of their investment portfolio grow over time.

In helping managers see how market information is linked to business strategy, all we do is ask them to remember that they wear two hats—a management hat *and* an investor hat. If the firm has developed a market-oriented business strategy, the interests of managers and investors should be similar. Both managers and investors will be interested in seeing the market value of their company's common stock increase.

To get managers to start thinking like investors, we typically ask the following two questions:

1. As an investor, would you buy stock in your own company?
2. As a manager, what are you doing to increase the value of your (shareholder's) investment in your company?

To a large extent, Chapters 9 through 12 are devoted to helping managers think like investors and to providing them with a way of integrating this investor perspective into the SPM we developed in Part One. The purpose of this chapter is to familiarize managers with the language of the market valuation process. Defining the basic terms used in discussions about market valuation is an important first step in helping managers see how their actions can affect the value of the shareholders' investment in the firm.

In the first part of this chapter, we will add some information about the market value of Wal-Mart's common stock to the summary version of the SPM. In keeping with the management philosophy underlying the DuPont executive charting system discussed in Chapter 1, we will look at what the market is telling us about its perceptions of Wal-Mart's financial performance.

In the second part of the chapter, we will look at Wal-Mart within the context of the broader capital marketplace. We will compare Wal-Mart's common stock performance with a "market basket" of other firms, as represented by the Standard & Poor's index of 500 firms (S&P 500).

In Chapters 10 and 11, we will take a closer look at the mechanics of how the market values a firm's debt and equity securities. In Chapter 12, we will return to the SPM and expand the model to incorporate key measures of market performance within a single management communications framework.

MARKET VALUATION AND THE STRATEGIC PROFIT MODEL

Figure 9.1 presents the summary version of Wal-Mart's SPM for the fiscal years ended January 31, 1990 and 2000, with one additional piece of financial information: the average market price of Wal-Mart's common stock for the fiscal years ended January 31, 1990 and 2000.

Figure 9.1   Wal-Mart Strategic Profit Model: Summary Version, Including Stock Price Performance (for the Fiscal Years Ended January 31, 1990 and 2000—Amounts in Millions)

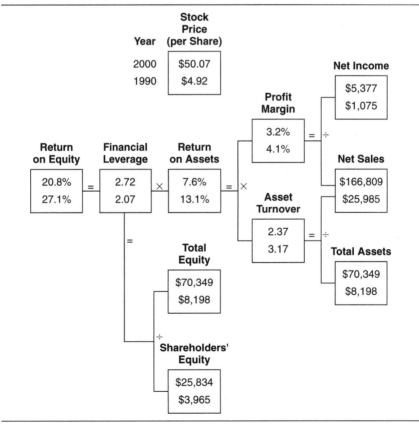

Figure 9.2 **Wal-Mart Strategic Profit Model: Summary Version (for the Fiscal Years Ended January 31, 1990 and 2000), Compound Annual Growth Rates (1990–2000)**

Market Information	
Stock Price	26.1%
Income Statement	
Net Sales	20.4%
Expenses (Net)	20.5%
Net Income	17.5%
Balance Sheet	
Assets	24.0%
Liabilities	26.5%
Shareholders' Equity	20.6%

Figure 9.2 presents the compound annual growth rates (CAGRs) for the ten-year period, including the growth rate for Wal-Mart's common stock. The CAGRs will be used to help us understand the capital market aspects of Wal-Mart's overall business strategy.

As we can see from the stock price information that has been added to Figure 9.1, the market value of one share of Wal-Mart's common stock increased from $4.92 in 1990 to $50.07 in 2000. From Figure 9.2, we can see that the market value of one share of Wal-Mart's common stock increased at a 26.1% CAGR.

On the surface, a 26.1% CAGR looks pretty good relative to other investments in the marketplace. As we can see from Figure 9.2, the other CAGRs associated with the income statement and balance sheet are mostly lower (net sales, 20.4%; net income, 17.5%; assets, 24.0%; shareholders' equity, 20.6%). Between 1990 and 2000, Wal-Mart's market performance outpaced its management performance, as reflected in the management measures of performance. These results give us a good indication that market has reacted positively to Wal-Mart's expansion and has high expectations of future growth and performance.

When we combine stock market performance measures with management performance measures, we are combining an orientation to past performance, as captured in the financial statements, with an orientation toward the future, as captured in the market value of the firm's common stock. In very general terms, if the market value of the firm's common stock is growing at a slower rate than the management performance measures, investors do not expect the firm to grow as fast in the future as it has grown in the past. Likewise, if the market value is growing at a faster rate than the management performance measures, investors expect the firm to grow at a faster rate in the future.

In Wal-Mart's case, this logic seems to make good common sense. Between 1999 and 2000, net income increased from $1.075 billion to $5.377 billion (a 17.5% increase). Between 1998 and 1999, net income increased from $3.526 billion to $4.430 billion (a 25.6% increase). Thus, even though Wal-Mart is the world's largest retailer, it has been growing faster recently than it has grown in the past.

The total market value of Wal-Mart's common stock outstanding also reflects this change in growth opportunities. The total market value (market capitalization of the company) equals the market value of one share of common stock times the total number of shares outstanding.[1]

Market Value = Stock Price × Shares Outstanding

2000: $22.288B = $4.92 × 4.5301B Shares

1990: $222.862B = $50.07 × 4.4510B Shares

For the entire ten-year period, the total market value of Wal-Mart's common stock outstanding increased from $22.3 billion to $222.9 billion, a $200.6 billion increase. However, the rate of increase between 1990 and 1991 was substantially slower than the rate of increase between 1999 and 2000.

Between 1990 and 1991, the total market value of Wal-Mart's common stock increased from $22.288 billion to $32.041 billion (a 43.8% increase). Between 1999 and 2000, the total market value of Wal-Mart's common stock increased from $137.982 billion to $222.862 billion (a 61.5% increase). It would appear that the market is adjusting the value of Wal-Mart's common stock to reflect increasing expectations of growth.

In order to support the statements we have just made about Wal-Mart's change in performance between 1990 and 1991 and 1999 and 2000, we need to fill in the blanks for the years not included in Figure 9.1. We need to see how management's performance and the market's assessment of that performance have been changing over time.

Figure 9.3 presents the relationships between the total market value of Wal-Mart's common stock, net income, and shareholder's equity as reported in Wal-Mart's income statements and balance sheets. As we can see from the bottom of the figure, the total market value of Wal-Mart's com-

Figure 9.3 **Wal-Mart Market and Management Measures of Performance (for the Years Ended January 31—Shares and Dollar Amounts in Millions)**

Year Ended January 13	Common Stock Outstanding	Market Value	Net Income	Shareholders' Equity	Average Annual Price
1990	4,530	$22,288	$1,075	$ 3,965	$ 4.92
1991	4,610	$32,042	$1,291	$ 5,366	$ 6.95
1992	4,610	$52,880	$1,609	$ 6,990	$11.47
1993	4,597	$65,513	$1,995	$ 8,759	$14.25
1994	4,597	$63,260	$2,333	$10,753	$13.76
1995	4,597	$56,362	$2,681	$12,726	$12.26
1996	4,594	$55,863	$2,740	$14,756	$12.16
1997	4,594	$56,322	$3,056	$17,143	$12.26
1998	4,516	$76,727	$3,526	$18,503	$16.99
1999	4,464	$137,982	$4,430	$21,112	$30.91
2000	4,451	$222,862	$5,377	$25,834	$50.07
CAGRs	−0.2%	25.9%	17.5%	20.6%	26.1%

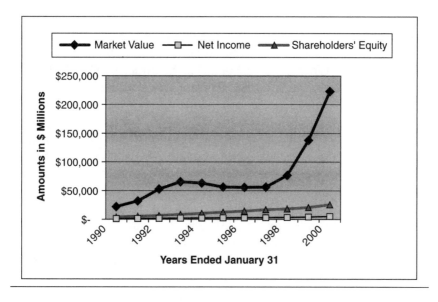

mon stock increased at a 25.9% CAGR over the entire ten-year period, compared with the 17.5% compound annual growth in net income and 20.6% compound annual growth in shareholders' equity.

However, as we can also see from the graphic presentation of Wal-Mart's actual performance over the ten-year period, the growth in market value was not anywhere near as smooth as the growth in net income and shareholders' equity. Up through 1998, the market value of Wal-Mart's common stock was increasing at a faster rate than net income and shareholders' equity. During this period, the market was not assigning a premium to Wal-Mart's common stock relative to the growth in net income and shareholders' equity. In more recent years, we can see a much faster rate of growth.

PRICE/EARNINGS AND MARKET/BOOK RATIOS

Market analysts frequently link share price information to the information found in the financial statements through two ratios: (1) the price/earnings (P/E) ratio and (2) the market/book (M/B) ratio. These ratios provide yet another way of looking at the relationship between management's performance and the market's assessment of that performance. Figure 9.4 presents Wal-Mart's P/E ratios and M/B ratios between 1990 and 2000.

Price/Earnings Ratio

The P/E ratio links the firm's common stock share price to the income statement. The ratio equals the market value of Wal-Mart's common stock divided by net income. In other words, the market price of the firm's common stock can be expressed as a multiple of the firm's net income. Wal-Mart's average P/E ratio of 26.4 between 1990 and 2000 means that the market value of its common stock has traded at 26.4 times its reported earnings.

Between 1990 and 2000, Wal-Mart's common stock traded, on average, at 26.4 times its earnings.

Figure 9.4 **Wal-Mart Price/Earnings and Market/Book Ratios (for the Years Ended January 31)**

Year Ended January 31	Price/Earnings (P/E) Ratio	Market/Book (M/B) Ratio
1990	20.5	5.6
1991	24.0	6.0
1992	32.8	7.6
1993	32.4	7.5
1994	27.0	5.9
1995	20.8	4.4
1996	20.3	3.8
1997	18.3	3.3
1998	21.8	4.1
1999	31.2	6.5
2000	41.4	8.6
Average	26.4	5.8

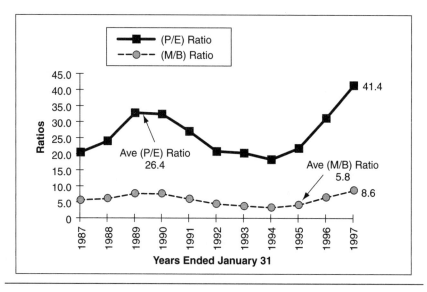

Source: Annual Value Line Investment Surveys.

However, as we can see from Figure 9.4, Wal-Mart's common stock has traded well above and well below the 26.4 average P/E ratio. In 1997, Wal-Mart's common stock was trading at 18.3 times its earnings; in 2000, Wal-Mart's common stock was trading at 41.4 times its earnings.

Market/Book Ratio

The M/B ratio expresses the relationship between the market value of a firm's common stock and the shareholders' equity section of the balance sheet. The M/B ratio equals the market value of the firm's common stock divided by the shareholders' equity reported in the balance sheet (the firm's book value). Since shareholders' equity equals the cumulative amount of common stock, retained earnings, and translation adjustments, the M/B ratio is typically much lower than the P/E ratio. The M/B ratio is another way of looking at the relationship between management's performance and the market's assessment of that performance.

Wal-Mart's average M/B ratio of 5.8 for the ten-year period between 1990 and 2000 means that the market value of its common stock has traded at 5.8 times its reported shareholders' equity.

Between 1990 and 2000, Wal-Mart's common stock traded, on average, at 5.8 times its reported shareholders' equity.

As we can see from Figure 9.4, Wal-Mart's common stock has traded well above and well below the 5.8 average M/B ratio. In 1997, Wal-Mart's common stock was trading at 3.3 times its book value; in 2000, Wal-Mart's common stock was trading at 8.6 times its book value.

As we can see from Figures 9.3 and 9.4, the market valuation process is not static. The market value for the common stock for all publicly traded firms, including Wal-Mart, ebbs and flows with the changes in expectations of what investors think the stock of a firm such as Wal-Mart is worth in the capital marketplace. From a business strategy perspective, managers need to focus on running the business with one eye toward the market. However, managers also have to realize that the market price of their firm's common stock is also affected by investor expectations about the financial performance of other firms.

To develop a better understanding of the broader capital marketplace, we are going to take a closer look at Wal-Mart as one part of a greater whole, as represented by the S&P 500. Within the context of the S&P 500, we will be able to see how well Wal-Mart has performed, compared with a market basket of 500 U.S. companies.

WAL-MART AND THE S&P 500

In addition to providing a full set of financial statements to shareholders on a quarterly and annual basis, firms are required by the Securities and Exchange Commission (SEC) to make additional disclosures to shareholders in the notice of the annual meeting of shareholders (typically referred to as the firm's proxy statement).

For our present purposes, we are most interested in the stock performance graph that presents the cumulative total shareholder return for each firm, as compared with the overall S&P 500 index and typically a more specific index consisting of firms in the same industry.

Figure 9.5 presents Wal-Mart's cumulative total return[2] compared with the S&P 500 index and the S&P retail stores composite index. The amounts reported in Figure 9.5 are based on the assumption that a shareholder invested $100 in Wal-Mart's common stock, $100 in a market basket of firms representing the entire S&P 500 index, and $100 in a more specific market basket consisting of all firms included in the S&P retail stores index.

As we can see from Figure 9.5, from 1995 through 2000, Wal-Mart outperformed both the S&P 500 index and the S&P retail stores index. Between these dates the average annual return on an investment in the S&P 500 would have equaled 27.9%; the S&P retail stores index, 25.6%, and Wal-Mart, 37.7%. In retrospect, it looks as if it would have been a good idea to invest in Wal-Mart stock in January 1995 rather than compared to the basket of S&P 500 stocks. However, as previously mentioned, the market price of Wal-Mart's common stock is now (May 2000) trading around $60.00 per share. If the stock price holds at $60.00 or increases even further, the performance graph included in the 2000 notice of annual meeting to shareholders will look substantially better.

From the standpoint of trying to understand the business through financial information, Figure 9.5 is interesting for several reasons:

- As investors, we are provided with information to help us assess how well we have done or might have done by investing or not investing in Wal-Mart's common stock. If we do not think that management is doing what it takes to turn things around, we just might want to invest our money elsewhere.
- As managers, we do not have the luxury of just selling our Wal-Mart stock and moving on. If some managers decided to leave Wal-Mart based on this information, the new managers would be faced with the problem of figuring out how to come up with a strategy to get Wal-Mart back on track in terms of creating value for its shareholders.

Figure 9.5   Comparison of Five-Year Cumulative Total Return* among Wal-Mart Stores, the S&P 500 Index, and the S&P Retail Stores Composite Index

Year Ended January 31	S&P 500	S&P Retail Stores	Wal-Mart Stock
1995	$100	$100	$100
1996	139	108	90
1997	175	129	106
1998	222	191	178
1999	295	313	387
2000	342	313	495
CAGR	27.9%	25.6%	37.7%

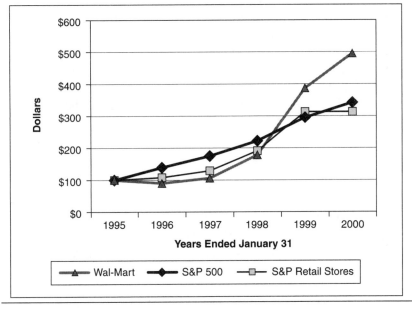

*Assumes dividends are reinvested at the prevailing market price.
Source: Wal-Mart Stores, Inc., Notice of Annual Meeting of Shareholders, June 2, 2000.

- As individuals trying to understand Wal-Mart's business, we might want to expand the horizon of our backward glance to see if a longer time horizon might provide a different perspective for thinking about how Wal-Mart's stock might perform in the future.

Our goal in this chapter has been to start the process of linking market information to the firm's overall business strategy. In the first part of this chapter, we added some information about the market value of Wal-Mart's common stock to the summary version of the SPM. In keeping with the management philosophy underlying the DuPont executive charting system discussed in Chapter 1, we tried to develop a basic understanding about the market's perception of Wal-Mart's financial performance.

In the second part of the chapter, we looked at Wal-Mart within the context of the broader capital marketplace. After defining the P/E ratio and the M/B ratio, we discussed how the market evaluated Wal-Mart's performance in terms of these two ratios. Given a basic understanding of this market terminology, we compared Wal-Mart's common stock performance with a market basket of other firms as represented by the S&P 500.

As we saw in Chapters 7 and 8 on the SFM, management relied on a combination of internal equity financing and external debt financing to grow the business between 1990 and 2000.

In Chapter 10, we will begin the process of seeing how the market establishes a price for a firm's long-term debt. The discussion in Chapter 10 will then serve as the foundation for the discussion in Chapter 11, where we will look at how the market values establish a price for a firm's common stock. In Chapter 12, we will then add what we have learned about the market valuation process to create a version of the SPM that integrates market- and management-based measures of financial performance into a single management system.

NOTES

1. The weighted average number of shares outstanding is reported in Wal-Mart's annual report and the Value-Line Investment Survey.

2. A firm's total return or the total return related to a stock index is based on the appreciation in the market value of the firm's common stock and dividend declarations. For the purpose of the total return calculation, any dividends declared are assumed to be reinvested in the firm's common stock.

CHAPTER 10

Market Valuation: Long-Term Debt

The markets for debt and equity securities are like the markets for producer and consumer products. It all boils down to prices and quantities. How much would we be willing to pay for a new computer, a new software package, or an exclusive contract with Michael Jordan to advertise our firm's consumer products? How much would we be willing to pay lenders for the right to borrow $100 million for the next fifteen years? How much would we be willing to pay for 100 shares of Wal-Mart's common stock? How much money would we be willing to invest in U.S. treasury bonds or in a mutual fund specializing in growth firms in Southeast Asia?

The old adage "buy low and sell high" reflects everyone's dream of making a good return on an investment. Customers want to pay the lowest price for the products they buy. At the same time, suppliers want to receive the highest price possible for the products they sell. A market transaction takes place when buyers and sellers agree on the price to be paid for the quantity of product to be exchanged. In the case of debt and equity securities of publicly traded companies, all we have to do is look in the business section of most daily newspapers and we can see the price investors actually paid for these securities the previous day.

In this chapter and Chapter 11, we are going to take a closer look at how the market establishes the price that investors pay for the privilege of owning the debt and equity securities of a particular firm—in our case, Wal-Mart. We will be looking at Wal-Mart from the perspective of a long-term creditor. As we shall see, the dynamics of the capital marketplace are based, in general terms, on two factors: (1) the logic of *risk and return* and (2) *growth.*

The greater the perceived risk associated with a particular investment, the greater the expected return. Firms that grow the business (through sales), grow earnings (net income), and grow cash flow to shareholders (through dividends) typically trade at higher prices than firms in the same industry that are not growing as fast.

We will begin our discussion of the market valuation process by looking at the issues associated with risk and return and then take a closer look at the issues associated with growth.

DEBT AND EQUITY SECURITIES

Firms such as Wal-Mart "buy" money on the capital markets to finance the growth of the business that cannot be financed from internal sources (internal equity financing). Management can buy money to finance the future of the firm by issuing long-term debt or common stock.[1] In the case of long-term debt, creditors lend money to the firm in exchange for the borrower's promise to pay interest and repay principal in the future. In the case of common stock, shareholders invest money in the firm in exchange for management's promise to be held accountable for the future success of the firm.

Debt financing: Management borrows money from lenders in exchange for its promise to pay interest and repay principal at some time in the future.

Equity financing: Management raises money from shareholders in exchange for its promise to be held accountable for the future success of the firm.

As we shall see in the remainder of this chapter, lenders "sell" money today in exchange for the right to receive money (a stream of cash flows) in the future. In Chapter 11, we will see that shareholders also sell money today in exchange for the right to receive money (a stream of cash flows) in the future. In the case of long-term debt, the stream of cash flows is more certain (and therefore less risky) than the stream of cash flows associated with common stock (which is therefore more risky).

Question: When we think about lending our money to someone, which potential borrower do you think is most likely to make the interest payments and repay the principal on that loan?

Answer: The U.S. government

Before taking a closer look at how the market values the long-term debt of firms such as Wal-Mart, it is helpful to see how the market values the long-term debt of the U.S. government. As we shall see, a very strong relationship exists between the interest rates associated with U.S. government debt (treasury bonds) and the market price of a firm's debt and equity securities. The interest on U.S. government securities represents the "risk-free" return on investment that investors use to determine what they would be willing to pay for more risky investments, such as corporate debt and equity securities.

In general, as interest rates on risk-free government bonds go up, investors demand higher returns on corporate debt and equity securities. And like any other products that are bought and sold at the market, prices vary with conditions and circumstances. When it comes to government securities, the price of U.S. treasury bonds varies with the general rate of inflation. As the rate of inflation goes up, the interest rate investors expect to receive on U.S. treasury bonds goes up. As the rate of inflation goes down, the interest rate investors expect to receive on U.S. treasury bonds goes down.

Figure 10.1 presents the general relationship between annual inflation rates in the U.S. economy and the interest rates on ten-year U.S. treasury bonds between 1990 and 2000. As we can see, the interest rates on U.S. treasury bonds were higher than the rate of inflation for each of these ten years.

Economists typically refer to the difference between interest rates and inflation rates as the *real* interest rate. For the year ended December 31, 1990, the real interest rate was 3.15% (8.55% interest rate minus the 5.40% inflation rate). For the year ended December 31, 1999, the real interest rate was 3.45% (5.65% interest rate minus the 2.20% inflation rate). Over the entire ten-year period, the average annual real interest rate was 3.66% (6.67% average interest rate minus the 3.01% average inflation rate).

Given this relationship between inflation rates and interest rates, it is not difficult to see why analysts and investors anxiously anticipate the quarterly announcements of changes in the consumer price index (CPI).

Figure 10.1   **U.S. Economy Inflation Rates and Interest Rates* (for the Calendar Years Ended December 31, 1990–1999)**

Year Ended	Inflation Rates	Interest Rates
1990	5.40%	8.55%
1991	4.21%	7.86%
1992	3.01%	7.01%
1993	2.99%	5.87%
1994	2.56%	7.09%
1995	2.83%	6.57%
1996	2.95%	6.44%
1997	2.30%	6.35%
1998	1.60%	5.26%
1999	2.20%	5.65%
Average	3.01%	6.67%

*Interest rates on ten-year U.S. treasury bonds. Inflation rates based on changes in the consumer price index.

Source: Economic Report of the President, February 2000.

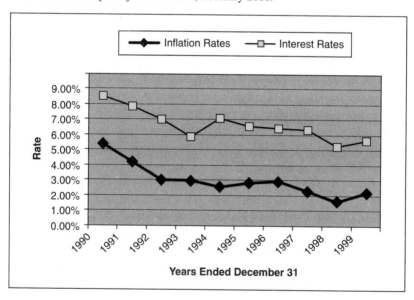

An increase in the CPI is likely to trigger a demand for higher interest rates on U.S. treasury bonds in order to maintain the same real interest rate. Since U.S. treasury bonds are supposed to be risk-free investments, with the effective interest rate tied to inflation, it should not be too hard to imagine the ripple effect on the interest rates of the more risky corporate debt.

Figure 10.2   Interest Rates on U.S. Treasury Bonds and Corporate Bonds*
(for the Years Ended December 31, 1990–1999)

Ten-Year Treasury Year	Corporate Bonds Bills	Corporate Bonds (Aaa)	Corporate Bonds (Baa)
1990	8.55%	9.32%	10.36%
1991	7.86%	8.77%	9.80%
1992	7.01%	8.14%	8.98%
1993	5.87%	7.22%	7.93%
1994	7.09%	7.96%	8.62%
1995	6.57%	7.59%	8.20%
1996	6.44%	7.37%	8.05%
1997	6.35%	7.26%	7.86%
1998	5.26%	6.53%	7.22%
1999	5.65%	7.04%	7.87%
Average	6.67%	7.72%	8.49%

*Ten-year treasury bonds and Moody's Aaa- and Baa-rated bonds.

Source: Economic Report of the President, February 2000.

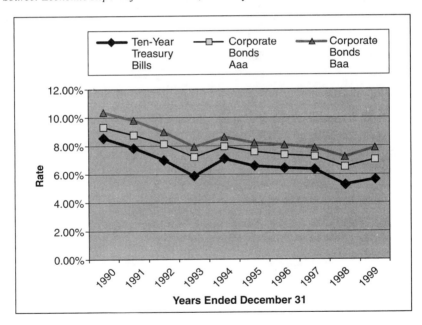

Figure 10.2 presents the relationships among ten-year U.S. treasury bonds and Moody's Aaa- and Baa-rated corporate bonds. Corporate bonds receiving Moody's Aaa rating represent the highest quality long-term corporate bonds or notes payable on the market. They are only slightly more

151

risky than investing in U.S. treasury bonds. Bonds rated Baa are considered investment-grade bonds and are slightly more risky than Aaa-rated bonds or notes and therefore carry a higher interest rate.

As we might expect, lower-rated bonds or notes carry higher interest rates to offset the higher perceived risk. As we can see from Figures 10.1 and 10.2, the average interest rate on U.S. treasury bonds was 6.67% between 1990 and 1999. The average interest rate on Aaa-rated corporate bonds was 7.72%, and the average interest rate on Baa-rated bonds was 8.49%. In terms of the language of risk and return, investors earned, on average, a risk premium of 1.05% on Aaa-rated corporate bonds over the U.S. treasury bonds. Investors earned, on average, another risk premium of 0.77% by investing in Baa-rated corporate bonds versus Aaa-rated corporate bonds.

In addition to the market information about the interest rates associated with corporate debt carrying different risk assessments, Moody's and Standard & Poor's rate the individual debt issues of publicly traded companies. For example, Moody's gives Wal-Mart's long-term debt an Aa rating, and Standard & Poor's gives Wal-Mart's long-term debt an AA rating. Both rating agencies consider Wal-Mart's debt to be high-quality. According to the Moody's and Standard & Poor's rating definitions, firms with Aa- and AA-rated debt have a very strong capacity to pay interest and repay principal. Aa- and AA-rated debt differ only slightly from Aaa- and AAA-rated debt, the highest ratings assigned by both rating agencies.

We can find all the information that we need to know about a firm's outstanding long-term debt in the debt footnote in its annual report. Market rates, for valuation purposes, are published monthly.[2] To value debt, we need to know the principal, or face amount, of the debt, the fiscal year when the debt was issued, and the year in which the principal is to be repaid. The stated interest rate represents the percentage of the principal that will be paid out in interest on an annual basis. Let's consider a simple example. Wal-Mart issued $500 million of 9.10%, 10 year long-term debt in 1991. Based on these terms, Wal-Mart would make annual payments to lenders of $45,500,000.

Interest Payment = Principal × Stated Interest Rate

$45,500,000 = $500,000,000 × 9.10%

Knowing the principal amount and the stated rate of interest, we can compute the contractual interest payment to be made. However, we cannot determine how much lenders are willing to pay in order to receive a 9.10% stated rate of interest and a principal payment of $500 million in the year 2000. In order to take this next step, we need to know the market rate of interest associated with the firm's long-term debt.

The market rates of interest associated with each of Wal-Mart's Aa-rated long-term debt issues can be found in Standard & Poor's or Moody's bond guides. For the $500 million of 9.10% long-term debt issued in 1991, the market rate of interest fluctuated between a high of 8.69% in 1991 and a low of 6.03% in 1994.

Given the relationship between inflation and interest rates on U.S. treasury bonds (Figure 10.1) and the relationship between U.S. treasury bonds and corporate bonds (Figure 10.2), the fluctuations in the market rates of interest for Wal-Mart's long-term debt make perfect sense. Even though the stated rate of interest and principal amounts remain the same, the market rate of interest varies with changes in the overall economy.

If we think of borrowing money in exchange terms, firms such as Wal-Mart "sell" a stream of cash flows to lenders, who pay a lump sum of money today to "buy" the right to receive this stream of cash flows in the future. The market interest rate on the day the bonds or notes payable are issued determines the amount of money the lender and borrower will give and receive in exchange.

MARKET VALUATION OF LONG-TERM DEBT

We will illustrate how the market valuation process works with respect to external debt financing using the $500 million of 9.10% long-term debt issued by Wal-Mart in 1991. For the initial example, we will assume that the market rate of interest equaled the stated rate of interest when Wal-Mart borrowed the money.

Figure 10.3 presents the stream of cash flows that Wal-Mart sold to lenders at the beginning of 1991 (shown as of the fiscal year ended January 31, 1990). As we can see, Wal-Mart agreed to pay lenders $955 million over a ten-year period in exchange for the $500 million needed to finance that part of the long-term investment plan not financed from internal sources in 1991 (see Chapter 8 for the discussion of internal equity and external debt financing).

Figure 10.3 Wal-Mart Schedule of Cash Flows, $500 Million, 9.10%
Long-Term Debt (Amounts in Millions)

Year Ended January 31	Principal Payment	Interest Payments	Total Cash Flow
1990		$0.0	$0.0
1991		$45.5	$45.5
1992		$45.5	$45.5
1993		$45.5	$45.5
1994		$45.5	$45.5
1995		$45.5	$45.5
1996		$45.5	$45.5
1997		$45.5	$45.5
1998		$45.5	$45.5
1999		$45.5	$45.5
2000	$500.0	$45.5	$545.5
Totals	$500.0	$455.0	$955.0

Determining the specific amount of money to be received by Wal-Mart and paid by the lenders is the responsibility of financial professionals working at Wal-Mart and the lending institutions. However, from a management perspective, all we need to understand is the logic of the time value of money underlying the market valuation process.

TIME VALUE OF MONEY

The essence of the market valuation process involves reducing a stream of future cash flows down to a single dollar equivalence amount that equates what borrowers will receive to what lenders will pay to make the deal happen. Both borrowers and lenders factor the time value of money into any decision to buy and sell money.

When we are concerned with the present value of a stream of future cash flows, we use present value analysis techniques. When we are concerned with the future value of a stream of future cash flows, we use future value analysis techniques.

▶

The present value of $1 to be received in the future will be less than $1 today.

The future value of $1 received today will be more than $1 in the future.

We use the market rate of interest to determine both present values and future values. In a sense, present values and future values are two sides of the same time value of money coin. If the market rate of interest is 9.10%, the present value and future value of $1 for one year are calculated as follows:

$$\text{Present Value of } \$1 = \$1 \div (1 + \text{Interest Rate})$$
$$\$.9166 = \$1 \div (1 + 9.10\%)$$
$$\text{Future Value of } \$1 = \$1 \times (1 + \text{Interest Rate})$$
$$\$1.091 = \$1 \times (1 + 9.10\%)$$

One dollar to be received one year from now is worth $.9166 today at 9.10% interest. Today's $1 will be worth $1.0910 at the end of the year at 9.10% interest. All that the present value and future value analysis techniques do is apply the logic of the time value of money over a longer time horizon—ten years in this example.

Since Wal-Mart is committed to paying out the stream of cash flows shown in Figure 10.3, we need to identify a present value factor and a future value factor to associate with the cash flowing from Wal-Mart to lenders each year. Figure 10.4 presents the present value and future value factors needed to determine how much Wal-Mart will receive and lenders will pay for the $955 million stream of cash that will be flowing from 1991 through the year 2000.

Under the market interest rates column, we have shown the 9.10% interest rate for each of the ten years associated with this long-term debt issue. Once we go beyond a simple example of the market valuation process, the market interest rate can be allowed to vary on a yearly (or monthly or daily) basis.

The single-period present value factors are shown to the left of the market interest rates. The future value factors are shown to the right. At 9.10% interest, the present value of $1 equals $.917 and the future value $1.091 (rounded to the nearest three decimal places). The factors do not change from year to year because the interest rate does not change.

Figure 10.4 Time Value of Money: Present Value and Future Value Factors, 9.10% Market Interest Rates

Year Ended January 31	Cumulative Present Value Factors	Present Value Factor 1 ÷ (1 + i)	Market Interest Rates (i)	Future Value Factor 1 × (1 + i)	Cumulative Future Value Factors
1990	1.000	1.000	0.000%	1.000	1.000
1991	0.917	0.917	9.100%	1.091	1.091
1992	0.840	0.917	9.100%	1.091	1.190
1993	0.770	0.917	9.100%	1.091	1.299
1994	0.706	0.917	9.100%	1.091	1.417
1995	0.647	0.917	9.100%	1.091	1.546
1996	0.593	0.917	9.100%	1.091	1.686
1997	0.544	0.917	9.100%	1.091	1.840
1998	0.498	0.917	9.100%	1.091	2.007
1999	0.457	0.917	9.100%	1.091	2.190
2000	0.419	0.917	9.100%	1.091	2.389

To the left of present value factors, we find the cumulative present value factors. To the right of the future value factors, we find the cumulative future value factors. As we can see, the cumulative present value factor associated with $1 to be received at the end of the year 2000 is 41.9¢. The cumulative future value of $1 is $2.389.

Heads: The present value of $1 to be received at the fiscal year ended January 31, 2000, is 41.9¢.

Tails: The future value for $1 to be received at the fiscal year ended January 31, 2000, is $2.389.

In Figure 10.4, the arrows connecting the present value factor column to the cumulative present values factor column show how each year's cumulative present value is determined.

The present value of $1 to be received at the fiscal year ended January 31, 1995, is 64.7¢.

64.7¢ = $1.000 × $.917 × $.917 × $.917 × $.917 × $.917

The arrows connecting the future value factor column to the cumulative future value factors column show how each year's cumulative future value is determined.

The future value of $1 to be received at the fiscal year ended January 31, 1995, is $1.546.

$1.546 = $1.000 × $1.091 × $1.091 × $1.091 × $1.091 × $1.091

Based on our experiences working in executive development programs, we know that managers appreciate a step-by-step buildup of the market valuation process. Even before we make any changes to this long-term debt example, managers can see that the cumulative present value and future value factors depend on the interest rates inserted into the market interest rates column of Figure 10.4.

LONG-TERM DEBT: MIND YOUR *P*s AND *Q*s

The old adage "mind your *P*s and *Q*s" refers to the advice tavern owners gave to the barmaids (and barmen?) in merry old England. *P*s and *Q*s referred to pints and quarts of beer. If we do not know how many pints and quarts were sold, we will not know how much to charge the customers. In today's global markets, we would give managers the same type of advice. Mind your *P*s (interest rates) and *Q*s (interest and principal payments).

When we combine the *P*s from Figure 10.4 with the *Q*s from Figure 10.3, we can determine the present values and the future values of the entire stream of cash flows, as shown in Figure 10.5. The total stream of cash flows that Wal-Mart has agreed to pay in interest and principal is shown in the middle column of Figure 10.5. The amounts shown in the cumulative

Figure 10.5   Wal-Mart Present Values and Future Values, $500 Million, 9.10% Long-Term Debt (Amounts in Millions)

Year Ended January 31	Cumulative Present Value	Cumulative Present Value Factors	Total Cash Flow	Cumulative Future Value Factors	Cumulative Future Value
1990	$0.0	1.000	$0.0	▲ 2.389	$0.0
1991	$41.7	0.917	$45.5	2.190	$99.6
1992	$38.2	0.840	$45.5	2.007	$91.3
1993	$35.0	0.770	$45.5	1.840	$83.7
1994	$32.1	0.706	$45.5	1.686	$76.7
1995	$29.4	0.647	$45.5	1.546	$70.3
1996	$27.0	0.593	$45.5	1.417	$64.5
1997	$24.7	0.544	$45.5	1.299	$59.1
1998	$22.7	0.498	$45.5	1.190	$54.2
1999	$20.8	0.457	$45.5	1.091	$49.6
2000	$228.3	▼ 0.419	$545.5	1.000	$545.5
Totals	$500.0		$955.0		$1,194.6

present value column equal the cash flow for the year times the cumulative present value factor for that year. For example, for 1995,

$$\$29.4M = 0.647 \times \$45.5M$$

The total cumulative present value equals $500,000.

The amounts shown in the cumulative future value column equal the cash flow for the year times the cumulative future value factor for that year. For example, for 1995,

$$\$70.3M = 1.546 \times \$45.5M$$

As we can see, the total present value of the $955.5 million in total cash flow equals $500 million, which Wal-Mart borrowed on January 31, 1990.

The total future value equals $1.1946 billion. In other words, lenders would be willing to pay $500 million to Wal-Mart for the right to receive the $955 million stream of actual cash flows shown in Figure 10.5. Over the course of the full ten-year period, the $955 million stream of cash flows would have accumulated to a total future value of $1.1946 billion by the year 2000 at 9.10% interest.

Figure 10.6 presents the same information, with one small difference. The initial $500 million that Wal-Mart received from lenders is shown as a negative amount. By adding the $500 million to the total cash flow column, we see that the totals for the cumulative present value column (the net present value) and cumulative future value column (net future value) equal $0.

▶───────────────────────────────────────

Question: What does it mean when the net present value and net future value equal $0?

Answer: You got what you paid for.

───────────────────────────────────────◀

Figure 10.6   Wal-Mart Net Present Values and Net Future Values, $500 Million, 9.10% Long-Term Debt (Amounts in Millions)

Year Ended January 31	Cumulative Present Value	Cumulative Present Value Factors	Total Cash Flow	Cumulative Future Value Factors	Cumulative Future Value
1990	($500.0)	1.000	($500.0)	▲ 2.389	($1,194.6)
1991	$41.7	0.917	$45.5	2.190	$99.6
1992	$38.2	0.840	$45.5	2.007	$91.3
1993	$35.0	0.770	$45.5	1.840	$83.7
1994	$32.1	0.706	$45.5	1.686	$76.7
1995	$29.4	0.647	$45.5	1.546	$70.3
1996	$27.0	0.593	$45.5	1.417	$64.5
1997	$24.7	0.544	$45.5	1.299	$59.1
1998	$22.7	0.498	$45.5	1.190	$54.2
1999	$20.8	0.457	$45.5	1.091	$49.6
2000	$228.3	▼ 0.419	$545.5	1.000	$545.5
Totals	$0.0		$455.0		$0.0

In today's highly sophisticated capital markets, we do not typically see how the logic of the time value affects what creditors will lend and borrowers will receive on any given day. However, even though managers cannot see the logic of the time value of money at work, it is always there.

FAST FORWARD SIX YEARS

Assume that it is January 31, 1996, and all of Wal-Mart's original lenders need cash. Furthermore, Wal-Mart has no desire to retire the debt until the year 2000.

▶ ──────────────────────────────

Question: What are these lenders to do?

Answer: Sell the rights to receive the remaining cash flows to someone interested in earning the current market rate of interest.

────────────────────────────── ◀

Assume that Wal-Mart's $500 million of 9.10% long-term debt had a market interest rate of 6.42% as of January 31, 1996. If the original lenders want to sell their rights to receive the remaining cash flows from Wal-Mart, they must use the 6.42% market interest rate to determine how much cash they will receive from the new holders of Wal-Mart's debt.

Figure 10.7 presents the schedule of cash flows remaining to be paid by Wal-Mart to January 31, 2000. Figure 10.8 presents the present and future value factors associated with a 6.42% interest rate. As we can see from these figures, the logic of the time value of money establishes what the current group of lenders will receive from the new group of lenders, who want to hold Wal-Mart's long-term debt.

Figure 10.7   Wal-Mart Schedule of Remaining Cash Flows, $500 Million, 9.1% Long-Term Debt (Amounts in Millions)

Year Ended January 31	Principal Payment	Interest Payments	Total Cash Flow
1997		$45.5	$45.5
1998		$45.5	$45.5
1999		$45.5	$45.5
2000	$500.0	$45.5	$545.5
Totals	$500.0	$182.0	$682.0

Figure 10.8 Time Value of Money—Present Value and Future Value
Factors, 6.42% Market Interest Rates

Year Ended January 31	Cumulative Present Value Factors	Present Value Factor $1 \div (1 + i)$	Market Interest Rates (i)	Future Value Factor $1 \times (1 + i)$	Cumulative Future Value Factors
1996	1.000	1.000	0.00%	1.000	1.000
1997	0.940	0.940	6.42%	1.064	1.064
1998	0.883	0.940	6.42%	1.064	1.133
1999	0.883	0.940	6.42%	1.064	1.205
2000	0.780	0.940	6.42%	1.064	1.283

As we can see, the cumulative present value of $1 to be received at the
end of four years is 78.0¢ at a 6.42% market rate of interest. The cumulative future value of $1 is $1.283. At a lower rate of interest (6.42% versus
9.10%), the present value of $1 decreases at a slower rate, and the future
value of $1 increases at slower rate.

Figure 10.9 presents the net present values and net future values associated with the rights to receive the remaining cash flows. At a 6.42% market interest rate, lenders should expect to receive $700.2 million in
exchange for their interests in Wal-Mart's long-term debt.

Figure 10.9 Wal-Mart Net Present Values and Net Future Values, $500
Million, 9.10% Long-Term Debt, 6.42% Market Interest
Rate (Amounts in Millions)

Year Ended January 31	Cumulative Present Value	Cumulative Present Value Factors	Total Cash Flow	Cumulative Future Value Factors	Cumulative Future Value
1996	$0.0	1.000	$0.0	1.283	$0.0
1997	$42.8	0.940	$45.5	1.205	$54.8
1998	$40.2	0.883	$45.5	1.133	$51.5
1999	$37.8	0.830	$45.5	1.064	$48.4
2000	$425.3	0.780	$545.5	1.000	$545.5
Totals	$546.0		$682.0		$700.2

When we use examples of Wal-Mart's long-term debt to introduce the time value of money concepts into the market valuation process, we have to be careful not to get caught up in the finer points of debt financing. We want managers to develop a feel for the role that the time value of money plays in valuing debt securities, so that we can move on to valuing equity securities—that is, common stock. All of the concepts that we have introduced in this chapter are a means to that end.

Figure 10.10 presents a more visual representation of the market valuation process, which we use to help managers see the time value of money at work.

When we look at how the market valuation process is applied to common stock in Chapter 11, the logic of the time value of money will not

Figure 10.10 **Wal-Mart Market Valuation Process, $500 Million, 9.1%**
Long-Term Debt, 6.42% Market Interest Rate
(Amounts in Millions)

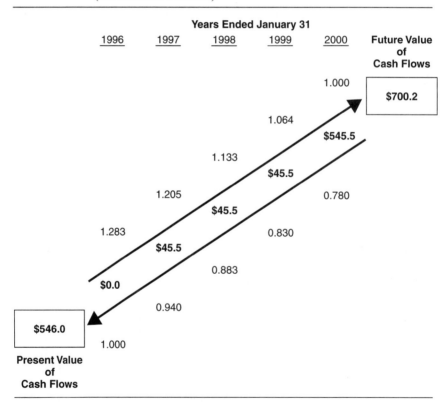

change. We will still use the same concepts to determine present values and future values. The main difference will revolve around how we incorporate risk into the calculation of present values and future values.

A second difference will involve the determination of the stream of future cash flows to be included in the valuation process. Cash flows associated with equity securities (common stock) involve more than the multiplication of a stated rate of interest by a known principal amount.

Question: What does not change in this analysis?

Answer: The logic of the time value of money analysis

NOTES

1. For this introduction to the market valuation process, we will not deal with preferred stock issues, convertible debt, or more complex debt and equity securities. In today's global financial markets, the number of ways of packaging deals to buy and sell money is virtually unlimited. The term *financial instruments* is used to focus attention on the similarities and differences among the various financial products on the market today. A detailed discussion of the different types of financial instruments is beyond the scope of this book.

2. Market rates of interest can be obtained from the monthly S&P bond guide.

CHAPTER 11

Market Valuation: Common Stock

In concluding our discussion, in Chapter 10, of how the market values a firm's long-term debt, we indicated that the logic of the time value of money remains the same when the market values the firm's common stock. In the case of long-term debt, when we know the timing of the principal and interest payments over the life of the loan, we can create a stream of future cash flows and discount those cash flows back to the present to determine the net present value. That net present value then represents the amount of money the lender would be willing to pay to the borrower.

When the market values a firm's common stock, several aspects of the valuation process become more problematic. The following are the three most significant differences between debt and equity valuation:

1. There is no market rate of interest associated with common stock, as there is with long-term debt. For common stock, financial analysts and investors use the term *cost of equity capital* to refer to the shareholders' expectations for a return on their investment in common stock.

2. Dividend payments are not the same as interest payments. Management is not obligated to pay a fixed dividend on a regular basis. Firms frequently change the amount and timing of their dividend payments. Some high-growth firms pay no dividends at all and reinvest all of their earnings into the business. Sometimes, when a firm is facing financial difficulties, management suspends the dividend payments until the firm returns to profitability.

3. When a firm issues common stock, the stock remains outstanding forever. There is no date when the principal comes due and management is required to repurchase the outstanding shares of common stock. Aside from any dividends the firm may pay to its shareholders, the only other way shareholders can get additional cash from their investment is to sell their shares of stock to another investor or back to the company.

Given these differences between long-term debt and common stock, it is not surprising that investors consider common stock to be a riskier investment than long-term debt, and, in exchange for assuming a greater risk, shareholders require a greater return on their investment.

Even though there is more uncertainty surrounding the returns associated with common stock, investors have reaped their rewards in the form of dividends and stock price appreciation over the years. Investments in common stock have consistently outperformed investments in corporate debt and U.S. treasury bonds.

In this chapter, we will see how financial analysts and investors go about the business of placing a value on a firm's common stock. We will begin by describing the cost of equity capital and relating the cost of equity capital to the risk-free return on U.S. treasury bonds.

COST OF EQUITY CAPITAL

As discussed in Chapter 10, the cost of corporate debt is higher than the cost of U.S. treasury bonds. Since the U.S. government is less likely than U.S. corporations to go out of business, the government incurs a lower cost of debt (lower market interest rate) than corporations when it borrows money. In a similar fashion, the cost of equity capital is higher than the cost of corporate debt. In exchange for a promise of contractual interest and principal payments, investors expect a lower return on corporate debt than the return they expect when they buy the firm's common stock. When firms are successful, the higher risk associated with common stock is offset by the higher rewards (dividends and stock price appreciation).

Most managers understand the concept of the cost of equity capital at an intuitive level. If investing in common stock is more risky than investing in a firm's long-term debt, why shouldn't investors demand a higher return?

An intuitive understanding of the cost of equity capital is typically sufficient until two specific events occur:

1. Managers, especially senior managers, are held accountable for increasing shareholder value (dividends plus stock price appreciation).
2. A significant portion of the managers' total compensation is tied to achieving the shareholder value target.

Suddenly, managers need to know the facts. Managers need to go beyond intuition and deal with concrete reality. The cost of debt is concrete. The cost of equity capital is somewhat less concrete.

Although individuals may differ in their personal risk preferences, a generally accepted procedure for calculating a firm's cost of equity capital does exist. The cost of equity capital is made up of three components:

1. The risk-free return associated with U.S. treasury bonds,
2. A general market risk premium associated with any common stock investment, and
3. A risk premium associated with a specific common stock relative to the overall stock market.

Figure 11.1 Overall Economy, Cost of Equity Capital Calculations (1990–1999)

Year	Ten-Year T-Bonds	Market Risk Premium	Cost of Equity Capital (CofC)
1990	8.55%	5.46%	14.01%
1991	7.86%	5.46%	13.32%
1992	7.01%	5.46%	12.47%
1993	5.87%	5.46%	11.33%
1994	7.09%	5.46%	12.55%
1995	6.57%	5.46%	12.03%
1996	6.44%	5.46%	11.90%
1997	6.35%	5.46%	11.81%
1998	5.26%	5.46%	10.72%
1999	5.65%	5.46%	11.11%
Average	6.67%	5.46%	12.13%

Source: Economic Report of the President, February 2000.

In working with managers to help them understand the business, we have found that it is much easier to understand the cost of equity capital concept if we can see how all of the components fit together for a particular firm.

Figure 11.1 presents the cost of equity capital for the overall economy and Wal-Mart for the ten-year period December 31, 1990, through December 31, 1999. As previously mentioned, we build the cost of equity capital for the economy and a particular firm on a foundation of the risk-free return associated with ten-year U.S. treasury bonds (T-bonds).

OVERALL ECONOMY

The cost of equity capital for the overall economy equals the risk-free interest rate on U.S. treasury bonds plus a market risk premium for investing in common stock.

Ten-Year Treasury Bonds

The risk-free interest rate on ten-year treasury bonds provides the foundation for estimating a firm's cost of equity capital. We have followed the common practice of using the ten-year treasury bond rate. However, the same type of cost of equity calculations can be made using rates associated with three-, five-, and thirty-year treasury bonds. As discussed more fully in Chapter 10, the market interest rate on U.S. treasury bonds rises and falls with changes in the inflation rate.

Market Risk Premium

The column for the market risk premium represents the historical returns earned by equity investors over and above the rate of return on ten-year treasury bonds. The estimate of 5.46% represents the additional return investors in the S&P 500 earned over treasury bonds for the period 1926 through 1999.[1]

For example, in 1990, investors in a market basket of S&P 500 common stocks were probably expecting a return of 14.01% on their investment. In 1999, those expectations had decreased to 11.11% on their investment.

Expected Return = U.S. T-Bond Rate + The Market Risk Premium
1990: 14.01% = 8.55% + 5.46%
1999: 11.11% = 5.65% + 5.46%

Like the market rate of interest on U.S. treasury bonds and long-term corporate debt, the cost of equity capital for the overall economy fluctuates from year to year in response to changes in the inflation rate.

While the overall cost of equity capital for the economy gives us a better feel for the relationship between U.S. treasury bonds and the risks associated with the stock market, we are still one step removed from understanding the cost of equity capital for a specific firm, such as Wal-Mart. To determine a firm's cost of equity capital, we must consider how risky the market considers a particular firm to be relative to the overall economy. In the next section, we shall see how Wal-Mart's cost of equity capital differs from the overall economy.

WAL-MART'S COST OF EQUITY CAPITAL

Wal-Mart's cost of equity capital equals the cost of equity capital for the overall economy plus a risk premium (expressed as a relationship to the overall economy) for investing in this firm.

Beta (β)

Beta (β) is a statistical measure of the volatility of the market rates of return on a particular common stock relative to the average rate of return of the market taken as a whole. Stocks with high Betas (greater than 1.00) are more volatile than the market taken as a whole. Stocks with low Betas (less than 1.00) are less volatile than the market taken as a whole. If the overall market is moving upward (a bull market), a firm with a high Beta is more likely to provide higher returns to investors than is a firm with a low Beta. However, if the overall market is moving downward (a bear market), a firm with a high Beta is more likely to experience a decline in value than is a firm with a low Beta.

168

For Wal-Mart or any other publicly traded firm, the firm-specific cost of equity capital is calculated in the following manner:

▶

Firm-Specific Cost of Equity Capital = Risk-Free Interest Rate + (Beta × Market Risk Premium)

◀

Figure 11.2 presents all of the information needed to make the cost of equity capital calculations for Wal-Mart. The overall market cost of equity capital is presented on the right-hand side of the figure for comparison purposes. As we can see from this figure, Wal-Mart's Beta has not remained constant over time. Between 1990 and 1999, Wal-Mart's common stock was more volatile than the market taken as a whole. However, in 1997, Wal-Mart's Beta fell to 1.00, indicating that Wal-Mart's common stock was increasing and decreasing along with the overall market. Between 1990 and 1999, investors expected the return on their investment in Wal-Mart's common stock to increase at a faster rate than the market as a whole.

Figure 11.2   Wal-Mart Cost of Equity Capital Calculations (1990–1999)

Year	Ten-Year T-Bonds*	Beta**	Market Risk Premium	Wal-Mart Cost of Equity Capital	Market Cost of Equity Capital (CofC)
1990	8.55%	1.25	5.46%	15.38%	14.01%
1991	7.86%	1.25	5.46%	14.69%	13.32%
1992	7.01%	1.25	5.46%	13.84%	12.47%
1993	5.87%	1.30	5.46%	12.97%	11.33%
1994	7.09%	1.25	5.46%	13.92%	12.55%
1995	6.57%	1.25	5.46%	13.40%	12.03%
1996	6.44%	1.10	5.46%	12.45%	11.90%
1997	6.35%	1.00	5.46%	11.81%	11.81%
1998	5.26%	0.95	5.46%	10.45%	10.72%
1999	5.65%	1.05	5.46%	11.38%	11.11%
Average	6.67%	1.17	5.46%	13.03%	12.13%

*Source: Economic Report of the President, February 2000.

**Source: Annual Value Line Investment Surveys.

The calculation of any firm's specific risk premium equals Beta multiplied by the overall market risk premium. Wal-Mart's risk premium for 1990 and 1997 are calculated as shown below:

▶
_____

Wal-Mart's Risk Premium = Beta (β) × Market Risk Premium
1990: 6.83% = 1.25 × 5.46%
1997: 5.46% = 1.00 × 5.46%

_____
◀

As we can see, Beta reflects the fact that the specific risk associated with a particular firm becomes less volatile as the market price of the stock increases and decreases with fluctuations in the overall market.[2]

Cost of Equity Capital

A firm's cost of equity capital represents the combination of the cost of equity capital for the overall economy plus a firm-specific risk premium. The following formula for determining the cost of equity capital:

▶
_____

Cost of Equity Capital = Risk-Free Interest Rate on U.S.
Treasury Bills + (Beta × Market Risk Premium)

_____
◀

For example, Wal-Mart's cost of equity capital for 1990 and 1997 and the average for the ten-year period is

▶
_____

1990: 15.38% = 8.55% + (1.25 × 5.46%)
1997: 11.81% = 6.35% + (1.00 × 5.46%)
Average: 13.03% = 6.67% + (1.17 × 5.46%)

_____
◀

Based on our experiences working with management groups, working through the calculation of a firm's cost of equity capital appears to be a necessary evil. However, once managers know how the cost of equity capital is calculated, their intuitive understanding of risk and return is strengthened. All that remains to be done is to show how a firm's cost of equity capital relates to the broader economy.

Figure 11.3 presents the cost of equity capital for the overall economy and for Wal-Mart compared with the inflation rate and the interest rate on ten-year treasury bonds.

Figure 11.3 Wal-Mart Inflation Rates, Interest Rates, and the Cost of Equity Capital (1990–1999)

Year Ended	Inflation Rates	Ten-Year T-Bonds	Economy CofC	Wal-Mart CofC
1990	5.40%	8.55%	14.01%	15.38%
1991	4.21%	7.86%	13.32%	14.69%
1992	3.01%	7.01%	12.47%	13.84%
1993	2.99%	5.87%	11.33%	12.97%
1994	2.56%	7.09%	12.55%	13.92%
1995	2.83%	6.57%	12.03%	13.40%
1996	2.95%	6.44%	11.90%	12.45%
1997	2.30%	6.35%	11.81%	11.81%
1998	1.60%	5.26%	10.72%	10.45%
1999	2.20%	5.65%	11.11%	11.38%
Average	3.01%	6.67%	12.13%	13.03%

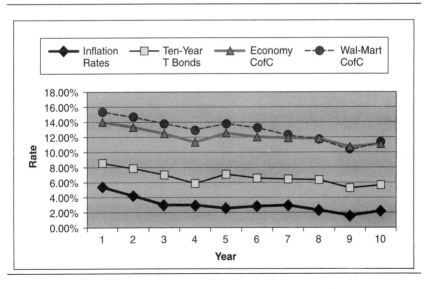

As we can see from Figure 11.3, the cost of equity capital for the economy taken as a whole and a particular firm rises and falls with changes in the inflation rate and interest rates on U.S. treasury bonds. As we can also see, in 1997 Wal-Mart's firm-specific risk premium disappeared. As the world's largest retailer, Wal-Mart represents a significant part of the U.S. economy. Wal-Mart is not the same high-risk company that went public back in 1970.

STREAM OF EQUITY CASH FLOWS

Once we calculate the cost of equity capital for any firm, we have jumped over our first hurdle. The cost of equity capital for common stock will be used to determine the present value factors and future value factors we will need to compute the net present value and net future value of a stream of equity cash flows.

As discussed in Chapter 10, the stream of cash flows associated with a firm's long-term debt equals the interest and principal payments specified in the debt agreement. Given the amount and timing of the interest and principal payments, the stream of cash flows can be discounted back to the present or accumulated into the future at the market rate of interest.

The equivalent stream of cash flows associated with a firm's common stock equals the periodic dividend payments plus an estimate of the terminal or residual value of the stock that investors might receive if they were to sell their shares in the future. The terminal value plays the same role in the valuation of a firm's common stock as the final principal payment played in the valuation of a firm's long-term debt.

Figure 11.4 presents the information about Wal-Mart's common stock (on a per-100-share basis) that we will use to illustrate the mechanics of the market valuation process.[3] For this illustration, we will be using 20/20 hindsight. We will go back to January 31, 1990, to see what investors might have been willing to pay for 100 shares of Wal-Mart's common stock. Of course, our perfect knowledge of all of the economic events that occurred between 1990 and 2000 was pure speculation at the beginning of this ten-year period.

At the end of fiscal 1991, Wal-Mart was earning 29¢ per share, paying 4¢ in dividends, and retaining the other 25¢ to grow the business. When we multiply the per-share data by 100 shares, we get the information presented in Figure 11.4.

Over this ten-year period, Wal-Mart earned a total of $650 on 100 shares of common stock, paid $100 in dividends, and retained $550 to grow the

Figure 11.4   Wal-Mart Earnings, Dividends, and Retained Earnings, 1991–2000 (per 100 Shares)

Year Ended January 31	Earnings	Dividends	Retained Earnings
1991	$29	$4	$25
1992	$35	$4	$31
1993	$44	$5	$39
1994	$51	$7	$44
1995	$59	$9	$50
1996	$60	$10	$50
1997	$67	$11	$56
1998	$78	$14	$64
1999	$99	$16	$83
2000	$128	$20	$108
Totals	$650	$100	$550

Source: Annual Value Line Investment Surveys.

business. Given these facts (which would have been predictions at the beginning of 1991), the question becomes one of using this information to put a value on Wal-Mart's common stock. How do we incorporate this earnings and dividends information into our time value of money calculations to estimate the present and future values of 100 shares of Wal-Mart's common stock?

As discussed in Chapter 1, net income equals net earned assets. The net assets *earned* by management on behalf of the shareholders can either be paid to shareholders in the form of dividends or reinvested in the business. When management declares and pays dividends, the shareholders must decide what to do with the money they receive. When management *retains* all or part of those earnings, management decides what to do with the money it retains.

From the investors' perspective, the only good reason for retaining or reinvesting all or part of the earnings is for management to grow the business and earn even more money on the shareholders' behalf. If management has no idea of how to grow the business and make more money on the shareholders' behalf, it might consider paying 100% of the earnings out in dividends. Theoretically, the firm that decided to pay out 100% of earnings in dividends would remain at its current size forever.

If at the end of 2000, Wal-Mart decided to pay 100% of earnings to shareholders in the form of dividends, the holder of 100 shares of common stock would receive $128 in cash each year forever. Since charges such as depreciation are included in the determination of net income, we can assume that management would use the money equal to the depreciation charges to replace productive assets as they wore out and to carry on other basic maintenance activities. Theoretically speaking and based on this set of assumptions, Wal-Mart would continue to generate $128 in earnings to be paid out in dividends every year from now until eternity.

As strange as paying out 100% of earnings in dividends may sound, this type of thinking is actually used to construct a stream of equity cash flows to be used in valuing a firm's common stock. As we shall see, financial analysts and investors typically make an assumption about when a firm will stop growing or start growing at a slower rate in the future. In the year the assumption of no growth is put into play, 100% of all future earnings are assumed to be paid out in dividends.

In Figure 11.5, we have converted the information contained in Figure 11.4 into a stream of dividend payments to shareholders for 1991 through 2000 and a single terminal or residual value for the end of 2000. This is the information we will use to see how much we might have been willing to pay for 100 shares of Wal-Mart's common stock at the beginning of 1991. We will also look to see how much that initial investment was expected to grow over the next ten years, assuming that investors were using Wal-Mart's 13.03% average cost of equity capital in the valuation process (review Figures 11.1, 11.2, and 11.3).

Dividends

If we had owned 100 shares of Wal-Mart's common stock since the beginning of 1991, we would have received a total of $100 in dividends over ten years. As we can see from Figures 11.4 and 11.5, Wal-Mart increased the amount of dividends paid to shareholders each year, but dividend payments still represented only 15.4% of earnings over the entire ten-year period—84.6% of those earnings were retained to grow the business.

Terminal Value

The terminal value shown for 2000 is calculated by dividing the earnings for 2000 by the cost of equity capital investors expected to earn on their investment over the ten-year period. As shown in Figure 11.2, Wal-Mart's average cost of equity capital equaled 13.03%.

Figure 11.5 Wal-Mart Dividends, Terminal Value and Total Cash Flows, 1991–2000 (per 100 Shares)

Year Ended January 31	Dividends	Terminal Value	Total Cash Flow
1991	$4		$4
1992	$4		$4
1993	$5		$5
1994	$7		$7
1995	$9		$9
1996	$10		$10
1997	$11		$11
1998	$14		$14
1999	$16		$16
2000	$20	$983	$1,003
Totals	$100	$983	$1,083

▶

Terminal Value = Net Income ÷ Cost of Equity Capital
$983 = $128   ÷ 13.03%

◀

Now that we know how the terminal value was calculated, we can begin to talk about what it means and how it fits into the market valuation process.

As mentioned at the beginning of the chapter, the terminal value or residual value is equivalent to the principal payment that the lender receives at the end of the loan period. In exchange for the final payment, the loan is canceled and the borrower's obligation to the lender terminated.

In this case, the terminal value represents the amount of money the shareholders would expect to receive in exchange for their 100 shares of common stock at the end of 2000. Since they wanted to earn a 13.03% return on their investment, they would have had to receive $983.

The terminal value represents an estimate of what 100 shares of Wal-Mart's stock would be worth if the company earned $128 in net income every year and paid 100% of those earnings out in dividends.

Terminal Value × Cost of Equity Capital = Net Income
$983 × 13.03% = $128

The $983 represents the amount an investor would be willing to pay to receive $128 per year from now until eternity. Whether financial analysts and investors follow this particular approach or some similar approach, the objective of the market valuation process is the same: to seek out stocks that will allow investors to earn their cost of equity capital and exceed their cost of equity capital when management performs at a higher level of performance than originally expected.

With a cost of equity capital in hand and a schedule of equity cash flows prepared, the time value of money analysis can now be applied to the valuation of common stock, following the same procedures we used to calculate the price of long-term debt in Chapter 10.

PRESENT AND FUTURE VALUES

Figure 11.6 presents the present value and future value factors we need to determine how much investors might have been willing to pay for 100 shares of Wal-Mart's common stock at the beginning of 1991 at a 13.03% cost of equity capital. As we can see from the figure, the present value of $1 to be received in 2000 was 30.3¢ as of January 31, 1990. The future value of $1 invested on January 31, 1990, would have accumulated to $3.40 as of January 31, 2000. If management had earned the investors' expected cost of equity capital, the $1 would have yielded a total return over the full ten-year period of 13.03%.

When we combine the present value and future value factors from Figure 11.6 with the schedule of total cash flows from Figure 11.5, we can determine the present values and the future values of the entire stream of cash flows, as shown in Figure 11.7.

Figure 11.8 presents the same information with one important difference: the total cumulative present value of $343.94 shown at the bottom of the cumulative present value column in Figure 11.7 is shown as a negative amount ($343.94) for 1989 in Figure 11.8.

As we can see from Figure 11.8, the total cumulative present value and total cumulative future value amounts equal $0 when we insert the $344 as a negative amount for 1990. We can see that an investment of $344 in 100

Figure 11.6 Time Value of Money, Present Value and Future Value Factors, 13.03% Cost of Equity Capital

Year Ended January 31	Cumulative Present Value Factors	Present Value Factor $1 \div (1 + i)$	Market Interest Rates (i)	Future Value Factor $1 \times (1 + i)$	Cumulative Future Value Factors
1990	1.000	1.000	0.00%	1.000	1.000
1991	0.911	0.885	13.03%	1.130	1.130
1992	0.806	0.885	13.03%	1.130	1.277
1993	0.713	0.885	13.03%	1.130	1.444
1994	0.631	0.885	13.03%	1.130	1.632
1995	0.558	0.885	13.03%	1.130	1.845
1996	0.494	0.885	13.03%	1.130	2.085
1997	0.437	0.885	13.03%	1.130	2.356
1998	0.387	0.885	13.03%	1.130	2.663
1999	0.342	0.885	13.03%	1.130	3.010
2000	0.303	0.885	13.03%	1.130	3.402

Figure 11.7 Wal-Mart Net Present Values and Net Future Values, 13.03% Cost of Equity Capital (per 100 Shares)

Year Ended January 31	Cumulative Present Value	Cumulative Present Value Factors	Total Cash Flow	Cumulative Future Value Factors	Cumulative Future Value
1990	–0–	1.000		3.402	–0–
1991	$3.64	0.911	$4.00	3.010	$12.04
1992	$3.22	0.806	$4.00	2.663	$10.65
1993	$3.57	0.713	$5.00	2.356	$11.78
1994	$4.42	0.631	$7.00	2.085	$14.59
1995	$5.02	0.558	$9.00	1.845	$16.60
1996	$4.94	0.494	$10.00	1.632	$16.32
1997	$4.81	0.437	$11.00	1.444	$15.88
1998	$5.41	0.387	$14.00	1.277	$17.88
1999	$5,47	0.342	$16.00	1.130	$18.08
2000	$303.44	0.303	$1002.66	1.000	$1,002.66
Totals	$343.94		$1,082.66		$1,136.50

Figure 11.8 **Wal-Mart Present Values and Future Values, 100 Shares of Common Stock at a 13.03% Cost of Equity Capital (per 100 Shares)**

Year Ended January 31	Cumulative Present Value	Cumulative Present Value Factors	Total Cash Flow	Cumulative Future Value Factors	Cumulative Future Value
1989	($343.94)	1.000	($343.94)	3.402	($1,136.50)
1990	$3.64	0.911	$4.00	3.010	$12.04
1991	$3.22	0.806	$4.00	2.663	$10.65
1992	$3.57	0.713	$5.00	2.356	$11.78
1993	$4.42	0.631	$7.00	2.085	$14.59
1994	$5.02	0.558	$9.00	1.845	$16.60
1995	$4.94	0.494	$10.00	1.632	$16.32
1996	$4.81	0.437	$11.00	1.444	$15.88
1997	$5.41	0.387	$14.00	1.277	$17.88
1998	$5.47	0.342	$16.00	1.130	$18.08
1999	$303.44	0.303	$1,002.66	1.000	$1,002.66
Totals	$0		$738.72		$0

shares of common stock might have generated future cash flows of $1,083 for a net cash flow of $739. This total stream of equity cash flows would have earned an investor the 13.03% cost of equity capital.

REALITY CHECK

A quick reality check on whether our valuation process makes any sense is to compare our results with the actual market price of Wal-Mart's common stock for fiscal 1990, the year before the cash flows associated with 100 shares of common stock would have started flowing to us.

▶

Question: If we had bought our hypothetical 100 shares of Wal-Mart's common stock on January 31, 1990, for $3.44 per share ($344 ÷ 100 shares), would the $3.44 have been even close to the actual market price for Wal-Mart's common stock?

Answer: Yes, it would have been in the ballpark.

For the fiscal year ended January 31, 1990, Wal-Mart's common stock traded between a low of $3.75 per share and a high of $5.92 per share.

Given the range of values that any firm's common stock trades at during any given year, it is not hard to see that investors differ to some degree in their assessments of a firm's expected future performance, their personal time horizons, and their estimation of cost of equity capital.

The market valuation process, as we have just described it, may not be perfect, but it does give managers a good understanding of what investors value: earnings and dividends. Even if we had paid the high price of $5.92 in 1990, we would have been very happy with our investment.

In Chapter 12, we are going to revisit the Strategic Profit Model to integrate what we have just learned about the market valuation process with our understanding of the firm's financial performance, as reported in the financial statements.

NOTES

1. Ibbotson Associates, *Stocks, Bonds, Bills and Inflation: 2000 Yearbook.*

2. Investment advisory services typically report a firm's Beta along with all of the other financial information they provide to their subscribers. The *Value Line Investment Survey* reports Beta for over 1,700 companies. These Betas are recalculated each time a new investment report is prepared for a company.

3. In order to make the discussion of the market valuation process relevant to managers, we will express all of the calculations in terms of 100 shares of common stock. For most managers, buying or selling 100 shares of common stock is easy to visualize.

CHAPTER 12

Market Valuation: Strategic Profit Model Revisited

In Part One of this book, we discussed how managers can use the information found in the financial statements to better understand the business. In the first three chapters of Part Two (Chapters 9–11), we outlined the fundamentals of how the market values debt and equity securities. Given the market interest rates on long-term debt and the estimates of shareholders' cost of equity capital, the basic logic and mechanics of the market valuation process were relatively straightforward.

The only trouble with looking at the firm from a market perspective is that managers find it difficult to translate the results of the market valuation process into their day-to-day responsibilities. That is where the Strategic Profit Model (SPM) comes back into the picture.

> If we add information about the total market value of the firm's common stock and the cost of equity capital to the SPM, we can go a long way toward integrating market and management measures of performance into a single, integrated management communications framework.

In Chapter 1, we used the concept of return on equity (ROE) to integrate margin management, asset management, and financial management concepts into an overall management communications framework. In the initial development of the SPM, we did not include any market measures of financial performance.

In this chapter, we will show how the SPM may be extended to integrate market measures of performance with the financial measures of management performance. In Chapter 11, we saw that the market price of a firm's common stock is based, in part, on expectations of future earnings and cash flows. In this chapter, we shall see that the market price is also related, in part, to past performance of the firm as captured by the ROE. Although achieving a high (and sustainable) ROE while growing the business does not guarantee a high market valuation for the firm, the common stock of firms with consistently high ROEs typically trades at higher prices than does that of firms with consistently lower ROEs.

We will begin the process of linking the market valuation process to management performance through the concept of "equity spread." We will examine Wal-Mart's performance from 1990 through 2000 through the concept of equity spread and see how the firm's equity spread can be integrated into the SPM. Once this is completed, managers can see how their performance and the performance of the entire firm fits into a broader market framework.

MANAGEMENT PERFORMANCE AND MARKET PERFORMANCE

By linking management's performance to the market's assessment of that performance, we will see the tension that almost always exists among managers, financial analysts, and investors. On the one hand, management must pay attention to the needs of customers, employees or associates, suppliers, and other creditors. On the other hand, management must be concerned about meeting the shareholders' expectations for a return on investment. Sam Walton highlighted the tension that every CEO of a publicly traded company confronts:

> What really worried me over the years is not our stock price, but that we might someday fail to take care of our customers, or that our managers might fail to motivate and take care of our associates.
>
> As business leaders, we absolutely cannot afford to get all caught up in trying to meet the goals that some retail analyst or financial institution in New York sets for us on a ten-year plan spit out of a computer that somebody set to compound at such-and-such a rate. If we

do that, we take our eye off the ball. But if we demonstrate in our sales and our earnings every day, every week, every quarter, that we are doing our job in a sound way, we will get the growth we are entitled, and the market will respect us in a way we deserve.

If we fail to live up to somebody's hypothetical projection for what we should be doing, I don't care. It may knock our stock back a little, but we're in it for the long run. We couldn't care less about what is forecast or what the market says we ought to do. If we listened very seriously to that sort of stuff, we never would have gone into small-town discounting in the first place.[1]

Rather than taking sides (with CEOs such as Sam Walton or a group of financial analysts or investors), we are going to use the concept of equity spread to illustrate this tension between management and the market.

CONCEPT OF EQUITY SPREAD

As discussed in Chapter 11, the firm's cost of equity capital is used to discount a stream of equity cash flows to estimate the market value of a firm's common stock. Based on this assessment of value, investors have two basic choices:

1. **Buy:** If they think that the current value of the firm is greater than the current market price
2. **Sell:** If they think that the current value of the firm is less than the current market price

In Chapter 11, we used the wisdom that comes from having 20/20 hindsight to value Wal-Mart's common stock. After creating a stream of equity cash flows and using Wal-Mart's average cost of equity capital (CofC) between 1990 and 2000, we estimated the value of 100 shares of common stock. As we saw, the value of $3.44 per share was relatively close to the average share price for the fiscal year ended January 31, 1990. In helping managers understand the business through financial information, we saw that a firm's cost of equity capital is a key measure of market performance.

When we link the market to management through the SPM, the cost of equity capital comes into play through the concept of equity spread. If a firm's ROE is greater than its CofC, management is said to be generating a positive equity spread. If the CofC is above the firm's ROE, management is generating a negative equity spread. As discussed in Chapter 11, the firm's CofC captures investor expectations by incorporating the effects of inflation, risk-free interest rates on U.S. treasury bonds, and market risk premiums into a single performance measure.

Since CofC is a measure of the market's expectations about a particular firm and since ROE is a measure of the firm's actual performance, there must be a way of combining these two measures into a single, more comprehensive performance measure. That is where the concept of equity spread demonstrates its value.

A firm's equity spread is defined in the following manner:

$$\text{Equity Spread} = \text{ROE} - \text{CofC}$$

Figure 12.1 presents Wal-Mart's equity spread for the years 1990 through 2000. As we can see from this figure, Wal-Mart generated a positive equity spread in each of these eleven years.

For every $1 of shareholders' equity, Wal-Mart generated 21.6¢ in profit in the years 1990 through 2000. Of that profit, 9.3¢ equaled Wal-Mart's cost of equity capital, while the remaining 12.3¢ represented the equity spread over and above the cost of equity capital.

The equity spread concept is a useful addition to the ROE concept for two reasons. First, the equity spread calculation starts with ROE. As discussed in Part One of this book, the concept of ROE allows managers to see how profit margins, asset turnovers, returns on assets, and financial leverage all come together through the SPM. Second, within an equity spread framework, management can see how well it is doing, compared with the shareholders' cost of equity capital.

In developing a comprehensive business strategy, management has to balance the tension between the shareholders' expectations for a return on their investment and the firm's ability to meet those expectations. Although

Figure 12.1   Wal-Mart Equity Spreads (for the Years Ended January 31, 1990–2000)

Year Ended January 31	Return on Equity	Cost of Capital	Equity Spread
1990	27.1%	14.0%	13.2%
1991	24.1%	14.0%	10.1%
1992	23.0%	13.3%	9.7%
1993	22.8%	12.5%	10.3%
1994	21.7%	11.3%	10.4%
1995	21.1%	12.6%	8.6%
1996	18.6%	12.0%	6.6%
1997	17.8%	11.9%	5.9%
1998	19.1%	11.8%	7.3%
1999	21.0%	10.7%	10.3%
2000	20.8%	11.1%	9.7%
Average	21.6%	12.3%	9.3%

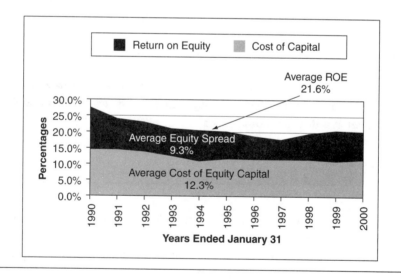

Wal-Mart exceeded the cost of equity capital in each of the ten years in our sample, the size of the spread declined over that period. Wal-Mart generated a 13.2% equity spread in 1990 but yielded only a 9.7% equity spread in 2000.

If the cost of equity capital had remained the same over the years 1990 through 2000 (14.0% in 1990), Wal-Mart's equity spread would have been only 6.8% in 2000. If management had been able to maintain the 27.1% ROE it was generating in 1990 while the cost of equity capital was falling, management would have generated a 16.0% equity spread in 2000. Over these years, Wal-Mart, like all other publicly traded firms, benefited from the effects of lower inflation rates and lower interest rates. As the data in Figure 12.1 suggest, if management had been able to stop or slow the decline in ROE that started to occur in 1991, Wal-Mart would have been able to reap the benefits of the substantial decline in the cost of equity capital that began in the same year.

From a management perspective, the firm's equity spread is made of one component that management can influence directly through its own actions (ROE) and a second component (the firm's CofC) that it can only influence indirectly. Management has no direct control over the inflation rate, the interest rate on U.S. treasury bonds, and how the market price of the firm's common stock fluctuates compared with the overall economy. However, management does have direct control over the firm's business, as measured by ROE. As previously mentioned, that is where the SPM becomes useful.

EXPANDED SUMMARY VERSION OF THE STRATEGIC PROFIT MODEL

Figure 12.2 presents an expanded summary version of Wal-Mart's SPM, which allows us to look at the business all the way from a customer perspective (net sales) to an investor's perspective (equity spread). In terms of this figure, management's job is to ensure that all of the bases are covered. Every component of the model is being managed or influenced to benefit the major stakeholders in the business—customers, employees, suppliers, creditors, and shareholders.

Within the context provided by Figure 12.2, we can see that the addition of Wal-Mart's cost of equity capital and equity spread represents a convenient and systematic way of bringing the market and investors into a comprehensive strategy framework.

As we can see from Figure 12.2, management grew the business from $25.99 billion in net sales in 1990 to $166.81 billion in 2000. However, this growth has come at a cost to the shareholders.

Figure 12.2   Wal-Mart Strategic Profit Model, Expanded Summary Version (for the Fiscal Years Ended January 31, 1990 and 2000—Amounts in Millions)

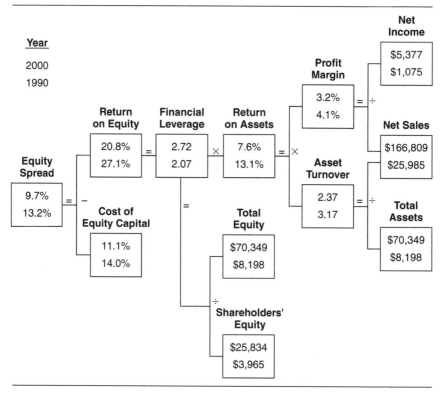

In 1990, Wal-Mart earned 27.1¢ for every $1 of shareholders' equity and generated an equity spread of 13.2¢ on behalf of the shareholders.

In 2000, Wal-Mart earned 20.8¢ for every $1 of shareholders' equity and generated an equity spread of 9.7¢.

Given that throughout this book we have used the Wal-Mart example to demonstrate how to understand the business through financial information, what aspects of the business would you focus on to reverse the decline in Wal-Mart's financial performance?

By adding market information to the SPM, managers can see how investors look at their firm relative to the stock of other publicly traded firms. Adding this market information accomplishes two objectives:

- Managers can see that they do not have to become financial analysts in order to understand what they have to do to create value for their shareholders. If management can increase the firm's ROE, they will have done everything under their control to increase the equity spread. The cost of equity capital is beyond their direct control.

- Once everyone on the management team sees the importance of growing the business and maintaining or improving the firm's ROE, managers can get back to the basics—improving margins and increasing asset turnover.

After using the financial information about Wal-Mart to help managers understand the business through financial information, we have come full circle. At this point, readers must decide where to go from here. One choice is to decide to learn more about the technical aspects of financial statement analysis and the market valuation process. The other choice is to go back to Chapter 1 and start the process all over again, only this time with your own company, a competitor, a supplier, or a potential investment opportunity.

Wal-Mart represents an example of how the models we have presented throughout this book may be used to understand any business through the use of financial information. The models presented in this book can be used to analyze any company. For publicly held companies, the information needed to complete the models is readily available to the general public.

Based on our experiences working with management groups, we know that the concepts underlying the SPM truly come to life when all of the members of a management team learn to speak the same language and use the SPM to help improve the financial performance of their firm.

NOTES

1. Sam Walton and John Huey, *Sam Walton, Made in America, My Story* (New York: Doubleday, 1992), 107–108.

Appendices: Case Studies

Introduction to Case Studies

As mentioned in the Introduction, this book is about helping managers tell a story about the financial performance of their firm. In order to tell a convincing story, managers need to have some idea of what users of financial information consider to be important performance indicators. Managers also need to know how their decisions and actions can affect the financial performance of the firm as captured by these performance indicators.

In Chapters 1 through 12, we used Wal-Mart's financial statements to introduce two business strategy models, which managers can use to help them make sense of the financial information found in those financial statements. The purpose of the case studies is to provide you with additional examples of how the principles of financial statement analysis presented in this book may be applied to other high-profile companies.

The Strategic Profit Model (SPM) shows how all of the elements found in a firm's balance sheets and income statements are integrated through the concept of return on shareholders' equity (ROE). We begin the analysis of any firm by starting with ROE and then breaking it down into its components parts:

- Profit margin
- Asset turnover
- Return on assets
- Financial leverage

The Strategic Financing Model (SFM) shows how all of the elements found in a firm's restructured balance sheets and financial flow statements allow us to understand the firm from a long-term investment and financing perspective. Given a basic understanding of this long-term perspective, we can then use the model to show how the firm's long-term financing and investment strategy is driven, in part, by the amount of internal equity financing generated by management. Generally speaking, a firm has access to three sources of long-term financing:

- External debt financing (creditors)
- External equity financing (shareholders)
- Internal equity financing (management)

As we saw in the discussion of Wal-Mart's financial performance, these two business strategy models, along with market information about a firm's stock price, provide a powerful framework for understanding the business through financial information. Once managers have a basic understanding of how to look at financial statements and market information from a business strategy perspective, practice makes perfect: by applying the principles of financial statement analysis to a few other well-known firms, managers develop their ability to analyze other companies, particularly their own firm.

In recent years, we have used the financial statements of Dell, Cisco, and Pfizer, among other U.S. companies, to help managers begin the process of understanding the business through financial information. Since virtually every manager has some working knowledge of the products and services provided by these high-profile companies, we can usually jump right into the financial statement analysis without having to provide much background information about these firms. In telling a story about Dell, Pfizer, and Cisco, we will focus on what we believe to be the most significant aspects of each firm's business strategy, as revealed through the two business strategy models.

Dell

Dell Computer Corporation is one of the world's leading sellers of computers. Dell has been credited with revolutionizing the computer systems industry with its direct-to-customer business model. It was one of the top performing stocks of the 1990s. A $10,000 investment on December 31, 1989, would have grown to an amazing $8,885,333 over the course of the decade.

Under leadership of CEO Michael Dell, Dell grew during the 1990s from a relatively unknown company to a well-established market leader. Between 1995 and 2000 alone, Dell's sales grew from $3.5 billion to $25.3 billion—a 48.7% CAGR (compound annual growth rate). It is an excellent example of a well-managed, high-technology company that has created tremendous wealth for its shareholders. By looking at Dell's financial performance between 1995 and 2000, we will see how the company balanced its sales growth focus with effective inventory management and conservative financial management practices.

Pfizer

Pfizer, Inc. is one of the world's leading pharmaceutical manufacturers. During the 1990s, Pfizer held a leadership position in the discovery and sale of new pharmaceutical products. During that decade, the company outpaced the sales growth in the pharmaceutical industry. Pfizer is a good example of a well-managed pharmaceutical company that has created tremendous wealth for its shareholders. By looking at Pfizer's financial performance between 1994 and 1999, we can see how the company balanced risk taking in research and development with aggressive sales growth, while maintaining conservative financial management practices.

Cisco

Cisco Systems is the worldwide leader in supplying networking equipment for the Internet. Cisco creates hardware and software solutions that link computer networks, so that people have easy access to information without regard to differences in time, place, or type of computer system. Cisco sells the products that manage and control the movement of data among users connected through local and global networks. Cisco was also one of the top performing stocks during the 1990s. A $10,000 investment on December 31, 1989, would have grown to $6,305,567 by December 31, 1999.

Between 1994 and 1999, Cisco grew sales from $1.2 billion in 1994 to $12.2 billion in 1999—a 57.8% CAGR. Under the leadership of CEO John Chambers, Cisco expects to sell $50 billion worth of products by 2004. Cisco expects to achieve this $50 billion goal through a combination of internal growth from existing product lines and new acquisitions.

CASE STUDY DEVELOPMENT

For each of the case study companies, we will analyze the financial statements and market information about the company in three steps:

1. We will use the quick overview of the SPM to make sense out of the financial information found in the firm's balance sheets and income statements. Based on what we find in this quick overview, we will indicate how you can take a closer look at the most important component or components of the SPM for that firm: the margin management, asset management, or financial management component of the model.
2. We will use the SFM to focus on the long-term investment and financing aspects of each firm's business strategy. As we shall see, the long-term financing and investment strategies differ across our three case study firms.
3. Using market value information about the S&P 500 and each firm's common stock, we will compare each firm's financial performance with the returns generated by the S&P 500.

The financial statement analyses of each case study firm closely parallel the thorough analysis of Wal-Mart that we used throughout the book. In order to keep each case study to a reasonable length, we have concentrated on the insights that can be gained from the summary versions of the SPM and SFM. We have also limited the discussion of the market valuation process for each firm's common stock.

We encourage you to conduct your own more in-depth analysis of each firm by referring to specific chapters in the text for additional guidance.

Dell Computer Corporation

Dell Computer builds and sells notebook and desktop computers, servers, Internet appliances, workstations, and storage systems. It is one of the world's leading sellers of computers and computer-related products. Dell revolutionized the personal computer industry with its direct-to-customer business model. It started as a company in the college dorm room of CEO Michael Dell in the 1980s. During the 1990s, Dell grew from a relatively unknown company to build market share and pass such well-established firms as Compaq and IBM. It has actively used information technology to expand the scope of its direct business model. Today, Dell relies heavily on the Internet to interact with customers, suppliers, business partners, and employees. In many respects, Dell is one of the best examples of a pure e-business.

Between 1995 and 2000, Dell increased sales at a 48.7% CAGR (compound annual growth rate). It is an excellent example of a well-managed, high-technology company that has created tremendous wealth for its shareholders. By looking at Dell's financial performance between 1995 and 2000, we can see how the company balanced sales growth with effective margin management, asset management, and financial management practices.

In telling a story about the company, we will draw on the financial information reported in Dell's balance sheets and income statements, along with market information about the company's common stock. We will focus on the most significant aspects of Dell's financial performance as captured by our business strategy models. As we shall see, all of the parts of Dell's financial performance fit together to form a unified whole. It is just one part—namely, margin management—that plays the greatest role in Dell's overall business strategy.

BALANCE SHEETS AND INCOME STATEMENTS

As mentioned in Chapter 2, a firm's balance sheets and income statements provide all of the information we will need to prepare the Strategic Profit Model and the Strategic Financing Model for any firm. In the case of the Strategic Financing Model, we restructure the balance sheets and create the financial flow statement before we do the analysis. However, all of the key financial performance indicators that we will use to begin understanding the business are included in the balance sheets and income statements in one form or another.

Balance Sheets

Figure A.1 presents Dell's balance sheets for the fiscal years ended January 31, 1995 and 2000.

Two specific aspects of Dell's balance sheets warrant special attention:

1. Accrued current liabilities and other long-term liabilities consist primarily of deferred revenues on warranty contracts.
2. Retained earnings include other equity adjustments.

Although reported separately in Dell's annual reports, these amounts are not material to understanding Dell's business operations.

We can now return to the overall comparison of 1995 with 2000 provided by Dell's balance sheet equations:

```
        Assets  =  Liabilities  +  Shareholders' Equity
1995: $1.594B  =  $ 943M       +  $651M
2000: $11.471B =  $6.163B      +  $5.308B
```

In terms of total assets, the Dell of 2000 is 7.20 times larger than it was in 1995. In terms of shareholders' equity, Dell is 8.15 times larger than it was in 1995.

**Figure A.1   Dell Computer Balance Sheets (Amounts in Millions),
Years Ended January 31**

	1995	2000
Assets		
Current Assets		
Accounts Receivable (Net)	$538	$2,608
Inventories	$293	$391
Cash	$43	$3,809
Other Current Assets	$596	$873
Total Current Assets	$1,470	$7,681
Productive Assets		
Property and Equipment	$208	$1,140
Accumulated Depreciation	($91)	($375)
Total Productive Assets	$117	$765
Other Assets		
Investments	$0	$2,721
Other Noncurrent Assets	$7	$304
Total Other Assets	$7	$3,025
Total Assets	$1,594	$11,471
Liabilities and Shareholders' Equity		
Current Liabilities		
Accounts Payable	$447	$3,538
Accrued Liabilities and Other	$304	$1,654
Total Current Liabilities	$751	$5,192
Long-Term Liabilities		
Long-Term Debt	$114	$508
Other Long-Term Liabilities	$78	$463
Total Long-Term Liabilities	$192	$971
Total Liabilities	$943	$6,163
Shareholders' Equity		
Common Stock*	$357	$3,583
Retained Earnings*	$294	$1,725
Total Shareholders' Equity	$651	$5,308
Total Equity	$1,594	$11,471

*Includes other equity adjustments

Income Statements

Figure A.2 presents Dell's income statements for the years ended January 31, 1995 and 2000.

Dell's income statements look very similar to Wal-Mart's income statements and differ in only two significant ways:

1. R&D (research and development) represents a material aspect of Dell's business strategy; therefore, the income statements disclose the amount of money the company spends on R&D ($65 million in 1995 and $374 million in 2000).

2. Purchased in-process R&D represents the expenses associated with the R&D efforts of acquired companies that will not be continued at Dell. In 2000, $194 million associated with the R&D effort of acquired companies would not be continued into the future and was therefore expensed immediately.

The expenses associated with both types of R&D will be reflected in the margin management component of the Strategic Profit Model.

Figure A.2 Dell Computer Income Statements (Amounts in Millions), Years Ended January 31

	1995	2000
Revenue		
Sales	$3,475	$25,265
Cost and Expenses		
Cost of Goods Sold	$2,737	$20,047
Selling, General, and Administrative Expenses	$423	$2,387
R&D Expenses	$65	$374
Purchased In-Process R&D	$0	$194
Total	$3,225	$23,002
Operating Income	$250	$2,263
Other Income (Expense)	($37)	188
Provision for Income Taxes	($64)	($785)
Net Income	$149	$1,666

Dell's balance sheets provide us with snapshots of the company at different points in time. The income statements provide us with information about Dell's financial performance on behalf of the shareholders in specific years. Dell's income statement equations for 1995 and 2000 provide us with basic information on how well management has performed on behalf of the shareholders:

▶

$$
\begin{array}{rcccl}
\text{Net Income} & = & \text{Revenue} & - & \text{Expenses (Net)} \\
1995:\ \$\ 149M & = & \$\ 3.475B & - & \$\ 3.326B \\
2000:\ \$1.666B & = & \$25.265B & - & \$23.599B
\end{array}
$$

◀

In 1995, Dell generated $3.475 billion in revenue and incurred $3.326 billion in expenses. The net income of $149 million represents the increase in net assets (assets − liabilities) earned by management on the shareholders' behalf during the year. In 2000, Dell generated $25.265 billion in revenue while incurring $23.599 billion in expenses. In 2000, management earned $1.666 billion in net assets on behalf of the shareholders. The net income reported for 2000 was 11.18 times larger than the net income reported in 1995.

Like our comparison of the two balance sheet equations, the comparison of the two income statement equations provides some initial insights into the business. When we add the return on equity (ROE) calculation to the analysis, we can begin to gain additional insights into the business by seeing how the balance sheets and income statements are interrelated. ROE provides the bridge between the firm's balance sheets and its income statements.

Return on Equity

Return on shareholders' equity (ROE) links Dell's income statements to its balance sheets. For the fiscal years ended January 31, 1995 and 2000,

▶

$$
\begin{array}{rcccl}
\text{ROE} & = & \text{Net Income} & \div & \text{Shareholders' Equity} \\
1995:\ 22.9\% & = & \$149M & \div & \$651M \\
2000:\ 31.4\% & = & \$1.666B & \div & \$5.308B
\end{array}
$$

◀

Stated in dollars and cents terms,

In 1995, Dell generated 22.9¢ in profit for every $1 of shareholders' equity. In 2000, Dell generated 31.4¢ in profit for every $1 of shareholders' equity.

By increasing ROE from 22.9¢ to 31.4¢, management was able to generate an additional $451 million in net income on shareholders' equity of $5.308 billion.

ROE represents a convenient way of linking the balance sheet to the income statement. ROE provides the anchor for taking a closer look at Dell through the Strategic Profit Model (SPM). No matter how deeply we drill into the details of Dell's financial performance, when we resurface, the ROEs for 1995 and 2000 will have remained the same–22.9% in 1995 and 31.4% in 2000.

The quick overview of the Strategic Profit Model shows how all of the financial aspects of Dell's business strategy fit into an integrated framework.

STRATEGIC PROFIT MODEL: QUICK OVERVIEW

Figure A.3 presents a quick overview of Dell's Strategic Profit Model for 1995 and 2000, using just four elements from Dell's income statements and balance sheets: sales, net income, total assets, and shareholders' equity.

In 1995, Dell generated 22.9¢ in profit on every $1 of shareholders' equity; in 2000, Dell generated 31.4¢.

In the process of growing the business over the last five years, Dell has experienced an 8.5¢ increase in ROE. With the quick overview provided by the SPM, we can now take a more in-depth look at the individual compo-

**Figure A.3   Dell Computer Strategic Profit Model: Quick Overview
for the Fiscal Years Ended January 31, 1995 and 2000
(Amounts in Millions)**

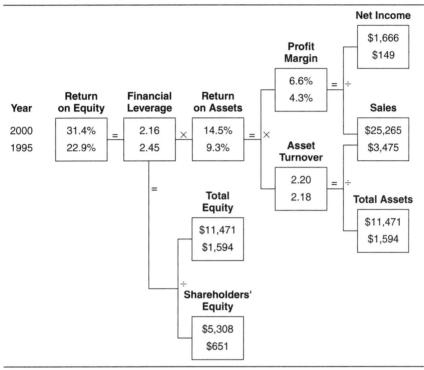

nents contributing to Dell's ROE in 1995 and 2000 and the 8.5¢ increase over the last five years.

As with Wal-Mart, we begin the discussion of the financial aspects of Dell's business strategy with the margin management component of the SPM.

Margin Management

As we can see from Figure A.3, Dell's profit margin increased from 4.3% to 6.6%. From a management perspective,

▶

Dell earned 4.3¢ in profit for every $1 of sales in 1995; in 2000, Dell earned 6.6¢ in profit.

◀

Between 1995 and 2000, Dell's margins have increased by 2.3¢ on every $1 of sales.

▶ ————————————————————————————————

> The 2.3¢ increase in profit margin translates into $583 million of net income on sales of $25.625 billion.

——————————————————————————————— ◀

Between 1995 and 2000, sales increased at a 48.7% compound annual growth rate (CAGR), net expenses increased by 48.0%, and net income increased by 62.1%. The 0.7 percentage point difference in growth rates for sales and net expenses translates into the 62.1% CAGR for net income and the 2.3¢ increase in profit margin.

If we took a closer look at the margin management component of the SPM, we would see that Dell's gross margin decreased slightly from 21.2% in 1995 to 20.7% in 2000, a 0.5 percentage point decrease. This decrease in gross margin was offset by decreases in S, G & A expenses from 12.2% to 9.4%. By reducing S, G & A expenses by approximately 2.8¢ for every $1 of sales, Dell saved $688 million on sales of $25.265 billion in 2000 relative to 1995 performance levels. Much of this reduction can be attributed to the efficiencies resulting from the increased use of technology and effective supply chain management.

Asset Management

As we can see from Figure A.3, Dell's asset turnover increased moderately from $2.18 in 1995 to $2.20 in 2000.

▶ ————————————————————————————————

> In 1995, Dell generated $2.18 in net revenue for every $1 of total assets; in 2000, Dell generated $2.20 in net revenue.

——————————————————————————————— ◀

All things considered, management (and shareholders) would prefer to generate more dollars of sales per $1 of assets than less. The greater the asset turnover, the greater the amount of customer financing management has generated with a given amount of assets.

Between 1995 and 2000, total assets increased at a 48.4% compound annual growth rate, compared with the 48.7% growth rate for sales. Any time sales increase faster than total assets, asset turnover increases. If Dell had not increased asset turnover from $2.18 to $2.20 per $1 of total assets, it would have required an additional investment of $118 million to support sales of $25.265 billion in 2000.

If we take a closer look at the inventory element of the asset management component of the SPM, the benefits of Dell's direct model become evident. Inventories increased from $293 million in 1995 to $391 million in 2000, a 5.9% CAGR. The 5.9% CAGR pales in comparison with the 48.7% CAGR for sales. Stated differently, in 1995 Dell held 30.8 days net sales in inventory, compared with 5.6 days in 2000. If Dell had not decreased days net sales invested in inventories by 25.1 days net sales, it would have required an additional investment of $1.739 billion to support sales of $25.265 billion in 2000. The financial information reported for inventories reinforces Dell's direct-to-customer business strategy. With the direct model, Dell has more money to invest resources in other areas of the business.

Return on Assets

As we can see from Figure A.3, Dell's return on assets (ROA) increased from 9.3% in 1995 to 14.5% in 2000.

In 1995, Dell earned 9.3¢ in profit for every $1 of total assets; in 2000, Dell earned 14.5¢.

The 5.2¢ increase in ROA reflects the combined effects of the 2.3¢ increase in profit margin and the 2.0¢ increase in asset turnover.

The key to operating success is a combination of Dell's margin management and asset management strategies.

Integration of Margin and Asset Management through ROA

To consolidate what managers are learning about Dell, it helps to return to the Strategic Profit Model "song" that we learned for Wal-Mart. In 2000,

For every $1 of assets, Dell generated $2.20 in sales, and,

For every $1 of sales, Dell earned 6.6¢ in profit.

Multiplying the profit margin by the asset turnover,

For every $1 of assets, Dell generated 14.5¢ in profit.

Compared with 1995, Dell has grown the business while increasing profit margins and asset turnover. Between 1995 and 2000, profit margins increased by 53.4%, while asset turnover increased by 0.9%. These increases together produced a 55.9% increase in ROA.

Financial Leverage

As we can see from Figure A.3, financial leverage decreased from 2.45 in 1995 to 2.16 in 2000.

In 1995, Dell utilized $2.45 in total equity for every $1 of shareholders' equity; in 2000, Dell utilized $2.16.

Like most firms in rapidly changing, highly competitive industries, such as the computer industry, managers must focus on the business risks associated with the competitive marketplace. Technologies change frequently. Innovation quickly redefines the marketplace. Managers do not want to make their job more difficult by taking on the additional financial risks associated with borrowing money.

Between 1995 and 2000, total equity increased at a 48.4% CAGR, total liabilities increased at a 45.6% CAGR, and shareholders' equity increased at a 52.1% CAGR. Based on these trends, we can see that the shareholders' interest in the business is growing at a faster rate than the interest of creditors.

Return on Equity: Closing the Loop

The concept of ROE provides us with the opportunity to interrelate all of the financial information included in the balance sheets and income statements into a comprehensive management framework. The Strategic Profit Model is then used to see how all of the parts fit together to form a greater whole. After managers see how all of the parts fit together, they can focus on developing their communication skills. For that part of the learning experience, we return to the Strategic Profit Model song. The 2000 version of Dell's SPM "song" goes something like this:

For every $1 of assets, Dell generated $2.20 in sales, and,

For every $1 of sales, Dell earned 6.6¢ in profit.

Multiplying the 6.6¢ profit margin by the $2.20 asset turnover, we see that,

For every $1 of assets, Dell generated 14.5¢ in profit.

Multiplying the 14.5¢ ROA by the $2.16 in financial leverage, we see that

Dell generated 31.4¢ in profit for every $1 of shareholders' equity invested in the business.

Between 1995 and 2000, Dell was able to grow sales at a 48.7% CAGR while growing net income at a 62.1% CAGR. Over the same period, total assets and total equity increased at 48.4% CAGRs, and shareholders' equity increased at a 52.1% CAGR.

STRATEGIC FINANCING MODEL

As discussed in Chapters 7 and 8, we restructure a firm's balance sheets to focus on the long-term investment and long-term financing aspects of the business. From the restructured balance sheets, we then create a financial flow statement, which shows how the long-term investment and long-term financing base changes over the five-year period.

**Figure A.4   Dell Computer Restructured Balance Sheets, Years Ended
January 31, 1995 and 2000 (Amounts in Millions)**

	1995	Change	2000
Long-Term Investment			
Current Assets			
Accounts Receivable (Net)	$538	$2,070	$2,608
Inventories	$293	$98	$391
Cash	$43	$3,766	$3,809
Other Current Assets	$596	$277	$873
Total Current Assets	$1,470	$6,211	$7,681
Current Liabilities			
Accounts Payable	$447	$3,091	$3,538
Accrued Liabilities and Other	$304	$1,350	$1,654
Total Current Liabilities	$751	$4,441	$5,192
Working Capital	$719	$1,770	$2,489
Gross Productive Assets	$208	$932	$1,140
Gross Other Assets	$7	$3,018	$3,025
Total Long-Term Investment	$934	$5,720	$6,654
Long-Term Financing			
External Debt Financing	$192	$779	$971
External Equity Financing			
Common Stock	$357	$3,226	$3,583
Stock Repurchases	$0	($3,843)	($3,843)
	$357	($617)	($260)
Internal Equity Financing			
Retained Earnings	$294	$1,431	$1,725
Accumulated Depreciation	$91	$284	$375
Stock Repurchases	$0	$3,843	$3,843
Total Internal Equity	$385	$5,558	$5,943
Total Long-Term Financing	$934	$5,720	$6,654

Restructured Balance Sheets

Figure A.4 presents Dell's restructured balance sheets for 1995 and 2000. As we can see, Dell's long-term investment is made up of working capital (current assets − current liabilities), gross productive assets, and gross other assets. Dell's long-term financing base consists of external debt financing, external equity financing, and internal equity financing.

Three aspects of Dell's restructured balance sheets are important to mention before discussing the SFM:

1. Gross productive assets exclude accumulated depreciation of $91 million in 1995 and $375 million in 2000.

2. Internal equity financing equals retained earnings plus accumulated depreciation and stock repurchases.

3. External equity financing equals common stock less stock repurchases charged to retained earnings.

As we shall see, these three observations will affect the way we interpret how Dell financed the business over the five-year period.

The following are the financial control equations underlying Dell's restructured balance sheets for 1995 and 2000:

Long-Term Investment = Long-Term Financing
1995: $ 934M = $ 934M
2000: $6.654B = $6.654B

In 2000, Dell's long-term investment and long-term financing base was 7.12 times larger than it was in 1995.

The only question that remains to be answered is *how* Dell financed the business over this period. As we saw with Wal-Mart, in order to answer that question it helps to explore the financial flow statement.

Financial Flow Statement

Figure A.5 presents Dell's financial flow statement for the five-year period ended January 31, 2000. As we can see, the financial flow statement differs from the restructured balance sheets in three ways:

1. The details included in the restructured balance sheets have been omitted from the financial flow statement.
2. The long-term financing activity has been placed above the long-term investment activity.
3. The financial flow statement includes a summary of the sales generated by Dell between the beginning of fiscal year 1996 and the end of fiscal year 2000—a total of $68.890 billion.

By focusing on the change column of Figure A.5, we can construct the financing the business component of the SFM, as presented in Figure A.6.

Figure A.5 **Dell Computer Financial Flow Statement for the Five Years Ended January 31, 2000 (Amounts in Millions)**

	1995	Change	2000
Long-Term Financing			
External Debt Financing	$192	$779	$971
External Equity Financing	$357	($617)	($260)
Internal Equity Financing	$385	$5,558	$5,943
Total Long-Term Financing	$934	$5,720	$6,654
Long-Term Investment			
Working Capital	$719	$1,770	$2,489
Gross Productive Assets	$208	$932	$1,140
Gross Other Assets	$7	$3,018	$3,025
Total Long-Term Investment	$934	$5,720	$6,654

Year	Sales
1996	$5,296
1997	$7,759
1998	$12,327
1999	$18,243
2000	$25,265
Five-Year Total	$68,890

As we can see from Figure A.6, Dell generated $5.558 billion in internal equity financing from $68.890 billion in sales and invested $5.720 billion for the long term. The difference between the internal equity financing and the long-term investment created a deficit of $162 million. This deficit, or requirement, had to be covered by external financing.

For every $1 of sales, Dell generated 8.1¢ in internal equity financing and increased long-term investment by 8.3¢, leaving a deficit of 0.2¢ for every $1 of sales.

Dell raised an additional 1.1¢ in external debt financing to cover the 0.2¢ deficiency and to reduce external equity financing by 0.9¢ for every $1 of sales.

Figure A.6   **Dell Computer Strategic Financing Model, Financing the Business, for the Five Years Ended January 31, 2000 (Amounts in Millions)**

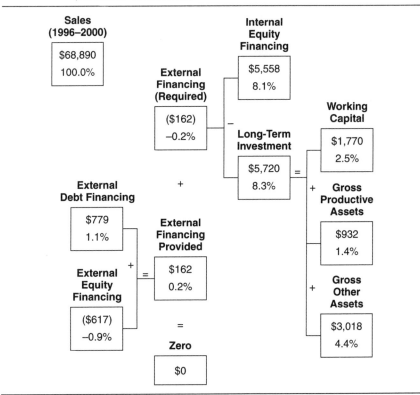

If we were to take a closer look at Dell's long-term investment base, we would see that the majority of the long-term investment has been invested in gross other assets $3.018 billion (4.4¢ for every $1 of sales). This increase is due primarily to investments in debt and equity securities. Increases in working capital and gross productive assets account for the remaining growth in long-term investment.

BUSINESS STRATEGY REVISITED

By using the quick overview from the Strategic Profit Model and the financing the business component of the Strategic Financing Model, we have been able to show how management increased Dell's ROE while growing the business. Dell increased its profit margin, asset turnover, and ROA while decreasing financial leverage and increasing ROE.

▶────────────────────────────────────

Between 1995 and 2000, sales increased from $3.475 billion in 1995 to $25.265 billion in 2000 (48.7% CAGR). Net income increased from $149 million to $1.666 billion (62.1% CAGR).

At the end of fiscal year 2000, Dell earned a 31.4% ROE, a ROE that is well above the 19.0% ROE for the similar period for the S&P 500.

Over this five-year period, Dell increased its long-term financing and long-term investment base by $5.720 billion (48.1% CAGR).

For every $1 of sales in years 1996 through 2000, Dell generated 8.1¢ in internal equity financing, and 8.3¢ was invested for the long-term.

The resulting 0.2¢ deficit in internal equity financing, plus the 0.9¢ reduction in external equity financing, was offset by the 1.1¢ increase in external debt financing for every $1 of sales over this five-year period.

────────────────────────────────────◀

Given this analysis of Dell's business strategy, we are well positioned to understand how the market valued Dell over this five-year period.

MARKET VALUATION

Figure A.7 presents the relationship between the market value of Dell's common stock and the two management measures of financial performance we used to calculate Dell's ROE—net income and shareholders' equity. With the benefit of hindsight, we can see that Dell's total market value (common shares outstanding times the market price per share) increased at a substantially faster rate than the increases in net income and shareholders' equity.[1]

Figure A.7   Dell Computer Market and Management Measures of Performance for the Years Ended January 31 (Shares and Amounts in Millions)

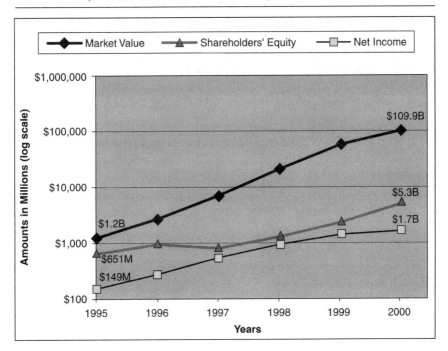

Years Ended January 31	Common Stock Outstanding	Market Value	Net Income	Shareholders' Equity
1995	2,475.5	$1,238	$149	$651
1996	2,539.5	$2,666	$272	$973
1997	2,990.3	$7,027	$531	$806
1998	2,768.8	$22,289	$944	$1,293
1999	2,576.0	$61,566	$1,460	$2,321
2000	2,543.0	$109,858	$1,666	$5,308
CAGR	0.5%	145.3%	62.1%	52.1%

As we can see from Figure A.7, Dell's common stock outstanding increased at a 0.5% CAGR between 1995 and 2000. Over this five-year period, the market value of the common stock outstanding increased at a 145.3% CAGR. During the same period, net income increased at a 62.1% CAGR, and shareholders' equity increased at a 52.1% CAGR.

As mentioned in Chapters 9 through 12, financial analysts and shareholders determine the value of a firm's common stock. The price of the firm's common stock is influenced by the recommendations of financial analysts at the major investment firms and what each of us is willing to pay for the firm's common stock. Firms such as Dell have no direct influence over the market price of their common stock, but they do have an indirect influence through their actions. For example, the expansion of product lines (e.g., offering Internet services or selling network servers) increases investors' expectations of future revenues and earnings.

From the quick overview of the Strategic Profit Model, we saw that Dell's ROE increased from 22.9% in 1995 to 31.4% in 2000. The average ROE for S&P 500 companies was around 17% in 1994 and 19% in 1999. For computer industry firms, the average ROE was around 21% in 1995 and 23% for 2000. Compared with these benchmarks, Dell's performance has been well above average.

From the Strategic Financing Model, we saw that Dell actually reduced the amount of external equity financing used in the business. The internal equity financing generated by management was more than enough to meet Dell's long-term investment needs and reduce external equity financing. The increase in external debt financing was also used to reduce external equity financing even more.

For the company as a whole, Dell has been a success in terms of both growth in market value and financial performance. The only question that remains to be answered is how well this performance has benefited individual shareholders relative to other firms (possible investments) in the capital marketplace.

Figure A.8 presents Dell's relative market performance, compared with the S&P 500 and the S&P Computer Systems Index (its industry peer group) between 1995 and 2000. The comparison is based on a hypothetical investment of $100 in a market basket of S&P 500 common stocks, the industry peer group, and Dell's common stock.

For every $100 invested in Dell's common stock, that investment would have increased to $5,693 (124.4% CAGR) by 2000. If that $100 were invested in the S&P Computer Systems Index, it would have increased to $687 (47.0% CAGR). If that $100 were invested in a market basket of

Figure A.8   Dell Computer, S&P Computer Systems Index, and the S&P 500, Cumulative Total Return, $100 Investment, as of January 31, 1995

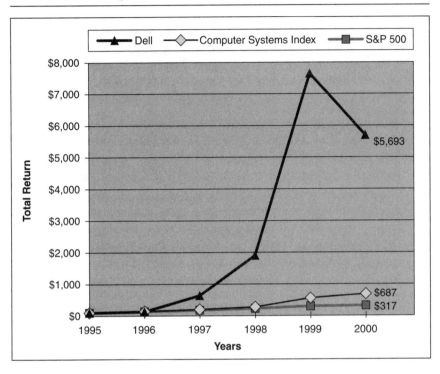

Total Return

Year	Dell	Computer Systems Index	S&P 500
1995	$100	$100	$100
1996	$131	$143	$136
1997	$633	$201	$175
1998	$1,901	$273	$228
1999	$7,642	$555	$295
2000	$5,693	$687	$317
CAGR	124.4%	47.0%	26.0%

S&P 500 common stocks, that investment would have increased to $317 (26.0% CAGR).[2]

This case study shows how the principles of financial statement analysis can help managers develop a better understanding of any business. If we were to go into a more in-depth analysis of Dell, we would return to the Strategic Profit Model and the Strategic Financing Model. We would take a closer look at each component of both models, as we did for Wal-Mart.

In the case study that follows, we will use the principles of financial statement analysis to see what we can learn about Pfizer, one of the leading pharmaceutical research and manufacturing firms in the world.

NOTES

1. We have plotted the relationship among market value, net income, and shareholders' equity using a log scale in order to present the information in a meaningful manner. If we did not use a log scale, the amounts reported for net income and shareholders' equity would barely get above the x-axis.

2. The total return for a $100 investment in the S&P Computer Systems Index or a market basket of S&P 500 common stocks assumes that any dividends received were reinvested to buy additional shares of common stock at the prevailing market price.

Pfizer, Inc.

Pfizer Inc. is one of the world's leading pharmaceutical manufacturers. During the 1990s, Pfizer held a leadership position in the discovery and sale of new pharmaceutical products. Every year of the 1990s, the company outpaced the sales growth in the pharmaceutical industry. Pfizer is a good example of a well-managed, pharmaceutical company that has created tremendous wealth for its shareholders. By looking at Pfizer's financial performance between 1994 and 1999, we can see how the company balanced risk taking in research and development with aggressive sales growth, while maintaining conservative financial management practices.

In telling a story about the company, we will draw on the financial information reported in Pfizer's balance sheets and income statements, along with market information about the company's common stock. We will focus on the most significant aspects of Pfizer's financial performance as captured by our business strategy models. As we shall see, all of the parts of Pfizer's financial performance fit together to form a unified whole. It is just one part—namely, margin management—that plays a greater role in Pfizer's overall business strategy than the other parts.

BALANCE SHEETS AND INCOME STATEMENTS

As mentioned in Chapter 2, a firm's balance sheets and income statements provide all of the information we need to prepare a Strategic Profit Model and a Strategic Financing Model for any firm. In the case of the Strategic Financing Model, we need to restructure the balance sheets and create the financial flow statement before we conduct the analysis. Nonetheless, all of the key financial performance indicators that we will use to begin understanding the business are included in the balance sheets and income statements in one form or another.

Figure B.1 Pfizer Balance Sheets (Amounts in Millions), Years Ended December 31

	1994	1999
Assets		
Current Assets		
Cash	$1,459	$739
Accounts Receivable	$1,665	$3,864
Inventories	$1,265	$1,654
Short-Term Investments	$921	$3,976
Other	$478	$958
Total Current Assets	$5,788	$11,191
Productive Assets		
Property, Plant, and Equipment	$4,993	$8,037
Accumulated Depreciation	($1,920)	($2,694)
Total Productive Assets	$3,073	$5,343
Other Assets		
Long-Term Investments	$724	$1,721
Other Noncurrent Assets	$1,514	$2,319
Total Other Assets	$2,238	$4,040
Total Other Assets	$11,099	$20,574
Liabilities		
Current Liabilities		
Accounts Payable	$525	$951
Accrued Liabilities	$2,081	$3,233
Current Debt Due	$2,220	$5,001
Total Current Liabilities	$4,826	$9,185
Long-Term Liabilities		
Long-Term Debt	$604	$525
Deferred Taxes	$212	$301
Other Long-Term Liabilities*	$1,133	$1,676
Total Long-Term Liabilities	$1,949	$2,502
Total Liabilities	$6,775	$11,687
Shareholders' Equity		
Common Stock	$685	$5,629
Treasury Stock	($1,753)	($6,851)
Employee Trusts	($749)	($2,888)
Retained Earnings**	$6,141	$12,997
Total Shareholders' Equity	$4,324	$8,887
Total Equity	$11,099	$20,574

*Includes postretirement benefits
**Includes other equity adjustments

Balance Sheets

Figure B.1 presents Pfizer's balance sheets for the fiscal years ended December 31, 1994 and 1999.

Two aspects of Pfizer's balance sheets are worth mentioning:

1. Other long-term liabilities include postretirement benefits.
2. Retained earnings include other equity adjustments.

Although reported separately in Pfizer's annual reports, these amounts are not material to understanding Pfizer's business operations.

We can now return to the overall comparison of 1994 with 1999 provided by Pfizer's balance sheet equations:

Assets = Liabilities + Shareholders' Equity
1994: $11.099B = $ 6.775B + $4.324B
1999: $20.574B = $11.687B + $8.887B

In terms of total assets, the Pfizer of 1999 was 1.85 times larger than the Pfizer of 1994. In terms of shareholders' equity, in 1999 Pfizer was 2.06 times larger than it was in 1994.

Income Statements

Figure B.2 presents Pfizer's income statements for the years ended December 31, 1994 and 1999.

Pfizer's income statements differ from Wal-Mart's income statements in one significant way:

R&D (research and development) represents a significant aspect of Pfizer's business strategy; therefore, the income statements disclose the amount of money the company spent on R&D ($1.139 billion in 1994 and $2.776 billion in 1999).

217

**Figure B.2   Pfizer Income Statements (Amounts in Millions),
Years Ended December 31**

	1994	1999
Net Revenue	$8,281	$16,204
Costs, Expenses, and (Other Income)		
Cost of Sales	$1,919	$2,528
Operating Expenses	$3,251	$6,351
Research and Development	$1,139	$2,776
Other Expense (Income)	$116	$126
Total	$6,425	$11,781
Income before Income Taxes	$1,856	$4,423
Provision for Income Taxes	$558	$1,244
Net Income	$1,298	$3,179

The expenses associated with R&D will be reflected in the margin management component of the Strategic Profit Model. As we shall see, a successful R&D pipeline is the lifeblood of Pfizer's long-term success.

Pfizer's balance sheets provide us with snapshots of the company at different points in time. The income statements provide us with information about Pfizer's financial performance on behalf of the shareholders in specific years. Pfizer's income statement equations for 1994 and 1999 provide us with basic information on how well management has performed on behalf of the shareholders:

▶

Net Income = Revenue − Expenses (Net)
1994: $1.298B = $ 8.281B − $6.983B
1999: $3.179B = $16.204B − $13.025B

◀

In 1994, Pfizer generated $8.281 billion in revenue and incurred $6.983 billion in expenses. The net income of $1.298 billion represents the increase in net assets (assets − liabilities) earned by management on the shareholders' behalf during the year. In 1999, Pfizer generated $16.204 billion in revenue while incurring $13.025 billion in expenses. In 1999, management earned \$3.179 billion in net assets on behalf of the shareholders. The net income reported for 1999 was 2.45 times the net income reported in 1994.

Like our comparison of the two balance sheet equations, the comparison of the two income statement equations provides some basic information about the business. ROE provides the bridge between the firm's balance sheets and its income statements. When we add the return on equity (ROE) calculation to the analysis, we can begin to gain additional insights into the business by seeing how the balance sheets and income statements are interrelated.

Return on Equity

Return on shareholders' equity (ROE) links Pfizer's income statements to its balance sheets. For the fiscal years ended December 31, 1994 and 1999,

▶───

$$\text{ROE} = \text{Net Income} \div \text{Shareholders' Equity}$$
1994: 30.0% = \$1.298B $\div$ \$4.324B
1999: 35.8% = \$3.179B $\div$ \$8.887B

───◀

Stated in dollars and cents terms,

▶───

In 1994, Pfizer generated 30.0¢ in profit for every \$1 of shareholders' equity. In 1999, Pfizer generated 35.8¢ in profit for every \$1 of shareholders' equity.

By increasing ROE from 30.0¢ to 35.8¢, management was able to generate an additional \$513 million in net income on shareholders' equity of \$8.887 billion.

───◀

ROE represents a convenient way of linking the balance sheet to the income statement. ROE provides the anchor for taking a closer look at Pfizer through the Strategic Profit Model. No matter how deeply we delve into the details of Pfizer's financial performance, when we resurface, the ROEs for 1994 and 1999 will have remained the same—30.0% in 1994 and 35.8% in 1999.

The quick overview of the Strategic Profit Model shows how all of the financial aspects of Pfizer's business strategy fit into an integrated management framework .

STRATEGIC PROFIT MODEL: QUICK OVERVIEW

Figure B.3 presents a quick overview of Pfizer's Strategic Profit Model for 1994 and 1999, using just four elements from Pfizer's income statements and balance sheets: net revenue, net income, total assets, and shareholders' equity.

Figure B.3 Pfizer Strategic Profit Model, Quick Overview, for the Fiscal Years Ended December 31 (Amounts in Millions)

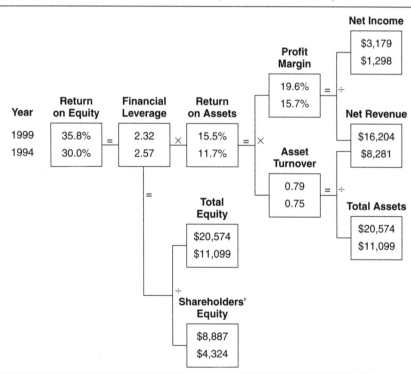

Stated in dollars and cents terms,

▶

In 1994, Pfizer generated 30.0¢ in profit on every $1 of shareholders' equity; in 1999, Pfizer generated 35.8¢.

◀

In the process of growing the business over the five-year period, Pfizer experienced a 5.8¢ increase in ROE. With the quick overview provided by the SPM, we can now take a more in-depth look at the individual components contributing to Pfizer's ROE in 1994 and 1999 and the 5.8¢ increase over the five years.

As with Wal-Mart and Dell, we begin the discussion of the financial aspects of Pfizer's business strategy with the margin management component of the SPM.

MARGIN MANAGEMENT

As we can see from Figure B.3, Pfizer's profit margin increased from 15.7% to 19.6%. From a management perspective,

▶

Pfizer earned 15.7¢ in profit for every $1 of net revenue in 1994; in 1999, Pfizer earned 19.6¢ in profit.

◀

Between 1994 and 1999, Pfizer's margins increased by 3.9¢ for every $1 of net revenues.

▶

The 3.9¢ increase in profit margin translates into $639 million of net income on net revenue of $16.204 billion.

◀

Between 1994 and 1999, net revenue increased at a 14.4% compound annual growth rate (CAGR), net expenses increased by 13.3%, and net income increased by 19.6%. The 1.1 percentage-point difference in growth rates for net revenues and net expenses translates into the 19.6% CAGR for net income and the 3.9¢ increase in profit margin.

If we were to take a closer look at the margin management component of the SPM, we would see that Pfizer's gross margin increased from 76.8% to 84.4%, a 7.6 percentage-point increase. This increase in gross margin was offset by an increase in R&D expenses from 13.8% to 17.1%. According to Management's Discussion and Analysis in the Pfizer's *1999 Annual Report,* the increase in R&D spending was necessary to support the advancement of an increasing number of potential drug candidates in all stages of development (from initial discovery through final regulatory approval).

Asset Management

As we can see from Figure B.3, Pfizer's asset turnover increased moderately from 0.75 in 1994 to 0.79 in 1999.

▶

In 1994, Pfizer generated $0.75 in net revenue for every $1 of total assets; in 1999, Pfizer generated $0.79 in net revenue.

◀

All things considered, management (and shareholders) would prefer to generate more, rather than fewer, dollars of net revenue per $1 of assets. The greater the asset turnover, the greater the amount of customer financing management has generated with a given amount of assets.

Between 1994 and 1999, total assets increased at a 13.1% compound annual growth rate, compared with the 14.4% growth rate for net revenue. Any time net revenues are increasing at a faster rate than total assets, asset turnover increases. If Pfizer had not increased asset turnover from $0.75 to $0.79 per $1 of total assets, it would have required an additional investment of $1.147 billion to support net revenues of $16.204 billion in 1999.

If we were to take a closer look at the asset management component of the SPM, we would see that, over the five years, there were substantial changes in the composition of total assets. Inventories (5.5% CAGR) and productive assets (11.7% CAGR) increased at a slower rate than net revenues (14.4% CAGR). Short-term investments (34.0% CAGR) increased at a substantially faster rate, and cash (-12.7% CAGR) actually decreased.

Return on Assets

As we can see from Figure B.3, Pfizer's return on assets (ROA) increased from 11.7% in 1994 to 15.5% in 1999.

In 1994, Pfizer earned 11.7¢ in profit for every $1 of total assets; in 1999, Pfizer earned 15.5¢.

The 3.8¢ increase in ROA reflects the combined effects of the 3.9¢ increase in profit margin and the 4¢ increase in asset turnover.

The key to operating success is a combination of Pfizer's margin management and asset management strategies.

Integration of Margin and Asset Management through ROA

To consolidate what managers are learning about Pfizer, it helps to return to the Strategic Profit Model song we learned for Wal-Mart. In 1999,

---

For every $1 of assets, Pfizer generated 79¢ in net revenue, and,

For every $1 of net revenue, Pfizer earned 19.6¢ in profit.
Multiplying the profit margin by the asset turnover,
For every $1 of assets, Pfizer generated 15.5¢ in profit.

Compared with 1994, Pfizer grew the business while increasing profit margins and asset turnover. Between 1994 and 1999, profit margins increased by 25.2%, while asset turnover increased by 5.6%. These increases together resulted in a 32.2% increase in ROA.

Financial Leverage

As seen in Figure B.3, financial leverage decreased from 2.57 in 1994 to 2.32 in 1999.

In 1994, Pfizer utilized $2.57 in total equity for every $1 of share-holders' equity; in 1999, Pfizer utilized $2.32.

Like most firms in rapidly changing, highly competitive industries, such as the pharmaceutical industry, managers focus on the business risks associated with the competitive marketplace. They do not want to make their job more difficult by taking on the additional financial risks associated with borrowing money.

Between 1994 and 1999, total equity increased at a 13.1% CAGR, total liabilities increased at an 11.5% CAGR, and shareholders' equity increased at a 15.5% CAGR.

Return on Equity: Closing the Loop

The concept of ROE provides us with the opportunity to interrelate all of the financial information included in the balance sheets and income statements into a comprehensive management framework. The Strategic Profit Model is then used to see how all of the parts fit together to form a greater whole. After managers see how all of the parts fit together, they can focus on developing their communication skills. For that part of the learning experience, we return to the Strategic Profit Model song. The 1999 version of Pfizer's SPM song goes something like this:

For every $1 of assets, Pfizer generated 79¢ in net revenue, and,

For every $1 of net revenue, Pfizer earned 19.6¢ in profit.

Multiplying the 19.6¢ profit margin by the 79¢ asset turnover, we know that,

For every $1 of assets, Pfizer generated 15.5¢ in profit.

Multiplying the 15.5¢ ROA by the $2.32 in financial leverage, we see that

Pfizer generated 35.8¢ in profit for every $1 of shareholders' equity invested in the business.

Between 1994 and 1999, Pfizer was able to grow net revenue at a 14.4% CAGR while growing net income at a 19.6% compound annual rate. Over the same period, total assets and total equity increased at 13.1% CAGRs, and shareholders' equity increased at a 15.5% CAGR.

STRATEGIC FINANCING MODEL

As discussed in Chapters 7 and 8, we restructure a firm's balance sheets to focus on the long-term investment and long-term financing aspects of the business. From the restructured balance sheets, we then create a financial flow statement, which shows how the long-term investment and long-term financing base changed over the five-year period.

Restructured Balance Sheets

Figure B.4 presents Pfizer's restructured balance sheets for 1994 and 1999. As we can see, Pfizer's long-term investment is made up of working capital (current assets − current liabilities), gross productive assets, and gross other assets. Pfizer's long-term financing base consists of external debt financing, external equity financing, and internal equity financing.

Three aspects of Pfizer's restructured balance sheets are important to mention before discussing the SFM:

1. Gross productive assets exclude accumulated depreciation of $1.920 billion in 1994 and $2.694 billion in 1999.
2. External debt financing excludes deferred taxes of $212 million in 1994 and $301 million in 1999.
3. Internal equity financing equals retained earnings plus accumulated depreciation and deferred income taxes (noncash charges to net income and retained earnings).

As we shall see, these three observations will affect the way we interpret how Pfizer financed the business over the five-year period.

The following financial control equations underlying Pfizer's restructured balance sheets for 1994 and 1999 are:

Long-Term Investment = Long-Term Financing
1994: $ 8.193B = $8.193B
1999: $14.083B = $14.083B

Figure B.4   Pfizer Restructured Balance Sheets, Years Ended December 31, 1994 and 1999 (Amounts in Millions)

	1994	Change	1999
Long-Term Investment			
Current Assets	$5,788	$5,403	$11,191
Current Liabilities	$4,826	$4,359	$9,185
Working Capital	$962	$1,044	$2,006
Gross Productive Assets	$4,993	$3,044	$8,037
Gross Other Assets	$2,238	$1,802	$4,040
Total Long-Term Investment	$8,193	$5,890	$14,083
Long-Term Financing			
External Debt Financing			
Long-Term Debt	$604	($79)	$525
Other Long-Term Liabilities	$1,133	$543	$1,676
Total External Debt	$1,737	$464	$2,201
External Equity Financing			
Common Stock	$685	$4,944	$5,629
Treasury Stock	($1,753)	($5,098)	($6,851)
Employee Trusts	($749)	($2,139)	($2,888)
Total External Equity	($1,817)	($2,293)	($4,110)
Internal Equity Financing			
Retained Earnings	$6,141	$6,856	$12,997
Accumulated Depreciation	$1,920	$774	$2,694
Deferred Taxes	$212	$89	$301
Total Internal Equity	$8,273	$7,719	$15,992
Total Long-Term Financing	$8,193	$5,890	$14,083

In 1999, Pfizer's long-term investment and long-term financing base was 1.72 times larger than it was in 1994.

The only question that remains to be answered is *how* Pfizer financed the business over this period. As we saw with Dell and Wal-Mart, in order to answer that question it helps to look at the financial flow statement.

Financial Flow Statement

Figure B.5 presents Pfizer's financial flow statement for the five-year period ended December 31, 1999. As we can see, the financial flow statement differs from the restructured balance sheets in three ways:

1. The details included in the restructured balance sheets have been omitted from the financial flow statement.
2. The long-term financing activity has been placed above the long-term investment activity.
3. The financial flow statement includes a summary of the net revenue generated by Pfizer over the five-year period.

By focusing on the change column of Figure B.5, we can construct the financing the business component of the SFM, as presented in Figure B.6.

Figure B.5 Pfizer Financial Flow Statement for the Five Years Ended December 31, 1999 (Amounts in Millions)

	1994	Change	1999
Long-Term Financing			
External Debt Financing	$1,737	$464	$2,201
External Equity Financing	($1,817)	($2,293)	($4,110)
Internal Equity Financing	$8,273	$7,719	$15,992
Total Long-Term Financing	$8,193	$5,890	$14,083
Long-Term Investment			
Working Capital	$962	$1,044	$2,006
Gross Productive Assets	$4,993	$3,044	$8,037
Gross Other Assets	$2,238	$1,802	$4,040
Total Long-Term Investment	$8,193	$5,890	$14,083

Year	Net Revenue
1995	$8,684
1996	$9,864
1997	$11,055
1998	$13,544
1999	$16,204
Five-Year total	$59,351

Figure B.6 **Pfizer Strategic Financing Model, Financing the Business, for the Five Years Ended December 31, 1999 (Amounts in Millions)**

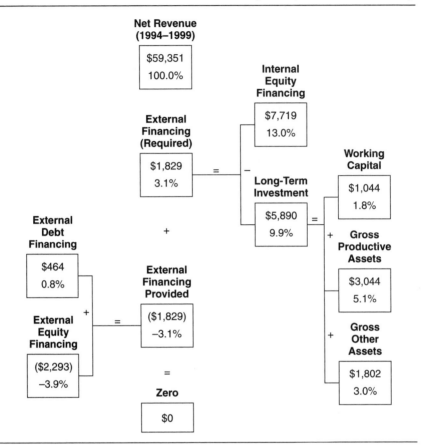

As seen in Figure B.6, Pfizer generated $7.791 billion in internal equity financing from $59.351 billion in net revenue and invested $5.890 billion for the long term. The difference between the internal equity financing and the long-term investment created an excess of $1.829 billion. This excess, or surplus, had to be used to reduce external financing.

▶

For every $1 of net revenue, Pfizer generated 13.0¢ in internal equity financing and invested 9.9¢ for the long term, leaving an excess of 3.1¢ for every $1 of sales.

Pfizer raised an additional 0.8¢ in external debt financing to complement the 3.1¢ excess and reduced external equity financing by 3.9¢ for every $1 of net revenues.

If we were to take a closer look at Pfizer's long-term investment base, we would see that the majority of the long-term investment was invested in gross productive assets $3.044 billion (5.1¢ of net revenue) and gross other assets $1.802 billion (3.0¢ of net revenue).

If we were to take a closer look at Pfizer's external equity financing, we would see that treasury stock purchases equaled $5.098 billion and purchases for employee trusts equaled $2.139 billion. To offset these repurchases, Pfizer issued $4.944 in common stock.

BUSINESS STRATEGY REVISITED

By using the quick overview of the Strategic Profit Model and the financing the business component of the Strategic Financing Model, we have been able to show how management increased Pfizer's ROE while growing the business. Pfizer increased its profit margin, asset turnover, and ROA while decreasing financial leverage and increasing ROE.

Between 1994 and 1999, net revenue increased from $8.281 billion in 1994 to $16.204 billion in 1999 (14.4% CAGR). Net income increased from $1.298 billion to $3.179 billion (19.6% CAGR).

At the end of 1999, Pfizer earned a 35.8% ROE, an ROE that is well above the 19.0% ROE for the S&P 500.

Over this five-year period, Pfizer increased its long-term financing and long-term investment base by $5.890 billion (11.4% CAGR).

For every $1 of sales, Pfizer generated 13.0¢ in internal equity financing, and 9.9¢ was invested for the long-term.

The 3.1¢ excess internal equity financing, plus 0.8¢ in external debt financing, was used to reduce external equity financing by 3.9¢ for every $1 of net revenues over this five-year period.

Given this analysis of Pfizer's business strategy, we are well positioned to understand how the market valued Pfizer over this five-year period.

MARKET VALUATION

Figure B.7 presents the relationship among the market value of Pfizer's common stock and the two management measures of financial performance we used to calculate Pfizer's ROE—net income and shareholders' equity. With the benefit of hindsight, we can see that Pfizer's total market value (common shares outstanding times the market price per share) increased at a substantially faster rate than did the increases in net income and shareholders' equity.[1]

As we can see from Figure B.7, Pfizer's common stock outstanding increased at a 0.6% CAGR between 1994 and 1999. A close examination of Pfizer's annual reports shows that the increase of 108 million shares was due primarily to employees' exercising stock options and buying additional shares through employee stock purchase plans less Pfizer's repurchases of common stock.

Over this five-year period, the market value of the common stock outstanding increased at a 39.0% CAGR. During the same period, net income increased at a 19.6% compound annual rate and shareholders' equity increased at a 15.5% compound annual rate.

As mentioned in Chapters 9 through 12, financial analysts and shareholders determine the value of a firm's common stock. The price of the firm's common stock is influenced by the recommendations of financial analysts at the major investment firms and what each of us is willing to pay for the firm's common stock. Firms such as Pfizer have no direct influence over the market price of their common stock, but they do have an indirect influence through their actions. For example, the release of new products (such as Viagra) increases investors' expectation of future revenues and earnings.

From the quick overview of the Strategic Profit Model, we saw that Pfizer's ROE increased from 30.0% in 1994 to 35.8% in 1999. The average ROE for S&P 500 companies was around 17% in 1994 and 19% in 1999. For pharmaceutical companies, the average ROE was around 25.1% in 1994 and 30.5% in 1999. Compared with these benchmarks, Pfizer's performance was well above average.

From the Strategic Financing Model, we saw that Pfizer actually reduced the amount of external equity financing used in the business. The

Figure B.7   Pfizer Market and Management Measures of Performance for the Years Ended December 31 (Shares and Amounts in Millions)

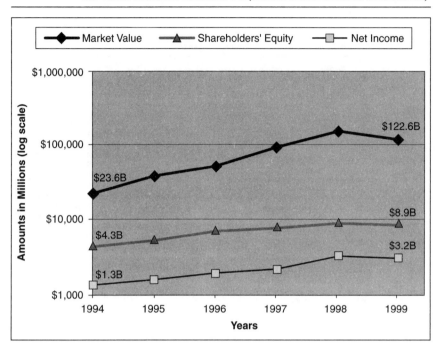

Year-Ended December 31	Common Stock Outstanding	Market Value	Net Income	Shareholders' Equity
1994	3,670	$ 23,635	$1,298	$4,324
1995	3,687	$ 38,714	$1,573	$5,506
1996	3,743	$ 51,766	$1,929	$6,954
1997	3,771	$ 93,709	$2,213	$7,933
1998	3,789	$157,888	$3,351	$8,810
1999	3,778	$122,558	$3,179	$8,887
CAGR	0.6%	39.0%	19.6%	15.5%

internal equity financing generated by management was more than enough to meet Pfizer's long-term investment needs and reduce external equity financing.

For the company as a whole, Pfizer has been a success in terms of both growth in market value and financial performance. The only question that remains to be answered is how well this performance has benefited

Figure B.8   Pfizer, Industry Peers, and the S&P 500, Cumulative Total
Return, $100 Investment, December 31, 1994

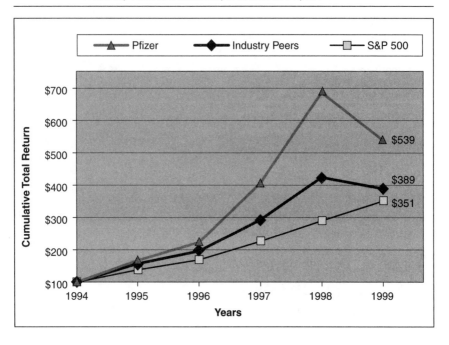

Total Return

Year	Pfizer	Industry Peers	S&P 500
1994	$100	$100	$100
1995	$167	$157	$138
1996	$223	$196	$169
1997	$406	$293	$226
1998	$686	$424	$290
1999	$539	$389	$351
CAGR	40.0%	31.2%	28.6%

Source: Pfizer, *Proxy Statement, 2000.*

individual shareholders relative to other firms (possible investments) in the capital marketplace.

Figure B.8 presents Pfizer's relative market performance compared with the S&P 500 and the pharmaceutical industry peer group between 1994 and 1999. The comparison is based on a hypothetical investment of $100 in a market basket of S&P 500 common stocks, the industry peer group, and Pfizer's common stock.

For every $100 invested in Pfizer's common stock, that investment would have increased to $539 (40.0% CAGR) by 1999. If that $100 were invested in the industry peer group, it would have increased to $389 (31.2% CAGR). If that $100 were invested in a market basket of S&P 500 common stocks, that investment would have increased to $351 (28.6% CAGR).[2]

As in the Dell case study, we have tried to show how the principles of financial statement analysis can help managers develop a better understanding of any business. If we were to go into a more in-depth analysis of Pfizer, we would return to the Strategic Profit Model and the Strategic Financing Model. We would take a closer look at each component of both models, as we did for Wal-Mart.

In Appendix C, we will use the principles of financial statement analysis to see what we can learn about Cisco, a technology firm with one of the highest market valuations in the world.

Cisco Systems

Cisco Systems is the worldwide leader in supplying networking equipment for the Internet. Cisco creates hardware and software solutions that link computer networks, so that people have easy access to information without regard to differences in time, place, or type of computer system. Cisco's products include routers, switches, dial-up access servers, systems network architecture, Internet services, network management software, and Cisco IOS software. In short, Cisco sells the products that manage and control the movement of data among users connected through local and global networks.

Between 1994 and 1999, Cisco grew sales at a 57.8% CAGR (compound annual growth rate). Under the leadership of CEO John Chambers, Cisco expects to sell $50 billion worth of products by 2004, compared with sales of $1.2 billion in 1994 and $12.2 billion in 1999. Cisco expects to achieve this $50 billion goal through a combination of internal growth from existing product lines and new acquisitions. Approximately two-thirds of Cisco's sales come from products it has developed and one-third from products it has acquired.

In telling a story about Cisco, we will draw on the financial information reported in the balance sheets and income statements, along with market information about the company's common stock. For this illustration of how to use the business strategy models to focus on the financial performance of Cisco's business operations, we will set aside Cisco's financial investments.

Given the amount of detail provided in Cisco's annual reports, we were able to separate the business operations from the financial investments controlled by the corporate financial organization.

Viewed as a holding company, with business operations and financial investments, a highly summarized version of Cisco's balance sheets and income statements for 1994 and 1999 appears in Figure C.1.

Figure C.1 Summarized Financial Statements (Amounts in Millions), Years Ended July 25 and July 31

	1994	1999
Assets		
Business Operations	$466	$5,424
Investments	$586	$9,301
Total Assets	$1,052	$14,725
Equity		
Business Operations	$466	$5,424
Investments	$586	$9,301
Total Equity	$1,052	$14,725
Income from Business Operations (Net)	$301	$1,880
Income from Investments (Net)	$14	$216
Net Income	$315	$2,096

We will use complete balance sheet and income statement information for Cisco's business operations to run through the Strategic Profit Model. We will then add back the information about Cisco's financial investments to run through the Strategic Financing Model. For the discussion of the market valuation process, we will use the financial information reported for the entire company.

As we can see from the highly summarized statements in Figure C.1, business operations accounted for 44.3% of total assets and 95.5% of net income in 1994 and 36.8% of total assets and 89.7% of net income in 1999. Investors and financial analysts are typically more concerned with Cisco's basic business operations than they are with Cisco's financial investments.

BALANCE SHEETS AND INCOME STATEMENTS

As discussed in Chapter 1, a firm's balance sheets and income statements provide all of the information needed to prepare a Strategic Profit Model and a Strategic Financing Model for any firm. In the case of the Strategic Financing Model, we restructure the balance sheets and create a financial flow statement before we do the analysis. However, all of the key financial performance indicators that we will use to begin understanding the business are included in the balance sheets and income statements in one form or another.

Figure C.2 Cisco Systems Balance Sheets (Amounts in Millions), Years Ended July 25 and July 31

	1994	1999
Assets		
Current Assets		
Accounts Receivable (Net)	$238	$1,242
Inventories	$28	$652
Cash	$54	$827
Other Current Assets	$58	$705
Total Current Assets	$378	$3,426
Productive Assets		
Property and Equipment (Net)	$77	$801
Other Assets		
Goodwill and Intangibles (Net)	$0	$460
Other Noncurrent Assets	$11	$1,197
Total Other Asssets	$11	$1,197
Total Assets	$466	$5,424
Equity		
Current Liabilities		
Accounts Payable	$32	$361
Accrued Expenses Payable	$88	$1,308
Other Current Liabilities	$84	$1,334
Total Current Liabilities	$204	$3,003
Long-Term Liabilities	$0	$0
Total Liabilities	$204	$3,003
Shareholders' Equity		
Common stock	$228	$5,568
Treasury Stock	($586)	($9,031)
Retained Earnings	$620	$6,154
Total Shareholders' Equity	$262	$2,421
Total Equity	$466	$5,424

Balance Sheets

Figure C.2 presents Cisco's balance sheets for business operations for the fiscal years ended July 25, 1994, and July 31, 1999.

Two aspects of Cisco's balance sheets are worth mentioning before we start the analysis:

1. As presented in Figure C.2, total assets have been reduced by the $586 million in investments in 1994 and the $9.301 billion in investments in 1999. We have assumed that Cisco sold these investments and repurchased common stock (reported as treasury stock in the equity section of the balance sheet).

2. We have included translation adjustments and other components of comprehensive income in retained earnings. Although reported separately in Cisco's annual reports, these amounts are not material to understanding Cisco's business operations.

We can now return to the overall comparison of 1994 with 1999 provided by Cisco's balance sheet equations:

Assets = Liabilities + Shareholders' Equity
1994: $ 466M = $ 204M + $262M
1999: $5.424B = $3.003B + $2.421B

In terms of total assets, the Cisco of 1999 was 11.64 times larger than the Cisco of 1994. In terms of shareholders' equity, in 1999 Cisco's was only 9.24 times larger than it was in 1994.

Income Statements

Figure C.3 presents Cisco's income statements for the fiscal years ended July 25, 1994, and July 31, 1999.

Figure C.3 Cisco Systems Income Statements (Amounts in Millions), Years Ended July 25 and July 31

		1994	1999
Revenue			
Sales		$1,243	$12,154
Cost and Expenses			
Cost of Sales		$413	$4,240
Sales and Marketing		$206	$2,447
General and Administrative		$47	$418
Research and Development		$89	$1,594
Purchased R&D		$0	$471
	Total	$755	$9,170
Operating Income		$488	$2,984
Provision for Income Taxes		($187)	($1,104)
Net Income		$301	$1,880

Cisco's income statements look very similar to Wal-Mart's income statements and differ in only two significant ways:

1. R&D (research and development) represents a significant aspect of Cisco's business strategy; therefore, the income statements disclose the amount of money the company spent on R&D ($89 million in 1994 and $1.594 billion in 1999).

2. Purchased R&D represents the expenses associated with the R&D efforts of acquired companies that will not be continued at Cisco. In 1999, $471 million associated with the R&D effort of acquired companies would not be continued into the future and was therefore expensed immediately.

The expenses associated with both types of R&D will be reflected in the margin management component of the Strategic Profit Model.

If Cisco's balance sheets provide us with snapshots of the company at different points in time, its income statements provide us with information about Cisco's financial performance on behalf of the shareholders in specific years. Cisco's income statement equations for 1994 and 1999 provide us with basic information on how well management has performed on behalf of the shareholders:

$$\text{Net Income} = \text{Revenue} - \text{Expenses (Net)}$$
$$1994: \$\ 301M = \$\ 1.243B - \$942M$$
$$1999: \$1.880B = \$12.154B - \$10.274B$$

In 1994, Cisco generated $1.243 billion in revenue and incurred $942 million in expenses. The net income of $301 million represents the increase in net assets (assets − liabilities) earned by management on the shareholders' behalf during the year. In 1999, Cisco generated $12.154 billion in revenue while incurring $10.274 billion in expenses. In 1999, management earned $1.880 billion in net assets on behalf of the shareholders. The net income reported for 1999 was 6.24 times larger than the net income reported in 1994.

Like the comparison of the two balance sheet equations, the comparison of the two income statement equations provides some initial insights into the business. When we add the return on equity (ROE) calculation to the analysis, we can gain additional insights by seeing how the balance sheets and income statements are interrelated. ROE provides the bridge between the firm's balance sheets and its income statements.

Return on Equity

Return on shareholders' equity (ROE) links Cisco's income statements to its balance sheets. For the fiscal years ended July 25, 1994, and July 31, 1999,

$$\text{ROE} = \text{Net Income} \div \text{Shareholders' Equity}$$
$$1994: 114.9\% = \$301M \div \$262M$$
$$1999:\ 77.7\% = \$1.880B \div \$2.421B$$

Stated in dollars and cents terms,

> In 1994, Cisco generated $1.149 in profit for every $1 of shareholders' equity. In 1999, Cisco generated 77.7¢ in profit for every $1 of shareholders' equity.
>
> Over this five-year period, net income increased by 525%, and shareholders' equity increased by 824%.
>
> Any time net income increases at a slower rate than shareholders' equity, a firm's ROE decreases.

ROE represents a convenient way of linking the balance sheet to the income statement. ROE provides the anchor for taking a closer look at Cisco through the Strategic Profit Model (SPM). No matter how deeply we delve into the details of Cisco's financial performance, when we resurface, the ROEs for 1994 and 1999 will have remained the same—114.9% in 1994 and 77.7% in 1999.

The quick overview of the Strategic Profit Model shows how all of the financial aspects of Cisco's business strategy fit into an integrated management framework.

STRATEGIC PROFIT MODEL: QUICK OVERVIEW

Figure C.4 presents a quick overview of Cisco's Strategic Profit Model for 1994 and 1999, using just four elements from Cisco's income statements and balance sheets: sales, net income, total assets, and shareholders' equity.

> In 1994, Cisco generated $1.149 in profit for every $1 of shareholders' equity; in 1999, Cisco generated 77.7¢.
>
> In the process of growing the business over the five years, Cisco experienced a 37.2¢ decrease in ROE.

Figure C.4   Cisco Systems Strategic Profit Model: Quick Overview, for the Fiscal Years Ended July 25, 1994, and July 31, 1999 (Amounts in Millions)

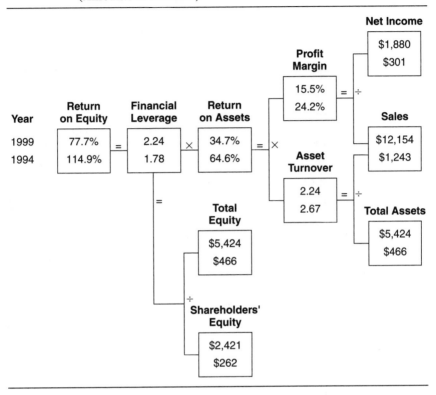

With the quick overview provided by the SPM, we can now take a more in-depth look at the individual components contributing to Cisco's ROE in 1994 and 1999 and the 37.2¢ decrease over the five years.

As with Dell, Pfizer, and Wal-Mart, we begin the discussion of the financial aspects of Cisco's business strategy with the margin management component of the SPM.

Margin Management

As seen in Figure C.4, Cisco's profit margin decreased from 24.2% to 15.5%. From a management perspective, see the following excerpt:

▶

Cisco earned 24.2¢ in profit for every $1 of sales in 1994; in 1999, Cisco earned 15.5¢ in profit.

◀

Between 1994 and 1999, Cisco's margins decreased 8.7¢ on every $1 of sales.

▶

The 8.7¢ decrease in profit margin translates into net income that is $1.1 billion less on sales of $12.154 billion earned if it could have maintained the 24.2¢ profit margin.

◀

Between 1994 and 1999, sales increased at a 57.8% compound annual growth rate (CAGR), net expenses increased by 61.3% CAGR, and net income increased by 44.3% CAGR.

From a financial perspective, growing net income at a 44.3% CAGR results from expenses (61.3% CAGR) increasing at a faster rate than sales (57.8% CAGR). This difference in growth rates translates into the 8.7¢ decrease in the profit margin.

If we were to take a closer look at the margin management component of the SPM, we would see that Cisco's gross margin decreased (as a percentage of sales) from 66.8% to 65.1% between 1994 and 1999. Sales and marketing expenses increased from 16.6% to 20.1% of sales. R&D increased from 7.2% to 13.1%, and general and administrative expenses decreased from 3.8% to 3.4%.

In Cisco's annual report (10-K) filed with the SEC, management attributed the decrease in gross margin to a change in product mix. In 1999, Cisco sold more products with lower gross margins, compared with 1994. The increase in sales and marketing expenses was attributed to an increase in the size of the direct sales force and related commissions, additional marketing and advertising costs associated with the introduction of new products, and the expansion of distribution channels.

Management attributed the increase in R&D expenses to Cisco's strategy of investing in technology to address potential market opportunities. Cisco also continues to purchase technology in order to bring a broad range of products to the market.

Asset Management

As we can see from Figure C.4, Cisco's asset turnover decreased from $2.67 in 1994 to $2.24 in 1999.

▶

In 1994, Cisco generated $2.67 in sales for every $1 of total assets; in 1999, Cisco generated $2.24 in sales.

◀

All things considered, management (and shareholders) would prefer to generate more dollars in sales per $1 of assets.

Between 1994 and 1999, total assets increased at a 63.4% CAGR, compared with the 57.8% CAGR for sales. Any time total assets increase at a faster rate than sales, asset turnover decreases. However, we must remember that any increase or decrease must be evaluated within the context of the firm's overall business strategy.

In Cisco's case, the decrease in asset turnover of 43¢ per $1 of assets resulted from a combination of offsetting effects. Current assets (55.4% CAGR), productive assets (59.7% CAGR), and other assets (155.5% CAGR) all increased at different compound annual growth rates.

If we were to take a closer look at the asset management component of the SPM, we would see that, over the five years, receivables decreased from 69.9 days net sales in 1994 to 37.3 days net sales in 1999, and other assets increased from 3.2 days net sales to 35.9 days net sales. The 32.6 days net sales decrease in receivables was almost completely offset by the 32.7 days net sales increase in other assets.

If we were to take a closer look at other assets, we would see that the goodwill and intangibles related to the acquisition of new companies increased from 0 days net sales in 1994 to 13.8 days net sales in 1999. Investments in strategic business partners and investments in leases also increased by 3.2 days net sales in 1994 to 22.1 days net sales in 1999. The investments in strategic business partners complement Cisco's overall business acquisition strategy.

Return on Assets

As we can see from Figure C.4, Cisco's return on assets (ROA) decreased from 64.6% in 1994 to 34.7% in 1999.

In 1994, Cisco earned 64.6¢ in profit for every $1 of total assets; in 1999, Cisco earned 34.7¢.

The 29.9¢ decrease in ROA reflects the combined effects of the 8.7¢ decline in profit margin and the 42.7¢ decline in asset turnover.

As mentioned at the beginning of the case study, all of the profitability relationships included in the SPM must be viewed within the context of Cisco's strategy to grow the business and achieve $50 billion in sales by 2004.

Integration of Margin and Asset Management through ROA

In order to consolidate what managers are learning about Cisco, it helps to return to the Strategic Profit Model song we learned for Wal-Mart. In 1999,

For every $1 of assets, Cisco generated $2.24 in sales, and,

For every $1 of sales, Cisco earned 24.2¢ in profit.

Multiplying the profit margin by the asset turnover,

For every $1 of assets, Cisco generated 34.7¢ in profit for every $1 of assets in 1999.

Compared with 1994, Cisco has grown the business while profit margins and asset turnover have declined. Between 1994 and 1999, the profit margin decreased 35.6%, and asset turnover decreased by 1.1%. These decreases together produced a 46.3% decrease in ROA.

Financial Leverage

As seen in Figure C.4, financial leverage increased from 1.78 in 1994 to 2.24 in 1999.

> In 1994, Cisco utilized $1.78 in total equity for every $1 of share-holders' equity; in 1999, Cisco utilized $2.24.

Since Cisco has no long-term liabilities, the 46¢ increase in financial leverage was due to current liabilities.

Between 1994 and 1999, total equity increased at a 63.4% CAGR, total liabilities increased at a 71.2% CAGR, and shareholders' equity increased at a 56.0% CAGR.

If we were to take a closer look at the financial management component of the SPM, we would see that the 46¢ increase in financial leverage was due to increases in accrued expenses (primarily commissions and bonuses) and deferred revenue (advances from customers). However, the increase in commissions and bonuses payable was due to Cisco's success in 1999. On the other hand, the increase in advances from customers represent prepayments for products to be delivered in the year 2000. Both increases in current liabilities are related to very positive aspects of Cisco's business strategy.

Return on Equity: Closing the Loop

The concept of ROE provides us with the opportunity to interrelate all of the financial information included in the balance sheets and income statements into a comprehensive management framework. The SPM is then used to see how all of the parts fit together to form a greater whole. The Strategic Profit Model song then allows managers to express their understanding in words. The 1999 version of Cisco's SPM song goes something like this:

> For every $1 of assets, Cisco generated $2.24 in sales, and,
>
> For every $1 of sales, Cisco earned 15.5¢ in profit.
>
> Multiplying the 15.5¢ profit margin by the $2.24 asset turnover, we see that,
>
> For every $1 of assets, Cisco generated 34.7¢ in profit.

Multiplying the 34.7¢ ROA by the $2.24 in financial leverage, we see that

Cisco generated 77.7¢ in profit for every $1 of shareholders' equity invested in the business.

◀━━◀

Between 1994 and 1999, Cisco was able to grow sales at a 57.8% CAGR while growing net income at a 44.3% CAGR. Over the same period, total assets and total equity increased at 63.4% CAGRs, and shareholders' equity increased at a 56.0% CAGR.

STRATEGIC FINANCING MODEL

As discussed in Chapters 7 and 8, we restructure a firm's balance sheets to focus on the long-term investment and long-term financing aspects of the business. From the restructured balance sheets, we then create a financial flow statement, which shows how the long-term investment and long-term financing base changed over the five-year period.

Restructured Balance Sheets

Figure C.5 presents Cisco's restructured balance sheets for 1994 and 1999. As we can see, Cisco's long-term investment is made up of working capital (current assets − current liabilities), gross productive assets, and gross other assets. Cisco's long-term financing base consists of external debt financing, external equity financing, and internal equity financing.

Three aspects of Cisco's restructured balance sheets are important to mention before discussing the SFM:

1. Gross other assets include the financial investments that were excluded from the balance sheets for Cisco's business operations ($586 million in 1994 and $9.301 billion in 1999).

2. External equity financing was increased $586 million in 1994 and $9.031 billion in 1999 to reflect the fact that Cisco did not sell its investment portfolio and repurchase common stock.

3. Internal equity financing equals retained earnings plus depreciation and amortization charges (noncash charges to net income and retained earnings).

**Figure C.5 Cisco Systems Restructured Balance Sheets
(Amounts in Millions), Years Ended July 25 and July 31**

	1994	Change	1999
Long-Term Investment			
Current Assets			
Accounts Receivable (Net)	$238	$1,004	$1,242
Inventories	$28	$624	$652
Cash	$54	$773	$827
Other Current Assets	$58	$647	$705
Total Current Assets	$378	$3,048	$3,426
Current Liabilities			
Accounts Payable	$32	$329	$361
Accrued Expenses Payable	$88	$1,220	$1,308
Other Current Liabilities	$84	$1,250	$1,334
Total Current Liabilities	$204	$2,799	$3,003
Working Capital	$174	$249	$423
Gross Productive Assets	$132	1,692	$1,824
Gross Other Assets*	$597	$9,993	$10,590
Total Long-Term Investment	$903	$11,934	$12,837
Long-Term Financing			
External Debt Financing	$0	$0	$0
External Equity Financing	$228	$5,340	$5,568
Internal Equity Financing			
Retained Earnings	$620	$5,534	$6,154
Depreciation	$55	$968	$1,023
Amortization	$0	$92	$92
Total Internal Equity	$675	$6,594	$7,269
Total Long-Term Financing	$903	$11,934	$12,837

*Includes investments

As we shall see, these three observations will affect the way we interpret how Cisco financed the business over the five-year period.

The following financial control equations underlying Cisco's restructured balance sheets for 1994 and 1999 are:

Long-Term Investment = Long-Term Financing
1994: $ 903M = $903M
1999: $12.837B = $12.837B

In 1999, Cisco's long-term investment and long-term financing base was 14.22 times larger than it was in 1994.

The only question that remains to be answered is *how* Cisco actually financed the business over this period. As we saw with Dell, Pfizer, and Wal-Mart, in order to answer that question it helps to look at the financial flow statement.

Financial Flow Statement

Figure C.6 presents Cisco's financial flow statement for the five-year period ended July 31, 1999.

As we can see, the financial flow statement differs from the restructured balance sheets in three ways:

1. The details included in the restructured balance sheets have been omitted from the financial flow statement.
2. The long-term financing activity has been placed above the long-term investment activity.
3. The financial flow statement includes a summary of the sales generated by Cisco over the five-year period.

By focusing on the change column of Figure C.6, we can construct the financing the business component of the SFM, as presented in Figure C.7.

As we can see from Figure C.7, Cisco generated $6.594 billion in internal equity financing from $33.127 billion in sales and invested $11.934 billion for the long term. The difference between the internal equity financ-

Figure C.6   Cisco Systems Financial Flow Statement for the Five Years Ended July 31, 1999 (Amounts in Millions)

	1994	Change	1999
Long-Term Investment			
External Debt Financing	$0	$0	$0
External Equity Financing	$228	$5,340	$5,568
Internal Equity Financing	$675	$6,594	$7,269
Total Long-Term Financing	$903	$11,934	$12,837
Long-Term Investment			
Working Capital	$174	$249	$423
Gross Productive Assets	$132	$1,692	$1,824
Gross Other Assets*	$597	$9,993	$10,590
Total Long-Term Investment	$903	$11,934	$12,837

Year	Sales
1995	$1,979
1996	$4,096
1997	$6,440
1998	$8,458
1999	$12,154
Five-Year Total	$33,127

*Includes investments

ing and the long-term investment created a shortfall of $5.340 billion. This shortfall, or deficiency, had to be financed from external sources. In this case, the external financing was provided by shareholders.

For every $1 of sales, Cisco generated 19.9¢ in internal equity financing and invested 36.0¢ for the long term, leaving a shortfall of 16.1¢ for every $1 of sales.

Cisco financed that shortfall with 16.1¢ of external equity financing.

Figure C.7 **Cisco Systems Strategic Financing Model, Financing the Business, for the Five Year Periods Ending July 25, 1994, and July 31, 1999 (Amounts in Millions)**

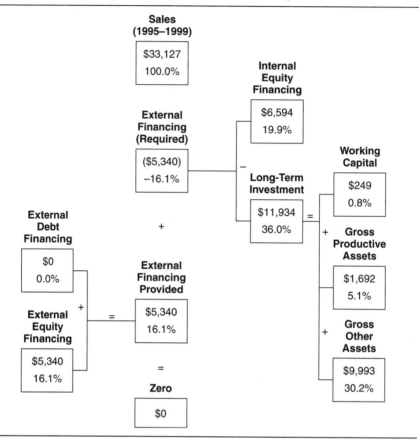

When we take a closer look at Cisco's long-term investment base, we see that the majority of the long-term investment has been in gross other assets. The increase in gross other assets includes an $8.715 billion increase in financial investments (26.3¢ for every $1 of sales). Working capital (0.8¢) and gross productive assets (5.1¢) show only modest increases over this period.

If we were to take a closer look at the 16.1¢ in external equity financing, we would see that the majority of the increase came from common stock issued to the shareholders of acquired companies. The second largest increase came from common stock issued in conjunction with stock options and employee stock purchase programs.

Business Strategy Revisited

By using the quick overview from the SPM and the financing the business component of the SFM, we have been able to show how Cisco managed the business from a financial perspective. Even though Cisco's profit margins, asset turnover, and ROA all decreased, these changes must be viewed within the context of Cisco's business strategy—currently, to increase sales to $50 billion by 2004.

Between 1994 and 1999, sales increased from $1.243 billion in 1994 to $12.154 billion in 1999 (57.8% CAGR). Net income increased from $301 million to $1.880 billion (44.3% CAGR).

At the end of 1999, Cisco earned a 77.7% ROE, a ROE that is well above that of firms in more established industries.

Over this five-year period, Cisco increased its long-term financing and long-term investment base by $11.934 billion (70.0% CAGR).

For every $1 of sales, Cisco invested 36.0¢ for the long term—19.9¢ came from internal equity financing, and 16.1¢ came from external equity financing.

Given this analysis of Cisco's business strategy, we are well positioned to understand how the market valued Cisco over this five-year period.

MARKET VALUATION

Figure C.8 presents the relationship among the market value of Cisco's common stock and the two management measures of financial performance we used to calculate Cisco's ROE—net income and shareholders' equity.[1] With the benefit of hindsight, we can see that Cisco's total market value (common shares outstanding times the market price per share) increased at a substantially faster rate than did the increase in net income and shareholders' equity.

As we can see from Figure C.8, Cisco's common stock outstanding increased at a 7.1% CAGR between 1994 and 1999. The majority of the

Figure C.8   Cisco Systems Market and Management Measures of Performance for the Years Ended July 31 (Shares and Amounts in Millions)

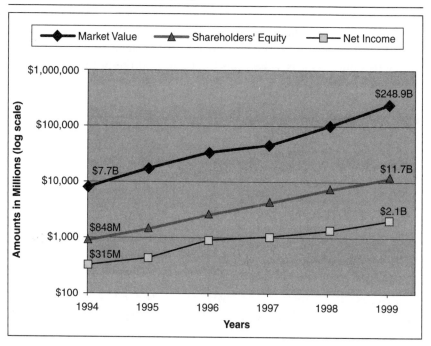

Year-Ended July 31	Common Stock Outstanding	Market Value	Net Income	Shareholders' Equity
1994	4,638.5	$7,654	$315	$848
1995	4,900.4	$16,661	$421	$1,379
1996	5,843.6	$32,724	$913	$2,620
1997	6,037.0	$45,579	$1,049	$4,290
1998	6,250.3	$103,755	$1,350	$7,107
1999	6,542.0	$248,923	$2,096	$11,678
CAGR	7.1%	100.7%	46.1%	69.0%

shares issued during this period (1.3 billion shares, 62% of the shares issued) were issued in conjunction with the acquisition of other companies. Another 800 million shares were issued in conjunction with employee stock option and stock purchase plans (38% of the shares issued).

Over this five-year period, the market value of the common stock outstanding increased at a 100.7% CAGR. During the same period, net income (including interest and other income) increased at a 46.1% CAGR, and shareholders' equity increased at a 69.0% CAGR.

As mentioned in Chapters 9 through 12, financial analysts and shareholders determine the value of a firm's common stock. The price of the firm's common stock is influenced by the recommendations of financial analysts at the major investment firms and by what we are willing to pay for the firm's common stock. Firms such as Cisco have no direct influence over the market price of their common stock, but they do have an indirect influence through their actions.

From the quick overview of the Strategic Profit Model, we saw that Cisco's ROE decreased from 114.9% in 1994 to 77.7% in 1999. However, this decrease has to be viewed within a broader economic context. The average ROE for S&P 500 companies was around 17% in 1994 and 19% in 1999. For technology companies, the average ROE was around 21% in 1994 and 24% in 1999. Compared with these benchmarks, Cisco's performance was outstanding.

The only question that remains to be answered is how well this performance has benefited individual shareholders relative to other firms (possible investments) in the capital markets.

Figure C.9 presents Cisco's relative market performance between July 25, 1994, and July 31, 1999, compared with the Hambrecht & Quist Technology Index (H&Q Index) and the S&P 500 index. The comparison is based on a hypothetical investment of $100 in a market basket of common stocks that make up the H&Q Index and S&P 500 index and a $100 investment in Cisco's common stock.

For every $100 invested in Cisco's common stock, that investment would have increased to $2,662 (92.8% CAGR) by 1999. If that $100 were invested in the H&Q Index, it would have increased to $526 (39.4% CAGR). If that $100 were invested in a market basket of S&P 500 common stocks, that investment would have increased to $321 (26.3% CAGR).[2]

As in the Dell and Pfizer case studies, we have tried to show how the principles of financial statement analysis can help managers develop a better understanding of any business. If we were to go into a more in-depth analysis of Cisco, we would return to the Strategic Profit Model and the Strategic Financing Model. We would take a closer look at each component of both models, as we did for Wal-Mart. Financial statement analysis is an ongoing process, which comes to life as we try to understand a business within the context of the firm's overall business strategy.

Figure C.9   Cisco Systems, H&Q Index, and the S&P 500, Cumulative Total Return, $100 Investment, on July 25, 1994

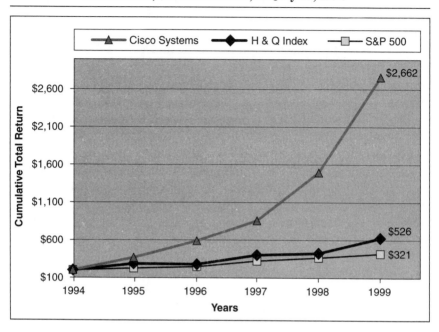

Total Return

Year	Cisco Systems	H&Q Index	S&P 500
1994	$100	$100	$100
1995	$267	$186	$126
1996	$489	$179	$147
1997	$759	$302	$224
1998	$1,396	$326	$267
1999	$2,662	$526	$321
CAGR	92.8%	39.4%	26.3%

Source: Cisco Systems Inc. *Definitive Proxy Statement, 1999.*

NOTES

1. We have plotted the relationship among market value, net income, and shareholders' equity using a log scale in order to present the information in a meaningful manner. If we did not use a log scale, the amounts reported for net income and shareholders' equity would barely get above the X-axis.

2. The total return for a $100 investment in the H&Q Index or a market basket of S&P 500 common stocks assumes that any dividends received were reinvested to buy additional shares of common stock at the prevailing market price.

Index